Learning English

Bayern

Unterrichtswerk für Realschulen

von
Paul Aston, Claudia Finkbeiner,
Rosemary Hellyer-Jones, Marion Horner,
Harriette Lanzer, Alan Posener, Rolf W. Roth,
Margaret Winck, Harold S. Wonham
sowie
Werner Beile, Alice Beile-Bowes,
Dorothea Kunz, Peter Lampater, Peter Pasch,
Helmut Slogsnat, Klaus Stenzel
und Dorit Stribel

Ernst Klett Verlag
Stuttgart Düsseldorf Leipzig

Learning English – *RED LINE* NEW **1** Bayern
für Klasse 5 an Realschulen

von
Paul Aston, Wells; Prof. Dr. Claudia Finkbeiner, Heilbronn; Rosemary Hellyer-Jones M.A., Ehingen (Donau); Marion Horner M.A., Cambridge; Dorothea Kunz, München; Harriette Lanzer B.A., London; Alan Posener, Berlin; Rolf W. Roth M.A., Idar-Oberstein; Margaret Winck B.A., Tübingen; Harold S. Wonham M.Litt., Stone, sowie Prof. Dr. Werner Beile, Alice Beile-Bowes M.A., Wuppertal und Iserlohn; Peter Lampater, Ehingen (Donau); Prof. Dr. Peter Pasch, Tübingen; Dr. Helmut Slogsnat, Neckargemünd; Klaus Stenzel, Bopfingen, und Dorit Stribel, Nürtingen

Beratende Mitarbeit
Falko Alig, Hitzacker (Elbe); Walter Düringer, Ketsch; Siegfried Kemmler, Calw; Brigitte Leber, Löffingen; Brunhilde Müller, Stuttgart; Manfred Nigmann, Donzdorf; Dr. Gudrun Steinbach, Halle; Heidrun Thieme, München; Wolfgang Weber, Lebrade; Gerhard Wildermuth, Esslingen; Gerlinde Wisiol, München

Visuelle Gestaltung
Elsie Lennox, London;
Kirsten Walther, Bochum (z. T. Grammatik, Vokabular)

 Kassetten und CDs zu diesem Band
Begleitkassette zum Schülerbuch für zu Hause und für den Unterricht
mit Unittexten, Liedern, Ausspracheübungen (Klettnummer 546402).
Die *Begleit-CD zum Schülerbuch* mit demselben Inhalt hat die Klettnummer 546499.
Lieferung durch jede Buchhandlung oder, wo dies auf Schwierigkeiten stößt,
zuzüglich Portokosten per Nachnahme vom Verlag.

 Kassette zum Hörverstehen für den Unterricht
mit den Hörverstehenstexten aller Werkteile (Klettnummer 546419).
Die *CD zum Hörverstehen* für den Unterricht hat die Klettnummer 546482.
Lieferung direkt an Lehrerinnen und Lehrer, Schulstempel erforderlich.

Software zu diesem Band:
Passend zu diesem Band gibt es ein Vokabel- und ein Grammatiktrainingsprogramm. Die Programme bieten abwechslungsreiche Übungsformen, zahlreiche Abfragevarianten, Leistungs- und Lernzielkontrolle und ein Lexikon mit dem Wortschatz der gesamten Lehrbuchreihe.

1. Auflage   A 1   5 4 3 2 1   1 2003 2002 2001 2000 1999

Alle Drucke dieser Auflage können im Unterricht nebeneinander benutzt werden,
sie sind untereinander unverändert. Die letzte Zahl bezeichnet das Jahr dieses Druckes.
© Ernst Klett Verlag GmbH, Stuttgart 1999.
Internetadresse: http://www.klett.de
Alle Rechte vorbehalten.

Redaktion: Christa Weck, Christa Meier, Jennifer Wood

Layout: Dieter Gebhardt, Graphic- und Foto-Design BFF, Asperg
Umschlaggestaltung: Christian Dekelver, Weinstadt
Satz: DTP-Verlag und Lihs GmbH, Medienhaus, Ludwigsburg
Reproduktion: Repro Maurer GmbH + Co, Tübingen
Druck: Wirtz Druck & Verlag, Speyer
ISBN: 3-12-546010-7

Inhaltsverzeichnis

Hallo!
Ich heiße Monny. Englischlernen macht Spaß – vor allem, wenn man es gemeinsam macht. Deshalb begleite ich dich durch dieses Buch und gebe dir ab und zu ein paar Tipps. Damit du dich in deinem Englischbuch leicht zurechtfindest, erkläre ich dir kurz, wie das Buch aufgebaut ist. Auf Seite 7 heißt es **Let's start**. Das bedeutet soviel wie: Jetzt geht's los. Dann kommen zehn **Units** (Kapitel) zu verschiedenen Themen. Am Ende jeder *Unit* kannst du auf einer **Let's check**-Seite überprüfen, was du in dieser *Unit* dazugelernt hast. Ab der Seite 124 findest du den **Grammatikanhang**. Das **Vokabular** beginnt auf Seite 147. Hier findest du alle neuen Wörter aus den *Units*. Wenn du einmal ein Wort aus einer früheren *Unit* nicht mehr weißt, kannst du in der **alphabetischen Wortliste** am Ende des Buches nachschlagen.
Alles klar? Na dann – **Let's start!** Viel Spaß!

Erläuterungen:

 Begleitkassette/CD zum Schülerbuch

 Kassette/CD zum Hörverstehen

 Hier kannst du über dich, deine Familie oder Freunde sprechen.

Partnerarbeit

Gruppenarbeit

 Wortschatzübungen

 Wiederholungsübungen

〈 〉 fakultativ (wahlfrei)

 schwierigere (wahlfreie) Aufgaben

 besonders für den fächerverbindenden Unterricht geeignet

Units/Steps	Kommunikative Schwerpunkte Arbeitstechniken (AT)	Strukturen (R = Revision/Wiederholung)	Seite

Let's start

1	In Nottingham	Jemanden begrüßen; sich vorstellen	I'm … .	7
2	Hello	Sich und andere vorstellen; darauf reagieren Informationen über sich und andere geben	What's your name?; My … . That's … . Is she/he …?; She's/He's … .	8
3	School!	Ein unbekanntes Wort erfragen AT: Ein Wortfeld anlegen	Am I …? Are you …? You're … .; How old are you?	10
4	Tutor group 7MD	Informationen über andere erfragen und geben	we're, you're (pl.), they're; her, his Where's …?; in, on, under	12
5	Haywood School	Informationen zum Thema Schule geben und erfragen; AT: Wortpaare sammeln	Kurzformen und Langformen von to be; isn't, aren't	14
6	The lesson	Aufforderungen äußern und darauf reagieren		16
7	Let's check			17

Unit 1 At home with the Burtons

A	Superdogs	Einfache mathematische Operationen	Grundzahlen 1 – 12	18
B	The Burtons	Besitzverhältnisse ausdrücken	our, your, their	19
	Two rooms	Beschreiben, welche Gegenstände eine Person hat	She's got …, He's got … . Has she got …? Has he got …? regelmäßige Pluralformen	20
	Good idea!	Einen Vorschlag machen Sich entschuldigen	I've got …, We've got … . We haven't got … .; Have you got …?	21
	Looking at the UK: Nottingham			22
C	Look!	Vorschläge machen und darauf reagieren	a – an; Let's … .; this – that	23
D	The frog			25
E	Let's check			27

Units/Steps	Kommunikative Schwerpunkte Arbeitstechniken (AT)	Strukturen (R = Revision/Wiederholung)	Seite

Unit 2   The Dixons

A Sarah and her family	Um etwas bitten	*man – men, woman – women, child – children;* Farben	28
B What a crazy family!	Jemanden auffordern, etwas zu tun	*family – families, shelf – shelves, knife – knives; its*	29
In the garage	Jemanden um etwas bitten	Kurzantworten mit *'to be'*	30
In Larwood Grove	Interesse bekunden	Kurzantworten mit *'have got'*	31
C Is that my new CD, Sarah?	Besitzverhältnisse klarstellen	*these – those*	32
D The ring	Zweifel ausdrücken		33
E Let's check			36

Unit 3   The new girl from Germany

A At the airport	Jemanden willkommen heißen Über verschiedene Nationalitäten sprechen	*There is/there are … .*	37
B In the car	Sagen, dass man etwas kann bzw. nicht kann; fragen, ob jemand etwas kann	*Can you …?/Can she/he …? Yes, (No,) she/he can (can't). Who's …?;* Fragewörter	38
At home in Sherwood	Verwandtschaftsbeziehungen ausdrücken	s-Genitiv	39
Let's say hello	Jemanden um etwas bitten	Objektpronomen *me, her, him; Can you help me? Sorry, I can't. I must … .*	40
Looking at the UK: How can you get there?			41
C Tea	Redemittel bei Tisch	*Can I help?; Can you pass me …? Here you are.; Oh, thank you.*	42
D The photo		R: Kurzantworten	43
E Let's check			45
⟨Christmas in the UK⟩			46

⟨Revision 1⟩	Wiederholung bisher geübter Strukturen und Sprechabsichten	Personalpronomen: Formen von *'to be'; Who …?;* s-Genitiv	47

Unit 4   Free time

A The alphabet	Vorschläge machen	*The alphabet*	48
B In the living-room	Fragen und sagen, was andere Personen gerade tun	*present progressive:* Verben mit regelmäßiger Schreibweise, 3. Person (Sg. und Pl.)	49
Mrs Croft	Sagen, was man selbst gerade tut	*present progressive:* 1. und 2. Person (Sg. und Pl.)	50
The idea	Um etwas bitten	*me, you, her, him, it, us, you, them*	51
Looking at the UK: Free time			52
C What's the weather like?	Das Wetter beschreiben	Gleichgeordnete Sätze mit *'and', 'or', 'but'*	53
D The flowerpot	AT: Kollokationen erkennen	R: *a/an;* Demonstrativpronomen	54
E Let's check			56

Units/Steps	Kommunikative Schwerpunkte Arbeitstechniken (AT)	Strukturen (R = Revision/Wiederholung)	Seite

Unit 5   Jenny's birthday

A A surprise party	Zahlenangaben machen	Grundzahlen 1 – 100	57
Jenny's letter	Monatsnamen benennen		58
B Everyone is very busy	Fragen und sagen, was eine Person gerade tut	*present progressive:* Verben mit unregelmäßiger Schreibweise	59
What is the date?	Auskünfte über Termine einholen und geben	Ordnungszahlen 1. – 100.; Datum	60
C What time is it?	Einladungen aussprechen	Uhrzeit; bestimmter Artikel	61
Looking at the UK: A British house			63
D A great birthday	Jemandem gratulieren	R: Possessivpronomen; s-Genitiv	64
E Let's check	AT: Ein Wortfeld erstellen		66
⟨Patrick's first day⟩			67
⟨Nottingham: what can you do there?⟩			68

⟨Revision 2⟩	Wiederholung bisher geübter Strukturen und Sprechabsichten	Objektpronomen; Kurzantworten mit *'to be', 'have got'; there is, there are*	69

Unit 6   In town

A In Nottingham	Sehenswürdigkeiten einer Stadt benennen		71
B Days of the week	Wochentage benennen	of-Genitiv; *Why …? – Because … .*	72
C At the Victoria shopping centre	Über Kleidung sprechen		73
Excuse me, please	Wegbeschreibungen	*Go down … . Turn right/left etc.*	74
David's grandma	Sich verabreden	weitere unregelmäßige Pluralformen R: *present progressive*	75
D Robert and Jenny in town	Vermutungen äußern; Zweifel ausdrücken	R: regelmäßige Pluralformen Fragewörter	76
E Let's check			78

Unit 7   School days

A Lunch time	Geldangaben machen		79
B Jenny's day	Sagen, was man gewohnheitsmäßig macht	*simple present* mit *'I, we, they'* (habitual usage)	80
Mark's day	Sagen, was andere Personen gewohnheitsmäßig machen	*simple present* mit 3. Person (habitual usage)	81
A busy day	Aufeinanderfolgende Handlungen schildern	Adverbien der Häufigkeit; Wort- stellung; *simple present (narrative usage)*	82
Looking at the UK: Haywood School			83
C The poster	Körperteile benennen		84
At the shops	Einkaufsgespräche führen	*a packet of, a pound of etc.*	85
D The healthy living prize		R: Uhrzeit	86
E Let's check			88
⟨Nottingham castle caves⟩			89

Unit 8   The accident

A Money and jobs	Über Taschengeld sprechen	*I like/want … .;* R: *simple present*	90
B Saturday morning	Vorlieben und Abneigungen ausdrücken	verneinte Aussagen mit *'don't'*	91
In Edward's Lane		*do, don't:* Fragen, Kurzantworten, verneinte Aussagen	92

Units/Steps	Kommunikative Schwerpunkte Arbeitstechniken (AT)	Strukturen (R = Revision/Wiederholung)	Seite
C In hospital	Jemandem gute Besserung wünschen Verbote ausdrücken	Get well soon. verneinter Imperativ; R: Präpositionen	93
Looking at the UK: Help!			95
D Fish fingers and ice cream			96
E Let's check	AT: Kollokationen bilden		98

Unit 9   A day at the seaside

A On the train	Vorschläge machen		99
B At Skegness	Fragen stellen und darauf antworten	does, doesn't: Fragen, Kurzantworten, verneinte Aussagen	100
At the boating lake	Fragen stellen und darauf antworten	do, don't, does, doesn't: Fragen, Kurzantworten, verneinte Aussagen	101
On the beach	Sich über etwas informieren	wh-Fragen mit 'do' und 'does'	102
Looking at the UK: At Skegness			103
C The sandcastle	Wünsche ausdrücken	want to + Infinitiv	104
At a souvenir shop	Einkaufsgespräche führen	How much does it cost? R: Mengenangaben	105
D Maxi's day at the seaside			106
E Let's check			108
⟨The fun run⟩			109

⟨Revision 3⟩	Wiederholung bisher geübter Sprechabsichten	present progressive; simple present; Fragen mit 'do'/'does'	111

Unit 10   On a Yorkshire farm

A Springfield Farm	Sich über Natur und Tierwelt informieren		113
B Jack's special friend	Gewohnheitsmäßige und zeitlich begrenzte Handlungen beschreiben	Gegenüberstellung: simple present und present progressive	114
The tractor	Tätigkeiten auf einem Bauernhof beschreiben	do/does; 'who' als Subjekt u. Objekt	116
C The seasons	Abläufe in den Jahreszeiten beschreiben	How much?/How many? not much/not many	117
D Problems on the farm		Untergeordnete Sätze mit 'because' R: Datum; Objektpronomen	118
E Let's check	AT: Gruppieren von Wörtern		121
⟨A holiday in Scotland⟩			122

Grammar   124

Grammar list   145

Vocabulary   147

Alphabetical word list   186

⟨In the classroom⟩   196

1 In Nottingham

Let's start

2 Hello

a) Becky: Hello.
Robert: Hello.
Becky: My name is Becky Burton.
Robert: I'm Robert. Robert Croft.
Sarah: Robert is new, Becky.
Robert: Yes. I'm from London.

b) Woof! Woof!

Robert: Oh hello, dog. What's your name?
Becky: Maxi. – And that's Mini.
Robert: Hello, Mini.

Woof! Woof!

what's = what is
that's = that is

Hello. I'm Monny.

1 My name

1. "Hello. I'm … ."
   – "Hello. I'm … ."

2. "Hello. My name is … ."
   – "Hello. My name is … ."

3. "Hello. What's your name?"
   – "… ."

4. "Hello. My name is … . What's … ?"
   – "… ."

2 I'm from Nottingham

1. Sarah: I'm Sarah. I'm from Nottingham.
2. Robert: … Robert. … from London.
3. Becky: … … Nottingham.

"I'm … . I'm from … ."

3 A song: Sarah Dixon

©Text: M. Horner, Melodie: trad.;
Gitarrenakkorde: M.Hauschild

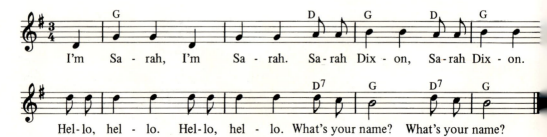

I'm Sa-rah, I'm Sa-rah. Sa-rah Dix-on, Sa-rah Dix-on.
Hel-lo, hel-lo. Hel-lo, hel-lo. What's your name? What's your name?

8 eight

c) Sarah: I'm at Haywood School.
Robert: Oh, that's my new school!
And Becky?
Is she at Haywood School?
Sarah: Yes. She's in my tutor group.

d) Sarah: Look. That's David Penrose.
He's in my tutor group, too.
Robert: Is he nice?
Sarah: Yes. He's a friend.
Hello, David!

Please look at page 123, too.

I'm = I am
she's = she is
he's = he is

4 That's Sarah

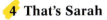

She's He's	from Nottingham. from London. at Haywood School.

1. That's Sarah. **She's** from Nottingham.
   She's at Haywood School.
2. That's … . **He's** from … . He's at … .
3. That's …   4. That's …

 "That's … . She's in my class."
"That's … . He's in my class."

5 My friend

1. Robert: **Becky** is my friend.
   Mrs Croft: **Is she** at your school?
   Robert: Yes. She's in my tutor group.

2. Robert: **David** is my friend.
   Mrs Croft: **Is he** at your school?
   Robert: Yes. … in my tutor group.

3. Robert: Sarah … .
   Mrs Croft: …
   Robert: …

6 A poster

 Make a poster.

nine **9**

Let's start

3 School!

a) *Sarah:* School, Becky!
Becky: I'm here. Am I late?
Sarah: Yes!
Robert: Look! Maxi is here, too.
Becky: Goodbye, Maxi.
Oh no! You crazy dog!
David: Your bag, Becky!

here's = here is

1 Here's your pen

1. Here's your pen, Becky. – Thank you.
2. Here's your book. – ... .
3. Here's your ... . – ... .

Please go on.

2 In your bag

Your teacher:
What's in your bag?
You: My folder

3 My English folder

4 Sound practice

Look, listen and say.

[aɪ]
M**y** dog is n**i**ce.
Am **I** late?
Goodb**y**e.

[æ]
M**a**xi is **a** dog.
Th**a**t's your b**a**g.
Th**a**nk you.

[əʊ]
Hell**o**.
A f**o**lder. A p**o**ster.
Oh n**o**!

10 ten

b) *Robert:* I'm twelve.
Are you twelve, too, David?
David: No. I'm eleven.
Robert: How old are you, Sarah?
Sarah: I'm eleven. And Becky, too.
Becky: I'm not eleven!
Sarah: Oh. Sorry, Becky. You're ten.
Becky: Ten? Sarah Dixon, you crazy girl.
I'm *twelve*.

you're = you are

5 How old?

Sarah	
Robert	11?
David	
Becky	12?

a) How old is Sarah? – She's ....
How old is Robert? – He's ....
How old is ... ? – ... *Please go on.*

10 – ten
11 – eleven
12 – twelve

b) "How old are you?" – "I'm ... ."
"How old is ...?" – "She's ... ."
"How old is ...?" – "He is ... ."

6 Are you new in Nottingham?

1. Are you new in Nottingham?
2. Am I late?
3. You're crazy!
4. Are you at Haywood School?
5. Hello, Becky.
6. You're a nice dog, Mini.

– Yes. That's my school.
– I'm not Becky. I'm Sarah.
– Yes. You're late.
– Woof! Woof!
– Yes. I'm new here.
– I'm not crazy!

7 Becky and Robert

a) Becky

1. Sarah? – Becky
   – Are you Sarah?
   – No, I'm not Sarah. I'm Becky.
2. eleven? – twelve
   – Are you eleven, Becky?
   – No, I'm not ... . I'm ... .

b) Robert

1. David? – Robert
   – ... you ...?
   – No, ... I'm ... .
2. from Nottingham? – from London
   – ...?
   – No, ...

8 I – you

Robert:
1. ...'m Robert. What's your name?
2. Are ... at Haywood School?
3. Oh, ...'m at Haywood School, too!
4. How old are ..., Sarah?
5. ...'re a crazy girl, Sarah!

9 he – she

Sarah:
1. Robert is new. ...'s from London.
2. That's Becky. ...'s in my tutor group.
3. David is my friend. Is ... your friend, too?
4. Is Robert late? Oh no. ...'s here.
5. How old is Becky? Is ... ten?

eleven **11**

4 Tutor group 7MD

a) *Robert:* Is that your teacher, David?
David: Yes. She's my English teacher. And she's my tutor, too. Her name is Mrs Dane. – Good morning, Mrs Dane.
Mrs Dane: Good morning, David. – Oh, are you the new boy?
Robert: Yes. I'm new here.
David: His name is Robert Croft.
Mrs Dane: Good morning, Robert. You're in my tutor group, too. That's tutor group 7MD.

she – **her**
he – **his**

1 Her name and his name

Is that | your tutor / girl in your tutor group / boy in your tutor group | ?
– Yes. Her name is
– Yes. His name is
Robert   Becky   David
Mrs Dane   Sarah

b) *Robert:* Becky! Sarah! You're in tutor group 7MD, right?
Becky: Yes. We're in 7MD.
Robert: That's my tutor group, too! Are the teachers OK?
Sarah: The teachers? They're …
Mr Cooper: Guten Morgen, girls and boys!
David: Guten Morgen. – That's Mr Cooper.
Robert: He's the German teacher, right?

we're = we are
you're = you are
they're = they are

2 What's the answer?

Teacher:
1. Good morning, girls and boys. – Good morning.
2. Becky Burton! David Penrose! – We're … .
3. You're late, boys! – …
4. Are you eleven? – …
5. Are you in tutor group 7MD? – … .

Sorry we're late.   We're here.
Good morning. ✓
Yes. We're eleven.
Yes. We're in 7MD.

3 Questions

1. Are Becky and Robert eleven? – No. **They're** twelve.
2. Are Sarah and David twelve, too? – No. … .
3. Are David, Sarah and Becky from London? – No. … from … .
4. Are they German? – No. … .
5. Are they at Greenwood School? – No. … at … .

c) *Sarah:* Hey, David! What's that?
David: What? Where?
On my desk?
Sarah: No. Under your chair.
David: Aaah! It's a snake!
Sarah: It's Sneaky Snake!
Here. Look.
David: Oh, Sarah!

it's = it is

4 What and where?

a) 1. Look! What's on the desk? – A pen and a book.
2. What's in the bag? – A ... . *Please go on.*
3. What's under the chair?
4. What's on the chair?
5. What's under the desk?
6. And under the bag? What's that?

b) Where's the biro? – It's on the ... .
Where's the comic? – It's ... .
Where's the ...? *Please go on.*

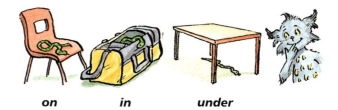

on   **in**   **under**

5 A game

Play the game.

Where's the ball?
Is it in the bag?
No.
Is it under the book?
No.
Is it on the chair?
Yes. Good!

6 Sound practice

[eɪ]
Please **say** your name.
That's **a** crazy game.
It's **a** snake.

[ð]
The boys are late.
They're in my
tutor group.
That's **the** teacher.

[w]
We're here, Mrs Dane.
What? **Where**?
Woof! **Woof**!

thirteen **13**

Let's start

5 Haywood School

a) Here is Haywood School.
It is in Nottingham.

The girls and boys in the picture are in year 7.
They are eleven or twelve.
They are at school in the morning and in the afternoon.

1 Please *say* the sentences

1. I am ten. ➤ **I'm** ten.
2. She is a teacher. ➤ **She's** a ... .
3. They are in year 7. ➤ ...
4. You are my friend. ➤ ...
5. He is a new boy. ➤ ...
6. I am from London. ➤ ...
7. We are from Nottingham. ➤ ...
8. You are late, boys. ➤ ...
9. It is a nice picture. ➤ ...
10. They are here. ➤ ...

I am – I'm
you are – you're
he is – he's
she is – she's
it is – it's
we are – we're
you are – you're
they are – they're

2 Make questions

is   am   are

1. **Is** Mr Cooper the German teacher?
2. ... I late?
3. ... they from Nottingham?
4. ... it a good comic?
5. ... you the new boy?
6. ... the girls and boys nice?
7. ... Sarah eleven?
8. ... we in your tutor group, Mrs Dane?

3 Let's learn words

Girl and boy, you and I,
Yes and no, hello and goodbye,
Her and his, desk and chair,
Words are easy in a pair!

Write the pairs in your folder.

question – answer
she – he
Mrs – Mr
my – your
morning – afternoon

b) *David:* Where's Sarah, Becky?
Becky: I'm not sure. She isn't here.
David: And Robert isn't here.
Becky: No. They aren't in the playground.
David: Hmm. – Chocolate, Becky?
Becky: Oh yes, please!

Robert: Chocolate?!
Sarah: Hello! We're here!

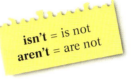

isn't = is not
aren't = are not

4 Where's Sarah?

1. Sarah?   Where's Sarah?
              – I'm not sure. **She isn't** here.
2. Mr Cooper?   Where's ...?
              – I'm not sure. **He isn't** here.

3. David?
4. Mrs Dane?
5. Becky?
6. Robert?

5 Crazy sentences

Maxi and Mini	are teachers.
David and Robert	are girls.
Mrs Dane and Mr Cooper	are eleven.
Sarah and David	are dogs.
Sarah and Becky	are boys.

a) 1. That's crazy! Maxi and Mini aren't teachers.
   2. That's crazy! David and Robert aren't ... .
   3. That's ... ! Mrs Dane and Mr Cooper ... .
Please go on.

b) *Find the right words.*
   1. Maxi and Mini are ... .
   2. David and Robert are ... . *Please go on.*

6 Listening practice: Thank you!

Listen and find the answer.

Becky: Where's my ... ?

David: It's under your ... .

7 Sound practice

[s]
Sorry, **S**arah.
Say yes.
A ni**c**e
pen**c**il ca**s**e.

[z]
Crazy dog**s**.
Where'**s** hi**s** pen?
Look here, plea**s**e,
girl**s** and boy**s**.

[s] – [z]
Ni**c**e dog**s**!
Sarah i**s** crazy.
Say hello, plea**s**e.

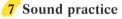

6 The lesson

The girls and boys are in the classroom.
Mrs Dane is late.

Sarah: Let's play a game!
I'm your teacher.
Becky: What's your name?
Sarah: Oh, I'm – Mrs Dixon.
David: You're funny, Mrs Dixon!
Sarah: Sit down, please.
Now, here's your homework.
Becky: Homework?
Robert: No, thank you!
David: Now you're the teacher, Robert.

Robert: OK. I'm the new teacher.
David, what's that on your desk?
David: It's a comic, Mr Croft.
Robert: A comic? In my lesson?
Bring the comic here, please.
David: It's my comic!
Sarah: Yes. It's his comic!
Robert: Quiet, please!
David, bring the comic here. –
Thank you. –
Oh good. It's a new comic.
David: You aren't the teacher now,
Robert.
I'm –
Mrs Dane: I'm the teacher now!
David: Oh! Mrs Dane!
Mrs Dane: Good afternoon. Sorry I'm late.

1 Right or wrong?

Are the sentences right or wrong?
Please correct the wrong sentences.

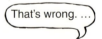

1. The girls and boys are in the playground.
   – That's wrong. The girls and boys are in … .
2. Mrs Dane is late.
   – That's … . *Please go on.*
3. Mrs Dixon is a funny teacher.
4. David is the new teacher.
5. It's a book on the desk.
6. Mr Cooper is the teacher now.
7. It's the afternoon.

16 sixteen

7 Let's check

1 In your classroom

Example: 1. *You:* Good morning. – *Your teacher:* Good morning. *Please go on.*

What's *Kugelschreiber* in English, please?

Here's my folder.

Good morning. ✓

Where's my book?

Sorry I'm late.

You:	Your teacher:
1.	– Good morning.
2.	– Thank you.
3.	– A biro.
4.	– On your desk. Look.
5.	– That's OK.

2 My, your, his or her?

1. *Robert:* Are Maxi and Mini your dogs?
   Becky: Yes. They're ... dogs.
2. *Sarah:* The new boy is from London.
   David: What's ... name?
3. *Becky:* Is Robert at Haywood School?
   Sarah: Yes. That's ... new school.
4. *Robert:* Is Mrs Dane your tutor?
   David: Yes. I'm in ... tutor group.
5. *Sarah:* What's that under your chair?
   David: Oh Sarah! You and ... snake!
6. *David:* Where's my comic?
   Robert: ... comic? It's on the desk.

3 Maxi and Mini   in   on   under

1. Mini is ... the folder.   2. Maxi is ... .   3. Mini ... . *Please go on.*

4 Find the right words

a) I'm   you're   we're

1. – Hello. ... David.
   – Hello, David.
2. – Becky! Sarah! Where are you?
   – ... here!
3. – Are we late, Mr Cooper?
   – Yes. ... late!
4. – Maxi, ... a crazy dog!
   – Woof! Woof!

b) he's   it's   she's   they're

1. Robert is new. ... from London.
2. David and Becky are from Nottingham. ... at Haywood School.
3. Haywood School is in Nottingham. ... a good school.
4. Sarah is eleven. ... in tutor group 7MD.
5. Mr Cooper is nice. ... the German teacher.

5 What's your answer?

Unit 1

At home with the Burtons

Step A

Superdogs

a) Becky is at home. She is with her brother Simon.

Becky: Look, Simon. Mini is a superdog. What's one and one, Mini?
Mini: Woof! Woo-
Becky: Clever dog! That's right. One and one is two.
Simon: Wow! Now you, Maxi! What's two and two?
Maxi: Woof! Woof! Woof! Woof! Woof! Woof!
Simon: No. That's wrong, Maxi. It's: Woof! Woof! Woof! Woof!

1 Let's play school

Find the answer.
Example: 5 + 3 = ?

What's five and three? Eight. That's right.

1. 9 + 2 = ?   2. 1 + 6 = ?   3. 5 + 5 = ?   4. 7 + 5 = ?   5. 4 + 2 = ?   Please go on.

2 Find the number

For Superkids!

1. 4 3 ? 1   2. 2 ? 6 8   3. 3 6 9 ?   4. 12 10 ? 6   5. 1 2 4 7 ?

b) *Simon:* Hm, where are my comics? – Oh yes, in my bag. Clever dog, Maxi. Thank you. – Now, let's look. Books, pens, my lunch box, a biscuit, a car. – Oh, here are my comics. But where's my new comic? – Clever dog, Mini. It's under my bed!

3 What's under the bed?

One comic, four books, ... Please go on.

4 Sound practice

[s]	[z]	[ɪz]
two book**s**	two girl**s**	two sentenc**es**
three desk**s**	three boy**s**	three pencil cas**es**
four comic**s**	four dog**s**	one box – two box**es**
	five friend**s**	

18 eighteen

Step B

The Burtons

Becky and Simon are in the kitchen.
Their mother and father aren't at home.
Their friend Robert is in the kitchen, too.

Robert: I'm hungry.
Becky: Where are our biscuits?
Simon: Here's a nice biscuit, Robert.
Robert: Thanks, Simon. – Hey, it's a dog biscuit! Here! – Oh, sorry.
Becky: Oh, hello Dad. Here's our new friend Robert.
Mr Burton: Your friend? Hm. Hello, Robert.

we – **our**
you – **your**
they – **their**

1 Becky and Simon

1. Becky and Simon
2. Their mother and father
3. Robert is
4. He's in
5. Their friend
6. Here's their father,

their new friend.
is hungry.
aren't at home.
Mr Burton.
are in the kitchen.
the kitchen, too.

2 Say it to the beat

○ Clap your hands.
○ (clap, clap, clap)
○ Stamp your feet.
○ (stamp, stamp, stamp)

Say it to the beat.
Say it to the beat.
Clap your hands
And stamp your feet.

We're OK.
Our friends are OK.
Let's go together
All the way.

Now all together.
Say it to the beat!

We're OK.
Our friends are OK.
Let's go together
All the way.

3 Our school

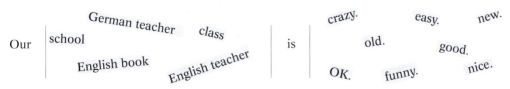

Step B

Two rooms

ⓐ Simon has got a football in his room.
And he has got a skateboard.
His radio is new.
Is that a CD player, too?

ⓑ Becky has got a computer in her room.
She has got a nice poster.
She hasn't got a radio.
But that's her new CD and – oh no!
Has Simon got her CD player? Brothers!

4 What has Simon got?

Look at the picture.
1. He's got a football.   2. He's got three cars.
3. He's got … .   *Please go on.*

*he has got = **he's got**
she has got = **she's got***

5 She's got a computer

a) Becky
1. She's got a computer.
2. She hasn't got a skateboard.
Please go on.

b) Simon
1. He hasn't got a computer.
2. He's got a skateboard.
Please go on.

She hasn't got a skateboard.
He hasn't got a computer.
Has she got a poster?
Has he got a football?

6 Becky or Simon?

Becky | a poster   a computer   a football   a skateboard   a new CD
Simon | a CD player   a box   a radio   **?**

1. Has Becky got a poster? – Yes. That's right.
2. Has Simon got a computer? – No. Becky has got a computer.
3. Has Becky got a football? – No. Simon … .   *Please go on.*

Step B

Good idea!

ⓐ *Robert:* Let's play football.
Becky: OK. – Oh sorry,
    I haven't got a ball.
Robert: Simon, have you got a ball?
Simon: Yes, I've got a *new* football.
    Look! Oops!
Becky: Oh no! Simon! My CD player!
Simon: Sorry, Becky. Let's play football
    in the garden.
Robert: Good idea.

I've got = I have got

7 Your room

What have you got in your room at home?
– "I've got ... ."

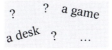

8 Brothers and sisters

Example:

Work with
a partner.

Have you got ... ?
I've got ... .
I haven't got ... .

ⓑ *Robert:* Hey, you've got a big tree.
    We haven't got a tree in our garden.
Simon: Oh yes, we've got a big tree and ...
    Oh, bad dogs, Maxi and Mini!
    Now we've got a hole in our garden.
Becky: Bad dogs? No, they're clever dogs.
    It's a nice big hole. Let's make
    a pond.
Simon: Good idea! Clever dogs! –
    Let's ask Mum.

9 Your classroom

What have you got in your classroom? What haven't you got?

We've got
We haven't got

a computer.

a radio.

a nice poster.

...

a football.

twenty-one 21

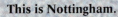

LOOKING AT THE UK:
Nottingham

Unit 1

This is Nottingham.

1 Nottingham

Look at the pictures.
1. This is … .
2. Nottingham is in … .
3. … is in Sherwood.
4. This is … .
5. This is … Road.
   The Burtons have got a house here.

2 My English folder

My home is in Stuttgart. This is our flat. It is in Ludwigstraße.

22 twenty-two

Step C

Look!

(a) Becky, Simon and Robert are in the garden. Now David is there, too.

David: What's this, Simon?
Simon: Hmmm – it's an apple.
Becky: Right. And what's this?
Simon: It's a ball. No. It's an egg – oops!
Robert: Yes. Look! It's an egg – a broken egg.

1 Sound practice

a pen	an apple	a nice apple	an English book
a biro	an egg	a broken egg	an easy question
a house	an idea	a big bag	an old football

2 WORD POWER

Play the game.

– What's this?
– Is it a   … ?
        an
– Yes. Right.
  No. Sorry.

(b)

Oh Maxi! This isn't your bed here. That's your bed over there. Look!

3 This isn't your chocolate!

1. Hey! This isn't your chocolate!
   That's your chocolate.   *Please go on.*

twenty-three 23

Step C

4 Role play: Let's make a pond

 Work with your partner.

Let's
- play football together.
- play a game.
- play with cars.
- play with the computer.
- make a poster.
- make a pond.

—

- Yes. Good idea.
- Oh no.
- Look. That isn't a good idea. Let's ....

5 In your classroom

Your teacher: Where's your **pen / homework / folder / book / biro ?**

You: Sorry, I haven't got my ... . Here it is.

6 Listening practice: A crazy morning

Listen and find the right words.
Becky: I haven't got a biro pen ball.
Robert: It's a book picture comic.
Sarah: I haven't got my homework folder pen.

7 What's your telephone number?

Robert: What's your telephone number, Becky?
Becky: Six nine o four seven two. What's your number?
Robert: My number is six seven double three five one.

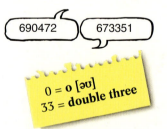

 What's your telephone number?

8 Listening practice: Telephone numbers

Listen, and write their telephone numbers:
David Penrose, Sarah Dixon, Robert Croft,
Becky and Simon Burton, Margaret Dane, Tim Cooper.

24 twenty-four

Step D

The frog

1. Sarah and Robert are on their bikes in Arnot Hill Park.

Sarah: Look, Robert. Is that a frog?
Robert: Where?
Sarah: There, look! Yes. It *is* a frog.
Robert: I've got an idea.
It's a nice frog – a frog for Becky.
Becky hasn't got a frog.

2. Becky and her mother are at home. Robert and Sarah are there, too.

Sarah: Hello, Mrs Burton! Hi, Becky!
Mrs Burton: Hello, you two!
What have you got there, Robert?
Robert: Hello, Mrs Burton.
This is for Becky. It's a frog.
Look, Becky – oops!
Your frog! Where's your frog?

3. Where is the frog?
It's under the table.
It's on a chair.
Where is it now?
Is it in the bag?

4. Now Becky has got the frog.

Robert: It's for your new pond, Becky.
Becky: Oh, Robert! We haven't got a pond.
Our pond isn't ready yet.
Poor frog!

5. Becky, Robert and Sarah are in the park.

Becky: Look frog. Now you're at home.
Sarah: Hey, look! More frogs! Two, three …
Robert: And there: four, five …
Becky: That's nice.
Our frog has got friends here.
Goodbye, frog.
Robert: Goodbye, frog. Sorry.

Step D

1 The frog

1. Sarah and Robert are — have got a frog for Becky.
2. Is that — at home in the park.
3. Robert and Sarah — on their bikes in Arnot Hill Park.
4. But the pond — friends here.
5. Now the frog is — a frog?
6. The frog has got — isn't ready yet.

2 A song: At the door

© Text: Alan Posener, Melodie: Petra Scheil

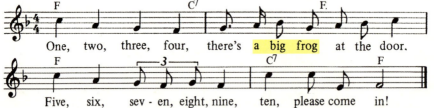

One, two, three, four, there's a big frog at the door.
Five, six, seven, eight, nine, ten, please come in!

an old dog
a new girl
a nice boy
a teacher
...

3 Sound practice

[ə]
That's a computer.
Mrs Dane is a clever teacher.
Simon and Becky are at home.

[r]
That's right, Sarah.
That's wrong, Robert.
This is my friend Superfrog.

4 Have you got a pen?

Have you got a pen? – No. Sorry.
...? – No. Ask .... She's got a pen.
He's ....
– Yes. Here your are. Please go on.

5 What have you got?

Write the answers.
Example:

Ilona: radio, bed, frog
Kemal: computer, pond, dog

a) You've got a house and a garden with three nice things. What are your things?
Write the words in a picture.

b) *Ask five friends. Example:*

What have you got in your house and garden?

I've got a radio, and a bed, and a frog.

c) What have your friends got?

Ilona has got ... .
Kemal ... .

26 *twenty-six*

Step E

Let's check

1 Has got or have got?

a) *Put in 'has got' or 'have got'.*
1. The Burtons *have got* a house in Arndale Road.
2. Simon *has got* a radio.
3. The frog ... friends in the park.
4. Becky ... a computer.
5. Maxi and Mini ... beds in the kitchen.
6. David ... a brother.
7. Sarah and Robert ... bikes.
8. The frogs ... a nice pond in the park.

b) *Write the sentences in a) with 'he's got', 'she's got', 'it's got' or 'they've got'.*
1. They've got a house in Arndale Road.
2. He's got ... .   *Please go on.*

2 WORD POWER

a) *Find the right words.*

b) *Write the words in groups.*

3 Our, your or their?

1. *Sarah:* Where are Becky and Simon?
   Mrs Burton: In ... rooms.
2. *David:* Hi, Becky! Hi, Simon! Where are ... dogs?
   Simon: In the garden.
3. *Simon:* Let's play football in the park.
   Becky: No. Let's play in ... garden.
4. *David:* Let's learn ... German words together.
   Robert: Yes. Good idea.
5. *Sarah:* Let's play with Becky and Simon.
   Robert: OK. What's ... telephone number?
6. *Robert:* Are ... mother and father at home?
   David: No. They aren't here yet.

4 In your classroom

1. I haven't got my book.
2. My biro is broken.
3. Let's work together.
4. Is this my book?
5. Where's my folder?

– Yes. Good idea.
– That's your folder over there.
– Here's a biro. I've got two.
– Here. Look at my book.
– No. It's my book. Here's my name.

twenty-seven **27**

Unit 2

The Dixons

Step A

Sarah and her family

ⓐ This is Sarah Dixon on her new bike. The poor man in the picture is her father. His name is Eddy and he is a bank clerk.

The woman in this picture is her mother. Her name is Janet and she is a vet's assistant. Here she is in the kitchen with their cat Tabby.

This is Sarah with her sister Kim. The children are in the garden. Sarah is in the tree. Tabby is in the picture, too – but where?

one man – two men   one woman – two women   one child – two children

1 What's in the pictures?

1. One child, … *Go on.*

 ⓑ Sarah and Kim are at home.

Sarah: Kim, have you got a red crayon for my German homework?
My pencil case is at school.
Kim: No, but I've got a blue crayon.
Sarah: OK, that's a good colour, too.
And have you got a green crayon?
Kim: No, but I've got a green biro.
Here you are.

2 What colour are the school bags?

a) Sarah has got a brown bag, and Kim has got a black bag. *Go on.*
b) What colour are the school bags?
– The school bags are brown and black. *Go on.*

3 My English folder

Draw your school things and write sentences.

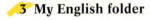

28 twenty-eight

Step B

What a crazy family!

a) In the morning.
Mr Dixon and the girls are in the kitchen.

Sarah: Where's my knife?
Hey, the knives and spoons aren't on the table, Kim.
It's your turn, today.
Kim: No, it's your turn, Sarah.
Mr Dixon: Girls, please! I've got the knives here.
Sarah: Thank you, Dad. –
Kim, where's my lunch box?
Mr Dixon: It's on that shelf over there.
Kim: And where's my apple?
Mr Dixon: Oh no! What a crazy family!

> family – famil**ies**
> shel**f** – shel**ves**
> kni**fe** – kni**ves**

1 Sound practice

[f]	[v]	[æ]	[e]
Where's my **kni**fe?	I've got **fi**ve **kni**ves.	That **m**an has got a **b**ag.	This **p**en is for my **fri**end.
The **f**unny **f**rog is	I've got twel**ve**	You're a **b**ad **c**at, **T**abby.	The **m**en are in the garden.
on the shel**f**.	shel**ves**.	What's **th**at, **D**ad?	Are you **rea**dy? – Let's check.

2 Sarah and her teachers

Find the words.
Sarah: I've got ten teachers at Haywood School, four and six . Two have

got big . For example, Mr Wood has got six ,

three boys and three girls. Mr Miller is nice. He's got chocolate and biscuits on the

 in his classroom. That's great!

b) In the afternoon. Sarah and Kim are at home. Their parents aren't there yet.

Kim: Look, Dad is very untidy.
His folders are on the chair.
Sarah: And Mum is very untidy, too.
Her books are under the chair.
And her new CD isn't in its box.
Kim: What a crazy family!

> he – **his**
> she – **her**
> it – **its**

3 The Dixons

Put in 'his', 'her' or 'its'.
1. Sarah and … sister are at home.
2. Kim has got an apple in … lunch box.
3. Mr Dixon is untidy. … folders are on the chair.
4. And Mrs Dixon? … books are under the chair.
5. That cat is crazy. … ball is under the bed.
6. And that CD? It isn't in … box.

Step B

In the garage

 Sarah and Robert are in the garage.

Robert: Let's go, Sarah. Are you ready?
Sarah: No, I'm not.
 My bike has got a flat tyre.
Robert: Where's your pump?
Sarah: Is it on that shelf over there, Robert?
Robert: No, it isn't.
Sarah: Oh – er – is it in that black box?
Robert: Yes, it is. Here you are.
Sarah: Thank you, Robert. …
Robert: Are you ready now?
Sarah: Yes, I am. Let's go and find Becky.

Yes, he is. – No, he isn't.
Yes, she is. – No, she isn't.
Yes, it is. – No, it isn't.
Yes, they are. – No, they aren't.

4 Questions and answers

1. Are Sarah and Robert in the garage?
2. Is the pump on the chair?
3. Are Mr and Mrs Dixon in the garage, too?
4. Is the cat there?
5. Is Robert there?
6. Is Sarah his sister?

No, they aren't.
Yes, she is.
No, it isn't.
Yes, they are.
No, she isn't.
Yes, he is.

5 What's your answer?

Yes, I am. – No, I'm not.
Yes, we are. – No, we aren't.

1. Are you at Haywood School?
2. Are you eleven?
3. Are you English?
4. Are you and your friends in class 5?
5. Are you at home now?
6. Are you from Berlin?

6 A question game

Throw the dice and look at the numbers.
Find the words and make questions.

Have you got two dice?
That's 'Würfel' in German.

Examples: ⚀ + ⚁ Are Sarah and Becky at Haywood School? – Yes, they are.
 ⚁ + ⚅ Are Mr and Mrs Dixon teachers? – No, they aren't.

⚀ Sarah and Robert	⚃ Robert and Becky	⚀ sisters	⚃ at Haywood School
⚁ Mr and Mrs Dixon	⚄ Kim and Sarah	⚁ ten	⚄ English
⚂ Sarah and Becky	⚅ the girls and boys in your class	⚂ German	⚅ teachers

+ between the two groups

30 thirty

Step B

In Larwood Grove

Sarah, Becky and Robert are in Larwood Grove.

Robert: Hey, Becky, have you got a new bag for your bike?
Becky: Yes, I have. It's from our shop.
Robert: Oh, have your parents got a bike shop?
Becky: Yes, they have.
Sarah: The bag is very nice. – Er, have your parents got yellow bags, too?
Becky: Yellow– er – no, they haven't. But they've got other colours. They've got red and blue and …
Robert: And have they got pumps, too?
Becky: Yes, they have.
Sarah: Let's go to the shop now.
Robert: Good idea.

Unit 2

Yes, they have. – No, they haven't.
Yes, he has. – No, he hasn't.
Yes, she has. – No, she hasn't.

7 What have they got?

a) Have the Dixons got a house in Larwood Grove? – Yes, they have.
Have the Burtons got a book shop?
Have Sarah and Becky got bikes?
Have the Burtons got blue bags?

b) Has Becky got a new bag?
Has Sarah got an old bike?
Has Robert got a bike, too?
Has Sarah got a blue bag for her bike?

8 What have you got?

Work with your partner.

Have you got

a bike
a bag for your bike
a red biro
a poster in your room
…

? –

Yes, I have.
No, I haven't.
Yes, we have.
No, we haven't.

9 Sarah and Mr Nosy

Sarah is in Larwood Grove with Mr Nosy, a neighbour. *What are her answers?*

Mr Nosy: Sarah:
1. Hello, Sarah.
   Is that boy your friend?   Yes, he is.
2. Is he from Nottingham?   …
3. Is he at your school?
4. Has he got a bike, too?
5. Have you got two dogs now, Sarah?
6. Oh, and the Burtons? Have they got two dogs?

thirty-one 31

Step C

 Is that my new CD, Sarah?

Sarah is in her room with Becky.
Kim is there, too.

Kim: Have you got my new CD, little sister?
Sarah: No, I haven't. This is my CD.
Becky: Hi, Kim.
Kim: No, it isn't. Look, Sarah.
That's my CD. – And those comics
over there are my comics, too.
Sarah: No, they aren't. They're …
Becky: Er – Kim, these are my comics.
Kim: Oh – sorry!

1 In the classroom

Work with a partner. Act the dialogues. Examples:

books ✓   crayons
pens   folders   pencils   biros

a) "Are these your books here?"
– "Yes, they are. Thank you."

b) "Are these my books here?"
– "No, those are your books over there."
– "Oh, yes. Thanks."

2 Are you ten?

a) Find a partner and ask questions.

	Jens
Questions	yes/no
Are you ten?	x
Have you got a brother?	x
Have you got a cat?	
Have you got a bike?	

Yes, I am. – No, I'm not.
Yes, I have. – No, I haven't.

b) Now talk about your partner:
Jens is ten. He hasn't got... .

3 Is that right?

1. Yellow is a nice colour.
2. Cats are funny.
3. English is OK.
4. Football is a good game.
5. Comics are funny.
6. Snakes are nice.

You:
Yes, it is./No, it isn't.
Yes, they are./No, they aren't.
Go on, please.

Look at this:
one woman [ʊ]
two women [ɪ]

 ### 4 Sound practice

[ʊ]
That's a good book.
Look at my football!
Kim is from Sherwood.

[uː]
She is in my tutor group.
She's at school this afternoon.
This is for you, too.

[ʊ] – [uː]
Good afternoon.
Let's play football at school.
That woman has got two dogs.

Step D

The ring

1. Sarah is at home with Robert, Becky and David. They are in the living-room.

Sarah: Look! My sister Kim has got a new ring. Isn't it nice?
Becky: Yes, it is.
David: Let's see the ring.
Sarah: Here you are. Be careful! – Oh no! Where is it?
David: Is it under the table?
Becky: No, it isn't.
Sarah: Are you sure? Let's look again. It isn't *my* ring!
Robert: Has Tabby got the ring?
Becky: Tabby? – No, that's silly. She hasn't got the ring.
Robert: Yes, I'm sure. Look, she's in the garden now.
David: Come on. Let's get Tabby.

2. The children are outside now.
Becky: Look, she's in that tree. Oh no, Kim is over there.
Robert: Come on. Let's get Tabby.
David: She's at the top of the tree now.
Robert: The silly cat!
Sarah: I've got an idea! Let's get those red boxes over there. Here, Tabby, Tabby! Come here. Good, I've got Tabby.
Robert: Has she got the ring?
Sarah: No, she hasn't. Where *is* it?
Robert: It's in Tabby, I'm sure.
Becky: What? Where?
Sarah: *In* Tabby?
David: Poor Tabby!

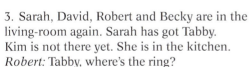

3. Sarah, David, Robert and Becky are in the living-room again. Sarah has got Tabby. Kim is not there yet. She is in the kitchen.
Robert: Tabby, where's the ring?
Becky: I'm sure she hasn't got the ring.
David: Hey, Sarah, look! What's that under those shelves over there?
Becky: What? Where? Is it the ring?
Sarah: Yes, it is. Oh, great! Let's put the ring in its box again.
Kim: Hello! – Hey, what's all this noise?
Sarah: Ha, ha. It's nothing, Kim. Everything is OK.

thirty-three **33**

Step D

1 Find the right answer

1. Where are the friends?
   Has Sarah got a new ring?
   Is the ring under the table?
2. Where is Tabby?
   Have the friends got blue boxes?
3. Where is the ring?
   Where is it now?
   Is Kim there now, too?

No, it isn't.
She is at the top of the tree.
The friends are in the living-room.
It is in its box again.
It is under the shelves.
No, Kim has got a new ring.
Yes, she is.
No, they have got red boxes.

2 WORD POWER

1. The Dixons are a ... .
2. Eddy Dixon is the ... .
3. Janet Dixon is the ... .
4. Kim and Sarah are their ... .
5. Mr and Mrs Dixon are the ... .
6. Kim and Sarah are ... .
7. Sarah hasn't got a ..., but she's got a sister.

3 My English folder

Draw your family in your folder and write about your family.

4 Where are my books?

a) *Put in 'this' or 'these'.*
Mr Dixon: Please put ... comics here in your room, Sarah.
Sarah: OK, Dad. Oh, and please put ... bank folder here on your desk.
Mr Dixon: Thank you, Sarah. And are ... your pictures here on the chair? And is ... your pencil under the table?

b) *Put in 'that' or 'those'.*
Mrs Dixon: Where are my books?
Mr Dixon: The green book is under ... chocolate biscuits on ... chair over there. And the new books are on ... shelves over there.

Step D

5 A song: Little boxes

Lit-tle box-es on the hill-side, lit-tle box-es made of tick-y-tack-y, lit-tle box-es, lit-tle box-es, lit-tle box-es all the same; there's a green one and a pink one and a blue one and a yel-low one, and they're all made out of tick-y-tack-y, and they all look just the same.

©Schröder Music, Essex GmbH Köln

6 Four families

Put in 'he's' or 'his'.

1. Simon   … ten and Becky is … sister. … parents have got a bike shop.
2. Mr Burton   Becky and Simon are … children.
3. Mr Dixon   … a bank clerk. … girls are at Haywood School.
4. Robert   He and … mother are from London. Sarah is … friend.
5. David   … in tutor group 7 MD. Becky and Sarah are … friends.

7 Listening practice: At the bike shop

Listen and find the colours.

1. The bag is … .
2. The box … . *Go on.*

thirty-five 35

Step E

Let's check

1 Colours

1. These apples are ..., ... and ... .

2. Chocolate is ... .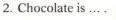

3. This car is ... and ... .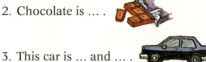

2 These or those?

1. *Sarah:* Hello, Mrs Burton. ... comics here are for Becky.
2. *Robert:* ... pictures here and ... posters over there are for our classroom.
3. *Mrs Dane:* Sarah, please put ... books here on my desk.
4. *Kim:* ... boys over there are in my tutor group.
5. *Mr Dixon:* Are my folders on ... shelves over there, Sarah?

3 Word Power

Four shelves, ...

4 Becky and Mr Nosy

Find the answers for Becky.

a) Is Robert your little brother? – No, he isn't.
   Are you new here in Nottingham?
   Are your friends at Haywood School?
   Are they eight?

b) Have your parents got a shop?
   Has your brother got a CD player?
   Has Robert got a dog?
   Have you got a black cat?

5 His, her or its?

1. *Becky:* Simon isn't here. He's in ... room.
2. *Mrs Dixon:* Please put the CD in ... box, Sarah.
3. *Simon:* Becky is outside with ... friends.
4. *Sarah:* Please put the ring in ... box, Becky.

The new girl from Germany

Step A

At the airport

a) These people are at Heathrow Airport in London. There are men, women and children. There is a girl with a big red bag. She is from Germany.

1 The people at the airport

Examples: There's a family with four children.
There's a man with ... .

There's ... .   There are ... .

There are two women with black bags.
There are three girls with ... .

b) Jenny Leinert is from Berlin. Her father is German, but her mother is British. She has got an aunt, an uncle and two cousins in England.

David: Hi, Jenny! We're here!
Mark: Jenny! Jenny!
Mrs Penrose: Hello, Jenny.
Mr Penrose: Welcome to England.
Jenny: Oh thank you. This is great!
David: Come on, Mark.
 Let's help Jenny with her bag.

2 I'm German

"Hi. I'm Christian. I'm German."
"My name is Laura. I'm Italian."
"I'm Maria and I'm Spanish."
"Melina is my name. I'm Greek."
"My name is Kemal. I'm Turkish."

a) *Talk about these people.*
 Start: Christian is German. Laura is ... .
b) "I'm ... ." [Ask your teacher for new words.]
c) *Ask your friends questions.*
 Example: "Are you German?"
  – "No, I'm not. I'm Italian."
  – "My parents are from Poland."

3 Sound practice

[tʃ]
Where's my lu**ch** box?
What's in the pi**ch**ure?
There are four **ch**ildren.

[dʒ]
Look at this pa**g**e.
My name is **J**anet.
Are you **G**erman?

[tʃ] – [dʒ]
The **ch**ild is from **G**ermany.
There's a big pi**ch**ure on this pa**g**e.
Thank you for the **ch**ocolate, **J**anet!

thirty-seven 37

Step B

In the car

The Penroses and Jenny are in the car.

David: You're lucky, Jenny. You can speak German and English.
Mrs P.: You can speak German, too, David.
Jenny: Oh, can you speak German now?
Mark: Yes, he can.
David: No, I can't. I can say one or two things, but –
Jenny: Hey, I can do your German homework!
David: Oh yes, that's a good idea.
Mrs P.: A good idea? I'm not sure. – What about Mr Cooper?
Jenny: Who's Mr Cooper?
David: He's my German teacher. He's OK.

1 Your English lessons

What can you and your friends do in English?
Example: We can ask questions in English.

We can — ask write play talk about make — sentences questions pictures posters dialogues answers games people … — in English.

2 Mark

1. write   2. draw   3. make   4. play   5. speak

a) *Make sentences with 'can' or 'can't'.*
1. Mark can't write his name. 2. He … draw a … . *Please go on.*

b) *Now make questions and answers.*
1. Can he write his name? – No, he can't.
2. Can he …? – Yes, he can. *Go on.*

Can he …? – Yes, he can.
            – No, he can't.

3 A name quiz

Who?

Who's from Berlin? – That's Jenny.
Who's a bank clerk? – That's Mr Dixon.
Who's …? – …

Make a name quiz with people from this book

4 Who can do what?

a) *Write questions with 'Can you …?'*

b) *Go to your friends. Ask the questions.*
"Can you speak Turkish, Nadine?"
– "No, I can't."

c) *Who can or can't do what? Tell the class.*
"Nadine can't speak Turkish, but she can … ."

38 thirty-eight

Step B

At home in Sherwood

(a) The Penroses are at home now.
Mark is in Jenny's room.

Mark: Is my mum your aunty, Jenny?
Jenny: Yes, she is.
Mark: Are we cousins?
Jenny: Yes, we are.
Your mother is my mother's sister.
So we're cousins.
Mark: Hey, what have you got in your bag? Presents?!

5 Jenny and the Penroses

Please make sentences. You can start:
1. Jenny is David's cousin.
2. She is ... cousin, too.
3. Mrs Penrose is ... . *Go on.*

Jenny Mrs Penrose Mr Penrose David Mark	is	Jenny's David's Mark's	aunt. uncle. cousin. brother. mother. father.

6 Listening practice: Presents

Please listen. What are their presents?
"Mrs Penrose's present is ... ."

(b)

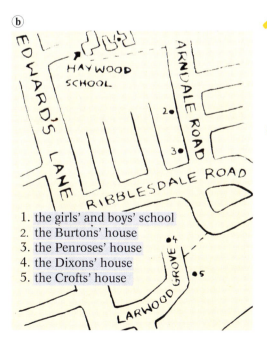

1. the girls' and boys' school
2. the Burtons' house
3. the Penroses' house
4. the Dixons' house
5. the Crofts' house

7 Where?

1. The girls' and boys' school is in Edward's Lane.
2. The Burtons' house is in ... . *Go on.*

my friend's house
my friends' house

8 Friends and neighbours

friends ✓   Burtons   parents   girls
           dogs   Dixons

What can David tell Jenny?
Write the right forms.
1. My friends' houses are in Sherwood.
2. There's Becky. Her ... bike shop is in Mansfield Road. 3. But the ... house is in Arndale Road. 4. Their ... names are Maxi and Mini. 5. The Dixons are a crazy family! Their ... names are Sarah and Kim. 6. There's Robert Croft, too. He and his mother are the ... neighbours in Larwood Grove.

Step B

Let's say hello

 ⓐ Becky is in Arndale Road. Sarah is with her.

Sarah: Can you give me your ball, please?
I've got an idea for a game, and –
Hey, look. David is in his garden.
Becky: Yes, I can see him.
And he's got a girl with him.
Sarah: It's his German cousin. Let's go and say hello to her.

Becky: Hi. I'm Becky. My German isn't very good.
Sarah: And I'm Sarah. My German is terrible!
Jenny: Oh! My name is Jenny. And it's OK – you can speak to me in English.
Sarah: Good! – Where's Robert, David?
David: I'm not sure. Maybe he's at home. Let's phone him.

I	–	me
she	–	her
he	–	him

9 Can you give me my ball, please?

Your friend has got your things. What can you say?

1. Can you give me my ball, please?
2. Can you give me my ..., please? *Go on.*

10 On the telephone

1. Robert? – not at home   2. Sarah? – at Becky's house   3. David? – at the Crofts' house
4. Jenny? – not here   5. Becky? – in the park with the dogs   6. Mark? – in bed

1. "Hello. Is Robert there? Can I speak to **him**, please?" – "Sorry. He isn't at home."
2. "Hello. Is Sarah there? Can I speak to **her**, please?" – "Sorry, she's at ... ." *Go on.*

 ⓑ Now the friends are at the Burtons' house.

Becky: Can you help me with the pond this afternoon?
David: Sorry, we can't. We must go to the shops.
Jenny: I must get my school uniform.
David: Jenny is at our school now.
Sarah: Oh, good. That's great.

11 Sorry, I can't

Can you { go to the park / play football / go to the shops / ... } with me? – Sorry, I can't. I must { do my homework. / help my parents. / phone my friend. / help in the garden. / ... }

Unit 3

40 forty

LOOKING AT THE UK:
How can you get there?

by plane

1 Look at the pictures

You can get there by plane.
You can get there by … .   *Go on.*

2 Look at the map

There are ferries from Belgium to England.
There are ferries from … to … .
There is a tunnel from … .   *Go on.*

by car and hovercraft

by train through the Channel Tunnel

by ferry

Go by train – you can see more!

3 Work with a partner

Make a poster for planes or trains or ferries – or for the Channel Tunnel. Find photos or draw pictures. What can you write on your poster?

Go by … . You can get there by … .
It's great by … . You can see more by … .

forty-one **41**

Step C

 Tea

It is late in the afternoon. Mr Penrose and Jenny are in the kitchen.

Jenny: Can I help, Uncle Colin?
Mr Penrose: Oh, thank you, Jenny.
Yes, you can help me with the tea.
Can you put the ham and the cheese on the table, please?
Jenny: Yes. – Er – is this the cheese?
Mr Penrose: Yes, that's right.
Jenny: English cheese is a funny colour.
Mmm – but it's nice.

1 Role play: Can I help?

How can you help at home?
"Can I help?"
– "Oh, thank you.
Can you help me in the kitchen, please?"

help me with the tea   go to the shops
put the bikes in the garage   make the beds
help me in the garden   …

2 WORD POWER

What's for tea?

– There's salad.
– And there's … .
– There are … .
– You can have … .
Can you go on?

3 What you can say at the table

Work in groups of four or five. Draw pictures of things for tea.
Put your pictures on the table. Now sit at the table and act little dialogues.

** 4 Sound practice**

[l]
Hello, Uncle Colin.
Can I help?
Can I have more milk, please?

[r]
It's brown bread.
Where are our CDs?
They're in my room.

42 *forty-two*

Step D

The photo

1. Sarah, Becky and Robert are with David. They are in the Penroses' garden. Robert has got his mother's camera with him.

Robert: It's a good camera. You can see the photos right away.
Becky: Let's take a photo of Jenny!
Sarah: Ha, ha. This is a great idea!
David: Yes, we can take a nice photo of her.
Becky: But where *is* Jenny?
Sarah: In the house. Let's go and find her.

2. Now Jenny is in the garden, too. She is in her new school uniform.

Jenny: Oh no, this isn't a good idea. This silly uniform –
Sarah: It isn't silly. It's – er –
Becky: It's very English.
David: And the photo is for your family in Berlin. Please, Jenny!
Jenny: Oh, OK. But you must all be in the photo with me.
Robert: Who can take the photo? Your father, David?

3. But they cannot find Mr Penrose. Here is little Mark. He can help. He is only four. This is great for him!
Mark: Are you all ready? Say 'cheese'!

4. Now they have got the photo.

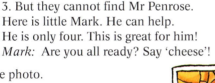

Robert: Oh no!
David: You can only see our legs!
Becky: Oh Mark, it isn't a very good photo.
Jenny: Yes, it is. It's a great photo. You can't see me in my uniform! Thanks, Mark!

Tell the story

Find the right sentences.

a) 1. The friends are in David's garden.

   2. ... But Jenny is in the house.

   3. ... Robert has got a camera.

   4. ... It is for a photo of Jenny.

b) 1. Now Jenny is in the garden.

   2. ... But Mark can help.

   3. ... Robert cannot take the photo.

   4. ... She is in her new school uniform.

What can you say about Mark's photo?

Step D

 2 Questions for Jenny

Jenny is new at Haywood School. *What can she tell the boys and girls there?*

1. Are you eleven, Jenny? – No, I'm not. I'm twelve.
2. Is your father German? – Yes, he ... .
3. Are David and Mark Penrose your cousins?
4. Is your mother German?
5. Are you from Hamburg?
6. Is Berlin big?
7. Are your parents in England, too?

3 Who and where?

a) 1. Who's that? – It's Jenny.
   Where is she? – She's in her room.
2. Who's that? – It's ... .
   Where is he? – He's in the ... .
   Go on. Make more questions and answers.

 b) *Draw a picture of a girl or boy in your class.*
Can the others say who it is?

4 Let's play   *me   her   him*

1. *Jenny:* Here's David. Let's play a game with ... .
2. *Mark:* Where am I? Can you find ...?
3. *David:* Jenny is under the table. Look at ... !
4. *Mark:* I can play football. Look at ... .
5. *David:* Jenny can draw good pictures. Have you got a crayon for ..., Mark?
6. *Jenny:* Mark can't write his name. But I can help ... .

5 Pictures from this unit

Can you find the pictures? Make sentences like this:
1. That's the Burtons' garden. 2. That's Mrs ...'s camera. 3. That's ...s' ... . Go on.

What's right?

6 What's right?

| you're – your | **You're** late. Is that **your** book? | it's – its | Look. **It's** Sarah's snake. What's **its** name? |

Sarah:
1. Oh good, Jenny. ... in our tutor group.
2. ... new uniform is OK.   3. ... lucky, David.
4. ... cousin is German.   5. She can do ... German homework!

Becky:
1. What's that? Oh, ... a frog.   2. Look at ... little green legs!   3. Where's ... home?
4. ... from the pond in Arnot Hill Park.
5. ... a funny frog!

Step E

Let's check

1 Find the right word   What?   Who?   Where?

1. ...'s that? – It's David's cousin.
2. ...'s your name? – Jenny.
3. ...'s Uncle Colin? – In the kitchen.
4. ...'s that? – It's a dog biscuit.
5. ...'s Jenny's home? – In Berlin.
6. ...'s the little boy? – Mark Penrose.

2 Pairs

Make sentences with these pairs.
You can start:
1. Becky is David's friend.
2. Tabby is the Dixons' ... . *Go on.*

1. Becky/David   2. Tabby/the Dixons   3. Jenny/Mark
4. Mrs Penrose/Jenny   5. Maxi/the Burtons
6. Kim/Sarah   7. Mr Cooper/the girls and boys

3 What can Maxi and Mini do? What can't they do?

play football   take a photo   speak German   make a hole   get a comic   draw a picture

1. Maxi **can** play football. 2. Mini **can't** ... . 3. Maxi ... . *Please go on.*

4 Me, her or him?

Jenny is on the telephone to her mother. *Can you find the right words?*

1. I'm at Haywood School now. The German lessons are easy for ... .
2. David is lucky. I can help ... with his German homework.
3. David's friend Becky has got two dogs. I can play with ... and with the dogs, too.
4. I've got a funny photo of ... and my friends. You can only see our legs!
5. Aunty Pat? No, sorry – you can't speak to ... . She isn't at home.
6. But here's Uncle Colin. You can speak to ... now.

5 WORD POWER

What's different?
Look at the two pictures. Make sentences. Start:
– In picture 1 there's one ball. In picture 2 there are two balls.

forty-five **45**

Christmas[1] in the UK

24th December[7]

It is Christmas Eve[2], and Mark and Jenny are upstairs.

Mark: Hey, Jenny, look! Here's my stocking[3].
It's for my presents from Father Christmas[4].
Jenny: A stocking? Oh, that's nice.
Mark: And here's a mince pie[5] for Father Christmas.
It's a long way[6] for him – so he's hungry.

25th December

It is Christmas Day[8]. Now they have all got their presents.

David: Christmas Dinner[9] – mmh! I'm hungry.
Jenny: What's for dinner?
Mr Penrose: Turkey[10]. And Christmas pudding[11].
Mark: Look, Jenny. Here are the crackers[12].
Let's pull[13] one.
David: No, Mark. We must wait[14] till[15] dinner.
Jenny: What's in the crackers?
Mark: A hat[16] and a present.

26th December

It is Boxing Day[17].

David: Can we go to the park?
Mrs Penrose: No! We've got tickets[18] for a pantomime[19] – 'Aladdin'[20].
Mark: Oh great!
Jenny: What's a pantomime?
David: A funny play[21]. With silly songs[22] and silly people. It's great fun[23].
Mrs Penrose: You can go to a pantomime at Christmas only.

A song: We wish[24] you a Merry[25] Christmas

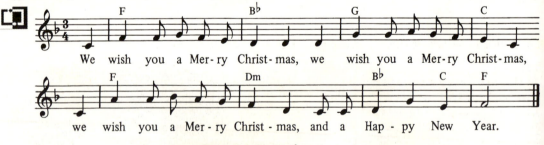

46   forty-six

⟨Revision 1⟩

1 Jenny at Haywood School

Put in 'am', 'is' or 'are'.

David: Here we ..., Jenny! This ... our classroom. – Mrs Dane! This ... my cousin, Jenny Leinert.
Jenny: Hello, Mrs Dane.
Mrs Dane: Hello, Jenny. ... you the girl from Germany?
Jenny: Yes, I ... .
Mrs Dane: Where ... you from in Germany?
Jenny: Berlin.
Mrs Dane: ... your parents German?
Jenny: Well, my father ... German. But my mother ... English. I can speak English, and German, too.
Mrs Dane: Ah! Good! You can help David with his German.
Jenny: Oh – ... I in David's group for German?
Mrs Dane: Yes, you ... . So David ... lucky!
David: Yes, I ...!

2 Who am I?

Now you are Becky Sarah Kim Simon Robert David Mark *or* Jenny .

Play the game with a partner. Example:
You: Who am I?
Partner: Are you a girl?
You: No, I'm not.
Partner: Are you David's brother?
You: Yes, I am.
Partner: Oh, are you Mark?
You: Yes, I am!

Are you — a girl/a boy — ten/eleven/twelve — from England/from Germany — David's cousin/brother — Becky's brother/friend — Simon's sister — ...'s ... ? – Yes, I am. No, I'm not.

3 At the Penroses' house   *the boy's football   the boys' football*

Example:
1. The boys have got a new football.
   – The boys' football is new.
2. David has got a big blue bag.
3. Mark has got a little red bag.
4. The Penroses have got a new CD player.
5. David has got an old radio.
6. Mrs Penrose has got a big computer.

forty-seven **47**

Unit 4

Free time

Step A

The alphabet

David and Jenny are at the Crofts' house. They are in Robert's room. Mark is there, too. He has got a new book.

Mark: Robert! Look at my new ABC book.
Robert: That's nice. – Can you say all the letters in the alphabet, Mark?
Mark: A – B – C – D. Er … E – F … er …
David: It's G! Let's make a rhyme. Then it's easy.
A – B – C – D – E – F – G –
Say the alphabet with *me*!
Jenny: Hey, that's good! Let's go on. Er …
H – I – J – K – L – M – N –
Mark can count from one to *ten*! – Can you, Mark?
Mark: Of course I can! One, two, three …
David: OK. – Now listen. *This* is clever …
O – P – Q – R – S – T – U –
Mark's new shoes are brown and *blue*.
Mark: No, they aren't. They're red and blue!
Jenny: OK. Mark's new shoes are *red* and blue. Now the last letters. Oh yes …
V and W – X – Y – Z –
Now it's late and time for *bed*!
Mark: No, it isn't. That's silly!
Robert: It's time for 'Camera box' now. Let's watch TV.
David: Oh, no. That's boring. Let's read our comics.
Jenny: Oh, you've got a kite, Robert.
Robert: Yes, but it's broken.
Jenny: Well, let's repair the kite and go to the park.

1 A is for APPLE

Find words for the letters in the alphabet. Work with a partner.
Example: Bettina: A is for APPLE.
Claudia: B is for BALL.
Bettina: C is for COMPUTER.
Go on.

2 Spell the words

Markus: Think of a word, Stefan.
Stefan: Apple.
Markus: Can you spell 'apple'?
Stefan: A – P – P – L – E.
Markus: Right. Now it's your turn.

'APPLE' has got two 'p's. So you can say: 'A – double P – L – E.'

 Can you spell your name?

3 Let's read our comics

Work with a partner.

Let's | watch | a salad for tea.
 | play | our comics.
 | read | your old camera.
 | listen to | football on TV.
 | repair | your new CD.
 | make | computer games.
 | | ….

Yes, | OK.
 | great!
 | that's a good idea.

No, | we haven't got time.
 | that's a silly idea.
 | not again!

48 *forty-eight*

Step B

In the living-room

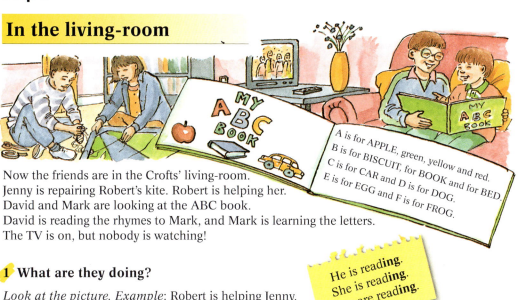

Now the friends are in the Crofts' living-room.
Jenny is repairing Robert's kite. Robert is helping her.
David and Mark are looking at the ABC book.
David is reading the rhymes to Mark, and Mark is learning the letters.
The TV is on, but nobody is watching!

1 What are they doing?

Look at the picture. Example: Robert is helping Jenny.

Robert		watching TV.
David		looking at the book together.
Jenny	is	reading the rhymes to Mark.
Mark	are	repairing the kite.
David and Mark		helping Jenny.
Jenny and Robert		learning the ABC.
Nobody		working together.

> He is read**ing**.
> She is read**ing**.
> They are read**ing**.

> **Is** he read**ing**?
> **Is** she read**ing**?
> **Are** they read**ing**?

2 In the evening

At the Burtons' house

4 At the Dixons' house

a) *Ask your friends questions.*
– What is Simon doing? – He's … .
– What are Mr Burton and Becky doing?
– They're … .

b) *Now ask different questions.*
– Is Simon working in the garden?
– No, he's … .
– Are Mr Burton and Becky …?
– No, they're … .

play a game   read a book   work in the garden   draw a picture   listen to the radio   watch TV

Unit 4

forty-nine 49

Step B

Mrs Croft

Becky: Hi, Robert! We're just going to our house. We've got an idea for the pond. Can you come, too?
Robert: In a minute. I'm just washing up.
Simon: Ugh, terrible.
Robert: Yes, but Mum is working late today. So it's my turn in the kitchen.
Simon: Ah! You're listening to Radio 1.
Robert: No, I'm not listening to Radio 1. It's Radio Nottingham. I'm listening to my mum.
Becky: Your mum? But she isn't at home. Robert, are you crazy or what?
Robert: Of course I'm not. Listen … .

… Hello there! And welcome to 'Tea and Talk', here on Radio Nottingham.

Simon: Hmm??
Robert: There! That's my mum. She's on Radio Nottingham. That's her job.
Becky: Hey, that's an exciting job!

I am work**ing**.
You are work**ing**.
We are work**ing**.

3 What are you doing?

1. *Mrs Penrose:* Colin! What are you doing?
   Mr Penrose: I'm working in the kitchen.

2. *Mrs Burton:* Becky, Simon! What …?
   Becky: We're … . Go on.

4 Let's play a game: What am I doing?

Think of an activity. Then act – and say, 'What am I doing?' Your friends must find out.

"Are you doing your homework?"
"No, I'm not."
"Are you reading a book?"
"No – but your question isn't bad!"
"Er … Are you reading a comic?"
"Right! Yes, I am."

You can play this game with a partner, too and act together

50 fifty

Step B

The idea

Becky and Simon are in their garden. They are looking at the hole. Robert is with them.

Robert: Oh, it's big now. – And what's your idea for the pond?
Simon: Big stones round it.

Robert: Stones? But where can you get them?
Becky: From the hole! – Look, we've got these stones here. And there are more stones in the hole. But we must get them out. And that isn't easy. Can you help us?
Robert: Of course I can help you. Give me the spade!

Unit 4

5 Please help

it   you   us   them

Please put in the right words.

1. *Mrs Croft:* I've got this ham for tea. Please put ... on the table, Robert.
2. *Simon:* These stones are terrible! We can't get ... out. Can you help ..., Robert?
3. *Mrs Burton:* Becky! Maxi and Mini are hungry. Please give ... their biscuits.
Becky: OK, Mum. Maxi! Mini! I've got biscuits for ...!
4. *Mr Penrose:* David! Mum and I are just going out. Can you and Jenny wash up for ..., please?
5. *Mark:* 'Playtime' is on TV. Please watch ... with me, Jenny!
6. *Becky:* Simon and Robert and I are working in the garden, Dad. Can you give ... your big spade?

6 Where are they?

Becky!

Where is / Where are | my lunch box / Dad / the chocolate biscuits / Mum / Maxi and Mini / my new shoes | ? I can't find | them him / it her .

7 Sound practice

[ʌ]
Your brother is funny.
One is my lucky number.
What colour is your pump?

[æ]
There's a black cat in the flat!
Dad! The apples are in that bag.
Pat hasn't got Tabby.

[ʌ] – [æ]
Can I come in?
I'm hungry.
– There's bread and butter with ham and salad.

fifty-one 51

LOOKING AT THE UK:
Free time

1 What are they doing?

In picture 1 they're playing tennis.
In picture 2 … .   *Go on.*

tennis ✓   football   computer games
   cricket   pop music

2 It's great!

Work with your partner.   Example: "Football is boring." – "Yes, it is."

Tennis		great.
Cricket		OK.
Football	is	exciting.
TV	are	boring.
Pop music		terrible.
Computer games		nice.
…		silly.

Yes, it is.
No, it isn't. It's … .
Yes, they are.
No, they aren't. They're … .
No idea.

3 WORD POWER

These are English words – but they are the same in German.
Think of more words like these.
Draw pictures – maybe you can find photos, too – and make a poster.

badminton   tennis   sweatshirt
   pop
       T-shirt   computer

52 fifty-two

Step C

What's the weather like?

In the morning

In the afternoon

In the evening

It's warm and sunny today, and Becky is playing cricket with David.

But now it's windy. Becky and Robert are out with their kites. Jenny is with them.

Becky is going for a walk with the dogs, but the weather isn't nice now. It's raining, and it's cold, too. The dogs are very wet.

Unit 4

1 What can you do today?

Example: It's sunny today. We can play football in the garden, **or** we can go to the park.
It's raining. We can't play outside, **but** we can … .

It's sunny today.		go for a walk. play outside.
It's raining.		listen to CDs. watch TV.
It's warm.	We can	play football
It's wet now.	We can't	sit in the garden. in the garden.
It's very windy today.		
It's cold here today.		play in the house. go to the park. …

2 A song: Sailing
© Polygram Songs Musikverlag GmbH, Hamburg

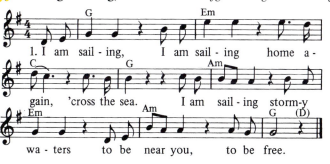

1. I am sailing, I am sailing home again, 'cross the sea. I am sailing stormy waters to be near you, to be free.

2. We are sailing, we are sailing
Home again, 'cross the sea.
We are sailing stormy waters
To be near you, to be free.

3 Listening practice: At home

Listen. Then answer the questions.
a) Where is Becky? And Simon? What's the weather like?
b) What is Robert doing? Is tea ready? Is Mrs Croft watching TV?

fifty-three 53

Step D

The flowerpot

1. It is Saturday morning, so there is no school today. The children are at Robert's house. The weather is cold, but it is not raining.
Robert: Let's go in and watch TV.
David: Oh no!
Sarah: Not again! TV is boring. Let's go out on our bikes.
David: But Jenny can't come with us – she hasn't got a bike here. Let's play football. We can play here.
Jenny: Oh yes! Sarah and I can be one team. And you boys can be the other team.
Robert: OK. We're Team A, and you're Team B. I've got a ball in the garage.

2. The game is exciting. The garage door is the boys' goal. Sarah has got the ball. She is good at football, and now she is kicking the ball.
Jenny: Great, Sarah! Goal!

3. Crash! There is a terrible noise. The ball is in the garage and Mrs Croft's big flowerpot is on the floor. It is broken.
Jenny: Oh, Sarah, look – the flowerpot!
Sarah: It's broken! Oh, sorry, Robert.
Robert: Oh no! Mum's pot! A present from Aunty Audrey.
David: Well, we must tell your mum.

4. Now Mrs Croft is there.
Mrs Croft: Hello!
Robert: Oh, Mum – your flowerpot from Aunty Audrey. It's broken.
David: We're very sorry, Mrs Croft. But we can get you a new pot.
Sarah: Or maybe we can repair it. I –
But Mrs Croft is laughing.
Mrs Croft: That big flowerpot from Aunty Audrey? It's a terrible old thing. I'm not angry about that – of course not.

1 The story

Put the sentences together.

1. It is Saturday today, and …
2. It is cold, but …
3. David and Robert are Team A, and …
4. Sarah has got the ball, and …
5. The ball is in the goal, but …
6. Maybe the children can repair it, or …
7. They are sorry, but …

she is kicking it now.
they can get a new pot.
there is no school.
Mrs Croft's flowerpot is broken.
Mrs Croft is not angry.
the girls are Team B.
the weather is OK for football.

54 *fifty-four*

Step D

2 Tell the story

Can you tell the story?

Start: The children are at Robert's house. They are outside. *Go on.*

children – at Robert's house / outside / cold – but – not raining / football – good idea / boys – Team A – girls – Team B / garage door – goal / now – Sarah – kicking – ball / Crash! / ball – in the garage – but – flowerpot – on the floor / broken / children – very sorry / must – tell Mrs Croft / but – Mrs Croft – laughing / flowerpot – Aunty Audrey – terrible old thing.

3 Can you help?

Put in 'me', 'you', 'him', 'her', 'it', 'us' or 'them'.

1. *Mr Penrose:* Mark can't find his shoes. Can you see … , David?
2. *Jenny:* I haven't got the telephone number for Germany. Can you tell … the number, please, Aunty Pat?
3. *Robert:* David and I can't do this German exercise. Jenny, can you help … with …?
4. *Jenny:* Can I play cricket with …, Robert?
5. *Mark:* Mum, where are my crayons?
   Mrs Penrose: Oh, David. They're on that shelf. Can you get … for …?
6. *Mrs Burton:* Becky is going to the shops, Simon. Can you go with …?

4 They're there – in their beds!

Please write this exercise.
Put in 'there', 'their' or 'they're'.

1. Where are Maxi and Mini? … here!
   … are two beds for them on the kitchen floor.
   They have got … dog biscuits in … beds.
2. Now … playing with Simon.
   Where is … new ball? – Look, … it is.
3. Now Maxi is in the living-room. Mini is …, too. … watching TV together.

5 A new ball – an old bag

'A' or 'an'? Example: This ball is new. – It's **a new** ball. *But:* This bag is old. – It's **an old** bag.

1. This ball is new. 2. This bag is old. 3. This stone is big. 4. This room is untidy.
5. This game is silly. 6. This book is exciting. 7. This kite is good. 8. This exercise is easy!

6 WORD POWER

Find the pairs.
Example: watch – TV.

kick   read   throw

watch ✓   draw   listen

fifty-five 55

Step E

Let's check

1 Robert's photos

Robert is talking about his photos. *Put in 'me', 'her', 'him', 'us' or 'them'.*

1. In this photo, you can see … with Mum.
2. This is Becky. In this picture, you can see … with Maxi and Mini.
3. This is David. Here you can see … with Mark.
4. Here are Sarah and Kim. In this photo you can see … with Tabby.
5. Here I am again! In this photo, you can see … with Jenny.
6. Jenny and I are in this photo, too. Here you can see … with Becky and Simon.

2 WORD POWER

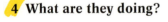

Put the opposites together in pairs. Example: 'Silly' is the opposite of 'clever'.

bad   boring   cold   wrong   good   everything   clever ✓   silly ✓   exciting   right   nothing   warm

3 A wet Saturday   …and… …but… …or…

Put two sentences together – and make one!

1. The weather is cold. It's raining.
2. It isn't nice outside. It's warm in the house.
3. We can play computer games in my room. We can watch TV in the living-room.
4. I haven't got a CD player. We can listen to the radio.
5. We can read comics. We can draw.
6. I've got two new pencils. My crayons are new, too.

4 What are they doing?

1. What's the weather like?
2. What are they doing?
   – Mrs Penrose is … . *Go on.*

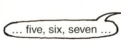

… five, six, seven …

56 *fifty-six*

Jenny's birthday

Step A

A surprise party

David, Becky and Sarah are outside the Penroses' house.

David: Jenny's birthday is in ten days. Let's have a surprise party for her.
Becky: Good idea! I can make the invitations.
David: Yes – we can invite six people from school.
Becky: That's six invitations.
David: Then there are you, Simon, Robert, Sarah, Mum and Dad, Mark, Jenny and me. That's nine people.
Sarah: Six and nine. That's fifteen. We must have a big cake then.
David: I can make it. That's no problem. And I can play the guitar, too.
Becky: Oh great! We can sing.
Sarah: And we can dance, too.

1 Numbers

1	one	(I'm 11) eleven	21	twenty-one	10	ten
2	two	12 twelve	22	twenty-two	20	twenty
3	three	13 thirteen	23	twenty-three	30	thirty
(I'm 4) 4	four	14 fourteen	24	twenty-four	(I'm 40) 40	forty
5	five	15 fifteen	25	twenty-five	50	fifty
6	six	16 sixteen	26	twenty-six	60	sixty
7	seven	17 seventeen	27	twenty-seven	70	seventy
8	eight	18 eighteen	28	twenty-eight	80	eighty
9	nine	19 nineteen	29	twenty-nine	90	ninety
10	ten	20 twenty	30	thirty	100	a/one hundred

(I'm 36)

2 Let's play a game with numbers

Think of a number from 1 to 100. Your partner must ask questions and find your number.

You:	What's my number?
Your partner:	Is it over twenty?
You:	No, it isn't.
Your partner:	Is it under ten?
You:	No, it isn't.
Your partner:	Has it got a five in it?
You:	No, it hasn't.
Your partner:	Has it got an eight in it?
You:	Yes, it has.
Your partner:	Then your number must be eighteen.
You:	Yes, that's right.

fifty-seven **57**

Step A

Jenny's letter

3 Arndale Road
Sherwood
Nottingham
NG5 3GT

Dear Mum and Dad,
How are you? I'm fine. What are you doing in Berlin now? Aunty Pat and Uncle Colin are at their friends' house. David and Mark are outside. It's raining, and they're playing football. How silly! Well, it's my birthday next month – my first birthday in England. That's nice. But it's my first birthday without you, and that's not so nice. But next February we can all have a party together in England.
That's all for now.

Love, Jenny

3 The months

January, February, March, April, May
Let's learn all the months today

June, July and August, too
all these names are new to you

September, October, November, December
but they are easy to remember.

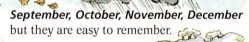

4 Find the months

Can you find the months?
Example: 1. They have got 31 days.
– January, March ... have got 31 days.
2. They have got 30 days.
– ... *Please go on.*
3. It has got 28 or 29 days.
4. These months are warm.
5. And these months are cold.
6. It has only got 3 letters.
7. They have got a 'y' in them.

5 Sound practice

[ən]
I've got‿an‿invitation for you.
I've got‿an‿idea.

[ðiː]
Here's the‿invitation.
The‿idea is very good.

[ə]
It's‿a nice‿invitation.
It's‿a good‿idea.

[ðə]
The new‿invitation is‿on the table
That's the new‿idea.

58 *fifty-eight*

Step B

Everyone is very busy

The children are getting everything ready for Jenny's surprise party. They are all sitting in the Burtons' kitchen. David is making a shopping list. Becky is writing invitations. And Sarah is helping her. Maxi is there, too. She is lying under a chair. She is playing with a balloon.

get – getting
sit – sitting
write – writing
make – making
lie – lying

1 Party invitations

Say what Becky is doing. Example: 1. *Becky is getting a pen. Go on.*

1	2	3	4	5
get a pen	sit at the table	make the invitation	draw a picture	write a name

2 In the afternoon

Example: 1. Mrs Burton: Is Becky playing with Maxi?
             Simon: No, she isn't. She's working with her computer. *Go on.*

Mrs Burton: – play with Maxi?   Mark: – make a cake?   Mr Burton: – do his homework?
Simon: Mrs Penrose: Becky:

Mr Dixon: – write a letter?   Jenny: – listen to the radio?   David: – work in the kitchen?
Kim: David: Mr Penrose:

fifty-nine 59

Step B

What is the date?

3 David's birthday list

first	1st
second	
third	2nd
fourth	3rd
fifth	4th
sixth	5th
seventh	6th
eighth	7th
ninth	8th
tenth	9th
	10th

	11th
eleventh	12th
twelfth	13th
thirteenth	14th
fourteenth	15th
fifteenth	16th
sixteenth	17th
seventeenth	18th
eighteenth	19th
nineteenth	20th
twentieth	

a) *Ask questions and give the answers.*
1. When is Mark's birthday?
   – His birthday is on the thirty-first of August.
2. When is Mrs Penrose's …? *Go on.*

b) *Now talk about all the birthdays in your family.*
– My mum's birthday is on the … .
   When is your mum's …?
– It's on … . *Go on.*

4 My English folder

Make a list with all the birthdays in your family. You can put your friends on the list, too.

twenty-first	21st
twenty-second	22nd
twenty-third	23rd
twenty-fourth	24th
twenty-fifth	25th
twenty-sixth	26th
twenty-seventh	27th
twenty-eighth	28th
twenty-ninth	29th
thirtieth	30th
…	…
hundredth	100th

sixty

Step C

What time is it?

Mark: What's this, Mum?
Mrs Penrose: It's Jenny's present from her parents. It's a surprise! David, can you put the present in my room, please? I must phone Jenny's mother now.
Mark: Can I say 'Guten Tag', Mum?
Mrs Penrose: OK, Mark. Let's see. What time is it?
David: It's quarter past six, Mum.
Mrs Penrose: Oh, then it's quarter past seven in Germany. Jenny's parents must be at home. Let's phone them now.

1 The time

It's four o'clock. It's quarter past four. It's half past four. It's quarter to five.

What time is it?

6.15	8.00	9.30	11.45
4.15	1.00	2.45	7.15
12.30	10.45	5.15	10.00

Unit 5

2 What time is it now?

It's ten to six.   It's four **minutes** to six.   It's twenty past six.

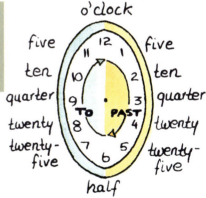

It's twenty past six. No, sorry, it's twenty-two minutes past six.

Can you tell the time?

| 2.15 | 2.22 | 3.20 | 11.10 | 8.05 | 10.25 |
| 11.30 | 4.57 | 9.35 | 1.30 | 7.18 | 10.40 |

sixty-one **61**

Step C

3 Role play: Can you come?

Can you come to / my house / my party / on the 14th / at 3 o'clock / on Saturday / today / this afternoon ?

On the 14th? Yes, I can. Thank you.
Sorry, I can't. It's my friend's birthday.
No, sorry. I haven't got time then.

4 In the classroom

Find the answer to these questions.

1. Sorry, what page are we on?
2. What exercise are we doing?
3. Can you help me with this?
4. Can I write in pencil?
5. What's our homework for tomorrow?
6. Must we do number 4, too?

Yes, number 3 and number 4.
Of course I can.
No, we must write in biro or pen.
We're doing exercise 6.
We're at the top of page 61.
Please do exercise 5 for tomorrow.

 5 Listening practice: A present for Jenny

That's right.   That's wrong.

a) *Right or wrong? Say what is right.*

1. It is 5th February.
2. Jenny is at Sarah's house.
3. Sarah and Robert have got crayons for Jenny.
4. David and Becky have got an idea: a T-shirt with 'Germany' on it.
5. It is quarter to five.
6. Becky must go to the shops.

 b) *Can you go on?*

1. It's Jenny's birthday in … .
2. David, Becky and Mark are talking about … .
3. Sarah and Robert have got … .
4. Now David and Becky have got a good idea: … .
5. They can get the present … .
6. Becky must go home. It's … .

Look. 'U' is the first letter in these words. The sound can be [ʌ] or [ju:].

 6 Sound practice

[ʌ]
[ən] Simon has got an **u**ntidy room.
      Jenny has got an **u**ncle in England.

[ju:]
[ə]   This is a **u**nit with numbers.
      There is a **u**niform at Haywood School.

[ʌ]
[ði:] Mini is in the **u**ntidy room.
      Colin Penrose is the **u**ncle in England.

[ju:]
[ðə] The **u**nit is about Jenny's birthday.
      The **u**niform is blue.

62 sixty-two

LOOKING AT THE UK:
A British house

These rooms are upstairs:

1 the children's bedroom
2 the bathroom and toilet
3 the parents' bedroom

These rooms are downstairs:

4 the living-room
5 the hall
6 the kitchen

Unit 5

1 **What are these rooms?**

1. You can have a bath in this room. It is the … .
2. In this room you can have breakfast or tea. It is … .   *Go on.*
3. You can sit and talk or play games in this room.
4. This room has got a big bed in it.
5. The children have got their things in this room.
6. This is the first 'room' downstairs in a house.

2 **My English folder**

*Draw a plan for a house or a flat.
Put in the rooms.*

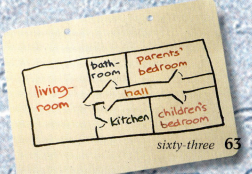

sixty-three **63**

Step D

A great birthday

1. It is 7th February. Robert is in the park with Jenny.
Robert: Are you having a good birthday, Jenny?
Jenny: Well, yes, it's nice, but very quiet.

2. At the Penroses' house. The friends are
5 getting everything ready for the surprise party.
David: Is everyone from school here now?
Sarah: Yes. – Wow! Your cake is great, David.
David: Thanks, Sarah. – What time is it?
Becky: It's five past three. Oh, look, there are
10 eleven candles on the cake – and it's
Jenny's twelfth birthday.
David, have you got another candle?
David: Oh, yes, there's a candle over there.
Sarah: Where's that present from Jenny's
15 parents?
Becky: Look, Robert and Jenny are coming
now. Ssh! Be quiet.

©Musikverlag Intersong GmbH, Hamburg

Hap-py birth-day to you! Hap-py birth-day to you!

Hap-py birth-day, dear Jen-ny. Hap-py birth-day to you!

3. *David:* Hey, Jenny, I'm in the living-
room. Can you come here?
Jenny: Yes, OK. Come on, Robert.
"Surprise, surprise!" "Happy birthday,
Jenny."
Everyone is there: her aunt,
her uncle, her cousins, her friends.
What a nice surprise!

4. *Mark:* Look, Jenny. More presents for you!
Jenny: Oh, thank you, everyone! What's
this? Is it a game? No, it's a book.
David: Well, there's another present for you.
30 *Jenny:* Thanks, David. Let's see.
Oh, a video. What is it?
David: I'm not sure, Jenny. Let's have a look.
Robert: Oh, yes, come on, Jenny.

5. The TV is on and the video
is playing.
Everyone is watching.
Jenny: Oh look, it's Mum and Dad!
And that's our flat!
Mark: That's Aunty Helen!
Jenny: Oh, what a great idea!
It's a great birthday.

64 sixty-four

Step D

1 The birthday

*Can you make sentences for the pictures?
Look at the pictures and at the words.
Example:* 1. Robert and Jenny are in the park.

singing friends are 'Happy Birthday' the

living-room Jenny are Robert in and the now

watching friends Jenny are and the her video

are park Robert in Jenny and the ✓

looking Jenny at her is presents

getting David cake is the ready

2 Where's Mum's CD?

my   your   his   her   its   our   their

1. *Mark:* Let's play a game. Mum's new CD is in the house. Where is it?
2. *Mr Penrose:* Is it in Jenny's room?
   Mark: No, it isn't in … room.
3. *David:* Is it in Mum and Dad's room?
   Mark: No, it isn't in … room.
4. *Jenny:* Is it in David's and … room, Mark?
   Mark: Yes, it's in … room.
5. *Mrs Penrose:* Is it under David's bed?
   Mark: No, it isn't under … bed.
6. *David:* Is it under … bed, Mark?
   Mark: Yes, it's under … bed.
7. *Mrs Penrose:* Is it in … box?
   Mark: Of course it is, Mum.
   Mrs Penrose: Good. Then please put it on the shelf in … living-room.

3 Where are their things?   's   s'

Example: 1. David**'s** cake is on the table. *Go on!*

sixty-five **65**

Step E

Let's check

1 Making a video

Mr Penrose is making a video. It is for Jenny's parents.
Write down what time it is and what Jenny is doing.

1. It's quarter past eight. Jenny is getting … . *Go on.*

get her things for school   go to school   make tea   write a letter   lie in bed

2 House numbers

Write these numbers in words, please.

3 Jenny's birthday list

When are their birthdays?
Example: Aunt Susi's birthday is on the tenth of April.
Go on, please.

4 Months and numbers

Find the months.

What is the | eleventh
first seventh
fifth tenth
ninth sixth | month ?

The eleventh month is November. *Go on.*

5 WORD POWER

Can you put these words in three groups?
1. Months:
2. Time:
3. Party things:

cake   two minutes   candle   March   half past three
December   4 o'clock   game   present   quarter past five
quarter to eight   August   balloon   July

66 *sixty-six*

⟨Patrick's first day⟩

Patrick is the new postman in Sherwood.
Today is his first day. It isn't easy: all the letters
must go to the right houses in the right roads.
He is very careful, but he has got a lot of letters
and packets in his bag. And it's late.
It's ten o'clock in the morning. Oh dear![1]

Now he is in Arndale Road. No letters for
Number 1. Good. The next house is Number 3.
What's this? There are a lot of letters for
Number 3. And four little packets, and a big
packet, too. Is there a birthday at Number 3?
Yes, all the letters and packets are for
"Jenny Leinert". All the letters are from Germany,
the four little packets and the big packet, too.
Is Jenny Leinert from Germany, too?

Patrick is at the door of 3 Arndale Road.
It's five past ten and nobody is at home. But what's that? "Woof, woof!" There's a dog.
Is it in the house? No, it's in the garden behind the house. "Woof, woof!"

There's a letter box in the door. All the letters can go in the letter box. Now all Jenny's letters
are in the house. That's no problem.

But what about the packets? The letter box isn't very big. Patrick can put two of the little
packets through the letter box. That's OK. But he has got two more little packets and a big
packet. What can he do with these packets? Patrick is a clever postman! He has got a great
idea. There's a dog in the garden behind the house. Maybe Jenny Leinert is there, too.
He can give her the packets – and he can say "Happy birthday", too!

Patrick can go round the house and into the garden. Oh, there's a door. Patrick can't open[2] it.
He can't get into the garden behind the house.

"Woof, woof. Woof, woof!" – it's Maxi! She is angry. There is a man at the door.
He is getting into the garden! "Woof, woof. Woof, woof!"

"Maxi! Maxi! What is it?" There is a boy on a bike. He is just coming round the corner.
It is David. "Hey, who are you? What are you doing here?"
"Sorry! I'm Patrick, the new postman. I have got three packets for Jenny Leinert.
I'm only doing my job."

"Oh, Jenny's my cousin. She's living with us. Be quiet Maxi!"
"Here you are." Now Patrick can give David the packets. "What about the dog? Is it always
here?"
"No." David is laughing now. "Maxi is Becky's dog. She's only here this morning.
We're going to the park now."
"Oh, good. And say 'Happy birthday' to Jenny."
"Thank you. It's her birthday tomorrow."

sixty-seven **67**

⟨Nottingham: what can you do there?⟩

It's half past nine on Thursday morning. It's Mrs Dane's English lesson.
The children are sitting in groups. There are five groups of five or six children.
Mrs Dane is talking to the children.
"We've got a very important job today. It's for Jenny. Jenny is new in Nottingham.
5 I think we can help her. We can tell her about all the nice places and things here.
What can she see? Where can she go? What can she do?"

That's a good idea. But how can the children do it?

Mrs Dane has got big pieces of paper for them and a lot of leaflets[1] with pictures
of Nottingham.
10 "You can take the photos out of these leaflets. They are not for children, but there
are nice photos in them. Or you can take photos or draw pictures of other places.
We can't do the posters in one lesson. We can go on next week and finish[2] them.
Oh, and you must write three or four sentences about every picture, too."

This is a nice lesson.

15 It's ten o'clock. The children are very busy. They are all working on their posters.
One group is doing a poster about Robin Hood. They have got a picture of the
Robin Hood statue. The statue is in front of Nottingham Castle. Round the statue
there are pictures of Robin Hood and his friends. The children haven't got photos
of those yet, but they can take them on Saturday.

20 Another group is writing about shopping. There are lots of nice shops in Nottingham.
You can buy[3] nice clothes[4] there. You can get books and comics and CDs – you can buy
everything in Nottingham.

The third group is making a poster
about museums[5] in Nottingham.
25 First of all they've got a list of museums
and a lot of questions.
They must find out the answers.
Then they can write them down
in the next lesson.

30 Two of the children in the fourth group are
football fans[6]. They have got a lot of photos
of Nottingham Forest football team.
That's their poster: football in Nottingham.

Where is the museum?

What can you see there?

Is it good?

Can you do things, too,
not just look at things?

When is it open?

Is it free?

Another group is making a poster about games[7].
35 You can do different games in Nottingham, not only football.
You can play tennis, badminton and hockey in Nottingham, too.
They've got pictures of these games and they are writing about them.

Jenny is very happy. You can see and do a lot of nice things in Nottingham.
She can go to a different place every Saturday or Sunday.

68 *sixty-eight*

⟨Revision 2⟩

1 The Sherwood video

Put in 'me', 'you', 'her', 'him', 'it', 'us' or 'them'.

a) *David:* The video from my aunt and uncle in Germany is very good. Now let's make a video for … !
Jenny: Great idea! 'The Sherwood video'! My parents can watch … on their TV.
Sarah: But we haven't got a camcorder.
Becky: Mrs Croft has! Maybe she can give … her camcorder for a day or two. Let's phone Robert and ask … .

b) It is OK. They can have Mrs Croft's camcorder. But everyone has got different ideas for the video!

Becky: Maxi and Mini are our superdogs. So we must have … in the video! Maxi! Mini! We're making a video – with … .
Sarah: Oh, Becky! OK, but the first scene must have Jenny in … . Then her parents can see … here in England right away.
Jenny: No, they must see … with all my new friends. Let's have everyone in the first scene.
Sarah: Everyone? But who can take the scene for …? Mark? So your parents can only see our legs again?
David: Oh, Sarah! My father can take … . He's in the kitchen now. Let's ask … .

2 All about Sherwood

Can you answer these questions about Sherwood – and the people there?

Examples: "Is there a school in Sherwood?" "Are there three dogs at the Burtons' house?"

– "Yes, there is." – "No, there aren't. There are two dogs at the Burtons' house."

1. Is there a pond in the Crofts' garden?
2. Is there a cat at the Penroses' house?
3. Are there frogs in Arnot Hill Park?
4. Are there four children in the Penrose family?
5. Is there a big tree in the Burtons' garden?
6. Is there a German cousin in the Dixon family?

3 All about Germany

Sarah has got a lot of questions for Jenny. *Can you give Jenny's answers?*

Are there / Have you got

good comics
tutor groups
British bikes
nice houses
school uniforms
chocolate biscuits
video shops
good pop groups

at German schools
in Germany
in German shops

? –

Yes, there are.
  we have.
No, there aren't.
  we haven't.
No idea.
I'm not sure.

4 A house puzzle

a) *Look at all the things.
Make three lists.*
1. upstairs: bed, ...
2. downstairs: telephone, ...
3. outside: car, ...

b) *Where can you put all the things?
Make dialogues with your partner.
Example:*
"Now, let's see. Oh yes!
We can put the telephone in the bathroom."
– "No, that's silly. Let's put the telephone in the hall."
"OK. – We can put ... ." *Go on.*

In town

Step A

In Nottingham

This is the Robin Hood statue. It is in front of Nottingham Castle.

Unit 6

Market Square is in city centre.

The Victoria shopping centre has got a lot of shops and restaurants.

Nottingham is a busy city. There are a lot of people in the streets.
You can see St Peter's Church in this picture. It is near Old Market Square.

1 The city centre

What can you say about Nottingham?
Example: There's a Robin Hood statue in front of Nottingham Castle.
There are a lot of people in the streets.

There's There are	a castle a church shops and restaurants a Robin Hood statue a big square a lot of people	in the city centre. in front of Nottingham Castle. in the Victoria shopping centre. near Old Market Square. in Nottingham. in the streets.

2 In your town

a) *Talk about your town.*
Examples: "We've got a nice market square."
"… is a little town, but it's got nice shops."
"We haven't got a castle, but we've got three churches."

b) *Now make a poster about your town. Find pictures for it and write about them.*

seventy-one 71

Step B

Days of the week

 ⓐ It is half past four on Friday, the last day of the school week.

Jenny: It's Saturday tomorrow, Becky. Let's go into town together. We can look at the shops, and then maybe we can go to the cinema.
Becky: OK. What time?
Jenny: Let's go at eleven o'clock.
Becky: Eleven is too late.
Jenny: Why?
Becky: Because it's so busy on Saturdays. What about ten o'clock?
Jenny: OK then.
Becky: We can get the 88 bus near the end of Larwood Grove.
Jenny: Oh, is it a double decker?
Becky: Yes, it is.
Jenny: That's great. You can see everything from the top of a double decker.
Becky: OK. Ten o'clock at the bottom of Arndale Road. Then we can walk to the bus stop together.

1 Can you go on?

pond ✓   road   week   book
town   tree   alphabet

Example: The little frog is at the bottom **of the pond**.
1. Saturday is the sixth day ... .
2. The cat is at the top ... .
3. The church is in the centre ... .
4. Our house is at the end ... .
5. B is the second letter ... .
6. David is reading. Now he is on the last page ... .

ⓑ
Monday "Oh no, school again!"
Tuesday "An easy day for me. We've got two German lessons."
Wednesday 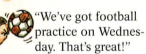 "We've got football practice on Wednesday. That's great!"
Thursday "My turn in the kitchen on Thursday!"

Friday "It's my guitar lesson on Friday. That's nice."
Saturday "The best day of the week – there's no school!"
Sunday "My favourite day of the week. Mum and Dad and David and Jenny are all at home."

2 Why?

Example: Why is Monday a bad day for Sarah?
– Because there's school again.
1. Why is Tuesday easy for Jenny?
2. Why is Wednesday a great day for Simon?
3. Why is Thursday a busy day for Robert?
4. Why is Friday a nice day for David?
– Because he's got ... .
5. Why is Saturday the best day for Becky?
6. Why is Sunday Mark's favourite day?

3 What day of the week?

Look at a calendar for this year. Then ask your partner questions.
Examples: "What day of the week is 1st April?"
– "It's a Monday this year."
"What day of the week is your birthday/your mum's birthday?"
– "It's a ...." Go on, please.

Step C

At the Victoria shopping centre

Becky and Jenny are at the
Victoria shopping centre.
They are trying on clothes in a shop.

Here is Jenny in jeans and in
a pullover. The jeans are OK,
but the pullover is very big!
Becky is wearing black trousers
and a yellow shirt. She is trying on
a yellow anorak. Yellow is her
favourite colour!

1 Clothes

a) What are Jenny and Becky wearing now?
Jenny is wearing a red and blue … .
Go on.

b) *What are you wearing?*
What is your teacher wearing?

2 My English folder

Draw your favourite clothes.
Then write about them.

3 A game: Who is it?

Think of a boy or girl in your class. Look at his or her clothes.
Then the others must ask questions about him or her. You can only answer with
'Yes' or 'No'. Example:

Julia:	I'm thinking of a girl in the class.	Sascha:	Then it must be Annette or Kathrin!
Patrick:	Is she wearing blue jeans?		Is she wearing a red pullover?
Julia:	No, she isn't.	Julia:	Yes, she is.
Melanie:	Is she wearing black jeans?	Nina:	Then it must be Annette.
Julia:	Yes, she is.	Julia:	Yes, it is.

4 Sound practice

[ət]
I'm at Haywood School.
Is Jenny at home?
Let's look at your
photos.

[əv]
That's the end of
the story.
Today is the first of May.
We've got a lot of apples.

[ət] – [əv]
Our house is at the bottom of
Old Street.
We're at the top of page ten.
There are a lot of people at the bus stop.

seventy-three 73

Step C

 Excuse me, please

David is in Old Market Square.
There are a lot of people there today.

Woman: Excuse me, please. Can you tell me the way to the castle?
David: Yes, I can. Go down Friar Lane. Go straight on to the end. Then turn left into Maid Marian Way. Then turn right into Castle Gate. Then you can see the castle on the left.

The way to the castle? I'm not sure.

5 Can you tell me the way?

Make dialogues. Here is an example:

1. Girl: Cinema in Mount Street?
   David: – down Beastmarket Hill and Angel Row. – turn left – Mount Street. – cinema – on right.

   Girl: Excuse me, please. Can you tell me the way to the cinema in Mount Street?
   David: Go down Beastmarket Hill and Angel Row. Then turn left into Mount Street. The cinema is on the right then.
   Girl: Oh, thanks!

2. Man: Victoria shopping centre?
   David: – down Market Street. – turn right – Parliament Street. – straight on – end of Parliament Street. – Victoria shopping centre – on left

3. Woman: St Peter's Church?
   David: – down South Parade. – straight on – end. – turn left – Exchange Walk. – turn left – St Peter's Gate. – church – on right.

6 A game: Draw a castle

Example: Blackstone Castle is very old. It is at the top of a hill. It is behind the trees. There is a road on the right. There is a statue at the bottom of the hill. It is near a tree. There is a pond on the right.

Now draw your picture of a castle. Put a hill, trees, a pond, a statue and a road in the picture. Then your partner must ask questions about it – and maybe draw it, too!

Example: "Is your castle at the top of the hill?" – "Yes, it is."
"Are the trees in front of the castle?" – "No, they're at the bottom of the hill." …

Unit 6

Step C

David's grandma

It is five o'clock on a Tuesday afternoon. David and Robert are at the Twinning Office in Nottingham. David's grandma has got a job there.

David: Hello, Grandma!
Grandma: Oh, there you are, David! Hello, Robert.
David: Can we go and eat at the 'Hot Potato'?
Grandma: Oh yes, that's a good idea. Their 'Hot Potato Special' is very good.
Robert: What's that?
Grandma: It's a big potato with ham and tomatoes and two eggs.
David: Great! – Can we go now?
Grandma: In a minute. I must phone Karlsruhe first.
Robert: Carl Srour? Who's that?
David: Oh, Robert! Karlsruhe isn't a person, it's a town. It's our twin town in Germany.
Robert: Oh!

potato – potatoes
tomato – tomatoes

7 At the Twinning Office

Example: Woman: Hello. Can I speak to Mrs Penrose, please?
Clerk: Sorry. Mrs Penrose … (talk – on telephone)
Mrs Penrose is talking on the telephone.

1. Man: Good morning. Is that Mrs Penrose?
   Clerk: No, sorry. She … (just have lunch). Can you phone again at 2 o'clock?
2. Woman: Hello! My name is Bauer. I'm phoning from Karlsruhe.
   Clerk: Oh, Frau Bauer! Mrs Penrose … (talk to – group of Germans). Please phone again this afternoon.
3. David: This is David Penrose. Is my grandma there, please?
   Clerk: Yes, she's here today. But she … (work – in another room). Phone again in ten minutes, David!
4. Mr Penrose: Colin Penrose here. Can I speak to my mother, please?
   Clerk: Oh, sorry, Mr Penrose. Your mother is busy. She … (phone – office in Karlsruhe). – Oh, she … (just say – goodbye)! – Here she is now!

8 In town

Look at the people in the picture. What are they all doing?
Example: A man and a woman are looking at a map. Go on, please.

Step D

Robert and Jenny in town

1. It is half past five on Saturday afternoon. Robert and Jenny are in Nottingham together.
Jenny: Let's get the bus back to Sherwood now. Our bus stop is near the Victoria shopping centre.
5 *Robert:* Look, Jenny. A bus is coming. Number 37.
It's going to Beeston. That's near Sherwood.
Jenny: Are you sure, Robert? The 88 and 89 are the Sherwood buses.
Robert: The 37 bus is OK, too. Beeston Park is near Sherwood.
Come on, Jenny. Let's get on.
10 *Jenny:* OK then.

2. Six o'clock.
Mr Penrose: It's six o'clock. Tea is ready. – Where's Jenny, David? Isn't she home yet?
David: No, she isn't. Maybe she's at the Crofts' house.
15 But Jenny isn't there. She and Robert are on the way to Beeston – on the 37 bus.

3. Robert and Jenny are sitting upstairs. They can see a big park on the right now.
Jenny: Robert, where are we? This isn't the way to Sherwood.
Robert: It's OK, Jenny. The bus is going a different way, that's all.
20 *Jenny:* Well, I'm not sure. Maybe we're on the wrong bus. Let's ask the driver at the next stop.

4. *Driver:* Yes, you're on the right bus for Beeston.
Jenny: And Beeston Park is near Sherwood?
Driver: Near Sherwood? Oh, no. Maybe you're thinking of Bestwood. Bestwood Park is near Sherwood.
25 *Jenny:* Oh, Robert, you are silly! It's Bestwood, not Beeston!
Robert: Oh, sorry, Jenny!
Jenny: Well, I must phone Aunty Pat. It's six o'clock now, and we're a long way from home.
Robert: No, let's get back to the city centre right away.

30 5. Mr and Mrs Penrose are worried now.
Mrs Penrose: It's half past six. Where can Jenny be?
David: Telephone! Maybe that's Jenny now.
But it is Mrs Croft on the telephone. She is worried, too.

6. Jenny and Robert are back in the city centre.
They are standing at the 88 bus stop.
35 *Jenny:* The next bus is in twenty minutes! That's terrible. I *must* phone Aunty Pat now!
Robert: Look. That red car over there is stopping.
Jenny: Oh, who is it?
40 *Robert:* Hey, it's David's grandma! Hello, Mrs Penrose!
Grandma: Hello, you two! Can I give you a lift?

Step D

1 Is that right?

Example: It is half past five. Robert and Jenny are at home.
– No, that's wrong. They're in Nottingham.

1. The bus to Beeston is number 37.
2. At six o'clock Robert and Jenny are at the Crofts' house.
3. The children can see a big park from the top of the bus.
4. They are on the right bus.
5. Beeston Park is near Sherwood.
6. The Penroses are worried because they aren't sure where Jenny is.
7. Robert and Jenny are on the 88 bus at half past six.
8. Now a red bus is stopping at the bus stop.
9. David's grandma is in the bus.
10. She can give the children a lift.

2  WORD POWER

What can you see in the kitchen?
Work in pairs, and make two lists:
1. a list of the things to eat
2. a list of the other things.
Then check your partner's list.

3 A lot of questions

What   Where   Who   Why   When

Put in the right words.
1. … is the castle? – It's at the top of the hill.
2. … has got a map of London? – I have!
3. … is the name of this road? – Park Lane.
4. … can't we go by car? – Because it's so busy in town on Saturdays.
5. … is the next bus? – At quarter past four.
6. … time is it now? – It's five past four.
7. … is the bus late? – No idea!
8. … is the bus stop? – At the end of this road.
9. …is market day? – On Wednesdays and Saturdays.
10. … can give us a lift into town?
    – My mum can!

4 Listening practice: People in town

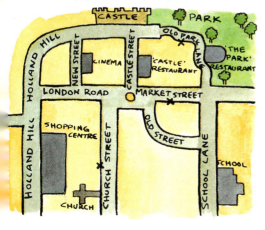

a) *Look at the map. Find the castle, the cinema, the restaurants, the shopping centre and the church.*

b) *Now listen to the first two dialogues. Can you find the way on the map?*

c) *Listen to the third dialogue now. Where is the woman going?*

d) *Now work with the map – with a partner. Ask the way and your partner must tell you.*
1. From School Lane – to the cinema.
2. From the castle – to the church.
3. From the shopping centre – to the castle.

Step E

Let's check

1 Sarah's clothes

Sarah's room isn't very tidy.
Look at all her clothes!
Her jeans are on the floor.
Her ... .
Go on, please.

2 What is different?

in   on   under   behind   in front of   near   round

Example: In picture 1, the apples are on the tree.
But in picture 2, they're under the tree.

3 WORD POWER

This is a letter from Jenny to her friend Sandra in Berlin. *Can you read it?*

78 *seventy-eight*

School days

Step A

Lunch time

ⓐ David: I'm hungry. Let's go to lunch.
Sarah: Hey, look at this. There's a competition.
Becky: A healthy living competition – you must make a poster. Oh, great.
Robert: Ugh, competitions are boring.
Becky: No, they aren't. Look, there are good prizes – a T-shirt, a sweatshirt, … .
Sarah: But I've got a lot of T-shirts and sweatshirts.
David: I'm very hungry. Can you lend me 50p for sausage and chips?
Sarah: How much? Er … No, sorry, I can't.
Becky: Here you are. I can lend you £1.
David: Great! Then I can buy a packet of crisps, too.
Becky: Sausage and chips and crisps for lunch again, David? That isn't very healthy!

ⓑ British money

(Reduced in size)

There are 100 pence (p) in a pound (£).

1 Listening practice: School lunch

Listen to the three dialogues.
How much money must Sarah, Becky and Robert give Mrs White?

seventy-nine **79**

Step B

Jenny's day

3 Arndale Road
Sherwood
Nottingham
NG5 3GT

Wednesday, 27th February

Dear Katharina,
My letter is from England – so it's in English!
Thanks for your letter. So lessons are boring without me? I'm sorry!
Haywood School (my new school) is OK. We start school at 8.45, so I get up at 8 o'clock every morning. That's nice and late for me.
I walk to school with David. Of course we wear school uniform – it's funny. We finish school at 3.30 every day. I come home, have tea and do my homework. In the evening, I play with David and Mark or go to Sarah's or Becky's house.
You see, it isn't boring here. – I must go now. Mark is in bed and I must read him a story. I read him a story every evening.

Love, Jenny

1 My school day

Talk about your school day.
Say when you get up every morning,
　　how you go to school every day,
　　when your lessons start,
　　what you do after school,
　　when you go to bed.

> I go to bed at … .
> Our lessons start at … .
> After school I go to my friend's house and we … or I … or I … .
> I get up at … every morning.
> I go to school by bus (by train) every day.
> I walk to school with … .

2 Free time

go　　play ✓　　play　　go　　make　　work

Say what they do in their free time.
Example: 1. Every Tuesday David and Jenny play tennis. 2. Every … . Go on.

Tuesday 1

Wednesday 2

Thursday 3

Friday 4

Saturday 5

Sunday 6

Step B

Mark's day

Mark gets up very early every morning. He goes into his parents' room.

At 8 o'clock Mr Penrose makes breakfast for the family. Mark helps him. He puts the cornflakes on the table.

At 8.30 Mark gets ready for nursery school.

At 8.40 Mark walks to nursery school with his father.

School finishes at 12.30. Mr Penrose collects Mark.

When Mark comes home, he has lunch. And then he does his 'homework'.

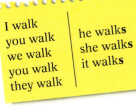

I walk
you walk
we walk
you walk
they walk

he walks
she walks
it walks

Look at these irregular forms.

I go – he, she, it goes
I do – he, she, it does

3 Jenny and Mark

Talk about their day.
Example: Jenny gets up at 8 o'clock every morning, but Mark gets up at 7 o'clock.
1. She walks to school with David every morning, but Mark … with his father.
2. Jenny has lunch at school every day, but Mark … lunch at home.
3. Jenny helps Mr Penrose with tea, but Mark … with breakfast.
4. Jenny listens to music in the evening, but Mark … in the morning.
5. Jenny goes to bed at 9.30, but Mark … at 7.30.

4 Every week

play   go   write   play   make   go   go ✓

Say what they do every week.
Example: Every week, Mr and Mrs Dixon go to the shops.

1. Jenny – a letter to her parents
2. David – to his guitar lesson
3. Becky – tennis at school
4. Mr and Mrs Penrose – a cake for Grandma
5. Sarah and Kim – to the shops
6. Mr and Mrs Burton – badminton

Step B

A busy day

 (a) What is it?
It sometimes goes to school,
  but it never goes to a lesson.
It often makes a noise,
  but it never says a word.
It sometimes has an upstairs,
  but it never has a hall.
It always takes people home and to town,
  because that is its job!
What is it? That's easy. It's a … .

 5 You and your family

Make sentences.
Example: My sister sometimes goes to the cinema.

Look at the word order!

I	always	go to the cinema ✓	draw pictures
My sister	often	listen to CDs	play football
My brother	sometimes	write stories	take photos
My parents	never	go for a walk on Sunday	
		read a book	write letters

 (b) Robert cannot finish his poster for the competition today. He must help in the house. After breakfast Mrs Croft goes to the shops. First Robert does the washing-up. Then he goes upstairs to his bedroom … oh dear, it is in a mess! First he makes his bed. After that he tidies up his desk. That is boring, but he finds an old comic there. He reads the first story. It is very good, so he sits down and reads the next story.

There is a noise downstairs. Mrs Croft is home again! Robert kicks his clothes under his bed and puts his skateboard behind the door. Then Mrs Croft walks in.
"Wow, Robert. Your room looks very tidy now. Well done!"
"Thanks, Mum," Robert says. "Housework isn't bad!"
"Good," says Mrs Croft. "Now we can tidy up the living-room!"

I tidy up – he/she tid**ies** up

6 Robert at home

Say what Robert does.

First Robert does the … .   Then … .   After that … .   After that … .   And then … .

82 eighty-two

Unit 7

LOOKING AT THE UK:
Haywood School

School starts at 8.45. There is an assembly every Monday morning.

Pupils play hockey at school.

Pupils usually have lunch in the school canteen.

Pupils wear school uniform at Haywood School.

There are a lot of activities for pupils at lunch time and after school. For example, they can go to a drama group.

1 My English folder

Here are some words about school.
Can you find more words?
Write them in your English folder.

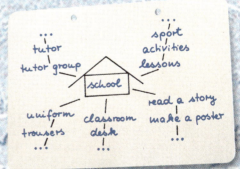

Unit 7

eighty-three **83**

Step C

 The poster

On Sunday the friends are in Becky's garage. They finish their healthy living posters. They go home for lunch. When they come back, they find Maxi and Mini in the garage.

Sarah: Oh, look! Maxi and Mini are on our posters!
Becky: Maxi! Mini! Get out! You're all wet!
David: Ugh! Our posters are all wet and dirty.
Sarah: Well – no prize for us now.
David: Look. Robert's poster is OK here. You can see his legs.
Sarah: Oh, yes. And there's your head, David. It's very big!
Robert: Ha, ha.
Becky: Hey, let's make *one* big poster together.
Sarah: Good idea.

1 WORD POWER

Look at the poster. Say what the numbers are.
Number 1 is Robert's leg. Number 2 is ... . *Go on.*

2 Beetle – a dice game

Take the dice and start the game. You must throw a six first and draw the body in your exercise book. Then it's your friend's turn. When your beetle has everything, you are the winner.

a head   a leg   an eye

a feeler a mouth a body

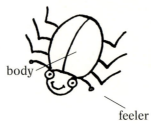
body
feeler

I've got a one (a six, a five ...).
Oh, no. I can't draw an eye.
I haven't got a head!
I can draw a leg now.
Can I have the dice, please?

3 A Song: Head and shoulders

(trad.; Gitarrenakkorde: M. Hauschild)

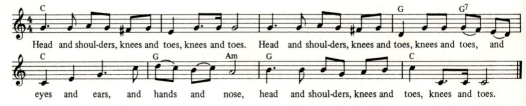

Head and shoul-ders, knees and toes, knees and toes. Head and shoul-ders, knees and toes, knees and toes, and eyes and ears, and hands and nose, head and shoul-ders, knees and toes, knees and toes.

Step C

At the shops

ⓐ *Assistant:* Hello. Can I help you?
Sarah: Hello. Can I have a pound of bananas, please?
Assistant: Yes, of course. Here you are. Anything else?
Sarah: Yes, this pint of milk, please.
Assistant: OK. That's £1.40, please.
Sarah: Thank you. Here you are. Goodbye.

ⓑ *David:* Excuse me. How much is this bottle of lemonade?
Assistant: That's 68p.
David: And how much is this bar of chocolate?
Assistant: 25p.
David: Oh, good. I've got £1. I can buy the chocolate, too.

4 What goes together?

a | bottle
  | packet
  | pound   of
  | bar
  | pint

Make pairs. Example:
A bottle of lemonade, a … of … .

5 Role play: At the shops

Work with your partner. Make dialogues and then act them.

Hello. Can I have a …, please? → Yes, of course. Here you are.

How much …? → It's … .

Here you are. Here's £… . → Thank you. Goodbye.

6 Listening practice: At the supermarket

Listen. What must Mr Penrose, Mark and David get? Find the right pictures.

Step D

The healthy living prize

1. It is Monday morning and the end of assembly. Mrs Benson, the headteacher, gets up and puts a big box on the table.
"Oh, look," David says. "Prizes for the
5 healthy living competition!"
Mrs Benson takes the prizes – a T-shirt, a sweatshirt and a football – and gives them to the three lucky winners – Peter Wall, Annabel Barker and Suvina Adib.
10 "Oh no!" David says. "There's no prize for us!"
"Oh, well," Sarah says. "Maybe next time!"
"Ssh," Jenny says. "Listen!"

2. Mrs Benson starts to talk again.
"I've got an extra prize today," she says.
"It's for a very funny poster. The prize goes to a group in 7MD. Come on, Becky, Robert, Jenny, Sarah and David. Come and get your prize!"
What a surprise for the friends!
They all stand up and walk to Mrs Benson and the box of prizes.

3. "Here you are," Mrs Benson says. "A funny prize for a funny poster. Well done!"
25 "Thank you," Becky says, and she takes the prize from Mrs Benson.
"What is it?" Sarah asks.
"Oh, no," Becky laughs. "Look! Five bars of soap and five bottles of bubble bath!"
30 "Hey, I can't see," David says.
"Be careful, David!" Mrs Benson says. But it is too late. David trips and falls over.

4. "Are you OK?" Jenny asks.
"I'm not sure," David says. "Oh no, my money is all over the floor."
"Here's 50p," Becky says.
"And here's 20p," Sarah says.
"And there's your packet of crisps," Mrs Benson says.
"Oh, no. I'm very sorry." David says.
"And that's your chocolate," Robert laughs.
"Well, David Penrose!" Sarah says,
"You aren't very healthy!"
"And you've got a healthy living prize! That's crazy!" Becky laughs.

Step D

1 Assembly

Put in the right names. Example: 1. Mrs Benson puts a big box on the table.

1. ... puts a big box on the table.
2. ... gives the prize to the winners.
3. ... says: "There's no prize for us!"
4. ... walk to Mrs Benson for the extra prize.
5. ... takes the prize from Mrs Benson.
6. ... get five bars of soap and five bottles of bubble bath.
7. ... trips.
8. ... sees David's packet of crisps.
9. ... finds David's bar of chocolate.

2 Your Sunday

sometimes   never   often   always

Write down what you do on Sunday.
Example:
On Sunday I often get up late.
Go on.

tidy up my room   watch TV
read a book   help Mum and Dad
go and see Grandma   play with my friends
write letters or birthday cards

3 Poor Simon!

Put in the verbs.   **go   buy   put   look   see   fall   go   take**

Tennis is on TV. But Simon can't watch it today. He must go to the shops. He ... the list from the kitchen table and ... at it. He ... to the supermarket and ... a packet of dog biscuits, a pint of milk and other things. After that he ... Becky. They ... back home together. Simon is happy now – he can watch TV. He ... the bag on the kitchen table. But, oh no! The bag ... to the floor. The dog biscuits are all over the floor. Poor Simon – he must tidy up the kitchen now.

4 Sound practice

[v]
David is eleven.
The vet is seventy-five.
Your pullover is very big.

[w]
He always walks to school.
March is always wet and windy.
Wow, you're the winner.

[v] – [w]
It's very warm in here.
Where is Larwood Grove?
We watch TV in the evenings.

5 What time is it?

Fill in the times. Example: 1. Let's play football at half past two.

1. Let's play football at ...
2. Oh no! It's ... and I'm late for school.
3. Can I phone my parents at ..., please?
4. I'm hungry! But it's only ... .
5. Oh, no. It's only ... and Mark is here.

Step E

Let's check

1 What is that?

That is a ... of ...

2 Their day

Correct the wrong sentences.

1. Mr and Mrs Dixon go to the park every Tuesday.
   – No, that's wrong. Mr and Mrs Dixon go to the shops every Thursday.
2. Robert helps his mum with the housework.
3. Becky goes to assembly every Friday.
4. Mark gets up at 9 o'clock every morning.
5. Mrs Penrose makes breakfast every morning.
6. David walks to school with his dad every morning.

3 Kim's activities

Write down what Kim sometimes/often/never/always does.
Example: Kim never makes her bed.

	sometimes	often	never	always
make her bed ✓			x	
go to the shops		x		
do the washing-up	x			
tidy up her bedroom				x
make tea		x		
repair Sarah's bike			x	
help in the garden	x			

 Say what you do in the house.
Example: I often tidy up my bedroom. *Go on.*

4 WORD POWER

Can you repair the broken words? Make a list.
Example: supermarket, ...

5 My mascot

Draw a funny mascot.
Give it a name. Then tell your friends about it.
Example: My mascot's name is Lucky. It has got two yellow legs, a big mouth and six black feelers. It hasn't got ... .

Unit 7

⟨Nottingham castle caves[1]⟩

Wenn du auf unbekannte Wörter im Text stößt, schau nicht gleich in das Vokabular. Lies weiter und versuche, die Wörter aus dem Zusammenhang heraus zu verstehen. So macht dir das Lesen bestimmt noch mehr Spaß.

One Saturday afternoon Sarah, Jenny and Robert meet[2] in front of Nottingham castle.
"What's the castle like?," Jenny asks.
"There are great caves under the castle," Robert says. "I've got my torch[3] with me, so –".
"Caves? Great! Let's go and explore[4] them!" says Jenny.
The three friends buy their tickets[5] and walk to the castle. There are a lot of other people there. The next tour[6] is in half an hour[7].
At 4 o'clock the tour starts. The guide[8] counts thirty people. "Please keep together[9]," the guide says. He takes them through a door and down some stone steps[10]. The stone is cold and wet. The guide tells the group stories about the caves. Sarah and Jenny think it is very exciting, and they walk near the guide and ask him questions. They forget[11] about Robert. They walk up steps and down steps, round corners[12] and into big, cold caves.
Robert is at the back[13] of the group. He thinks the stories are boring. "Good. I've got my torch with me. So I can go and see what's behind those steps over there. Maybe I can find a new cave or treasure[14]."
Suddenly[15] Robert sees something[16] on the floor. It's a bracelet[17]. "Great!," he thinks. "My lucky day! It must be very old. Maybe I can find more treasure." Then Robert sees other steps.

He goes up and round a corner. It is dark[18] and wet there. Robert suddenly trips and falls. He drops[19] the torch. He looks for it on the floor. At last[20] he finds it, but it is broken. It is very dark. "What can I do?" he thinks. "I can't see the way … ."
It is the end of the tour now. The guide counts all the people. "Twenty-eight, twenty-nine … twenty-nine?"
"Where is Robert?" Jenny asks.
"Please, I think our friend is in the caves," Sarah says to the guide.
"Oh no! Silly boy!" says the man. But he is worried. "I must go and look for[21] him."
Sarah and Jenny are worried, too. There is only one other person with them, a woman. But she isn't very happy. "My bracelet," she says. "I can't find it. It must be down in the caves. It's a present from my grandma."
At that moment the guide comes back with Robert. He has the broken torch in one hand, but he is smiling. "Hey, you two. Look what I've got! Old treasure: a very old bracelet." But Jenny, Sarah and the woman are smiling. "I'm sorry," says the woman. "It isn't treasure. It's my bracelet, you see." "Oh," Robert says. "No treasure for me today, only a broken torch. Here's your bracelet." "Thank you," the woman says. "Let's go and have tea together."

Unit 8

The accident

Step A

Money and jobs

ⓐ Sarah always gets her pocket money on Fridays.
She often buys sweets or magazines with it.
She never saves her pocket money!

1 You and your money

Talk about your money.

- I often buy crisps.
- I sometimes save my pocket money.
- I always get comics with my pocket money.
- I sometimes buy a CD.

ⓑ Kim has got a Saturday job.
She sells clothes in a jeans shop.

Sarah: Hey, I like your new shirt, Kim.
Kim: Thanks, Sarah. It's from the jeans shop.
Sarah: You're lucky. You've got a Saturday job.
Kim: Yes. I can buy nice things with the money.
Sarah: I want a job, too. I need money for a new CD.
Kim: Well, you can't be a shop assistant. You're only eleven.
Sarah: I know. Hm. Maybe I can do jobs for the neighbours. I can repair bikes.
Kim: Oh, right! Sarah the bike mechanic!

2 I like it

Has your friend got nice things? What can you say?

- I like your T-shirt. / new pen. / bag. / ring. / pullover. / …
- Oh, thank you. It's a present from … . …

3 People and their jobs

repair   help   work in   work with   sell

What can you say about these people?

1. This woman is a mechanic. She repairs cars.
2. This woman is a … . She … cats and dogs.
3. This … . *Go on.*

90   ninety

Step B

Saturday morning

Kim: Oh no – not 'Two'n'Two'!
Sarah: I like 'Two'n'Two'. They're my favourite group.
Kim: Well, I don't like them. They're terrible.
Sarah: They aren't! They sing great songs.
Kim: Sing? They don't sing – they make a noise!
Mr Dixon: Girls, please! – Look at the time, Kim.
Kim: Oh yes. I must go. – Bye, Dad. Bye, Sarah. Have a nice day with 'Two'n'Two'!

1 Sisters

Sarah is eleven, and Kim is sixteen. So the two girls don't like the same things.
Make sentences about them.
Example: They don't listen to the same music.

They don't | listen to ✓ | | magazines | music ✓
| like read wear | the same | things on TV pop groups
| watch do | | activities clothes

2 Everyone likes different things

Say what you like and don't like.
Examples: "I like red, but I don't like black."
"I like football, but I don't like tennis."

colours	activities & games	pop groups
red	tennis	
yellow	TV	...
brown	computer games	
...	...	

3 Your school

What can you tell an English friend about your school in Germany?
Say what you do and what you don't do.
Examples: We don't wear school uniform. We get homework.

wear school uniform — get homework — finish school at lunch time — have lunch at school — go to school on Saturdays — learn English — work with computers — have assembly — play ... .

Unit 8

ninety-one

Step B

In Edward's Lane

David is on his bike, and Jenny has got Mrs Penrose's bike. They see Sarah with a packet of sweets and a new magazine.

Jenny: Hello, Sarah!
Sarah: Hello, you two.
Here. Do you want a sweet?
David: Oh yes, please.
Jenny: No, thank you, Sarah.
Oh, you've got a music magazine. Do you buy it every week?
Sarah: No, I don't. But this week there's a good poster in it.
David: Do people in Germany listen to English pop music, Jenny?
Jenny: Yes, they do. A lot of English groups are very popular.

David: Hey, Jenny. Look at the time. We must go home for lunch. Come on
Jenny: OK. Bye, Sarah. – Careful, David. Be careful with your bike! – Oh!
David: Aaah!
Sarah: Are you OK?
Jenny: Yes, I'm OK, thanks.
David: Oh, my leg … .
Sarah: Oh, David!

Do you …? – Yes, I do.
            – No, I don't.

4 Do you want a sweet?

Make dialogues. Your answer can be 'Yes, please' or 'No, thank you'.
Example: "Do you want a cake?" – "No, thank you."

5 What about you?

1. Do you listen to English pop music?
2. Do you and your friends like football?
3. Do you and your family watch TV every day?
4. Do your parents like pop music?
5. Do you save all your pocket money?
6. Do a lot of people in Germany play cricket?
7. Do you speak Turkish (Spanish, …)?

	I	
Yes,	we	do.
No,	they	don't.

6 What's popular?

a) *Write 4 questions about different activities.*

Questions	YES	NO
1. Do you read a lot of comics?	IIII	I
2. Do you play badminton?	I	III
3. Do you like computers?	II	II

listen to pop music   watch a lot of TV
play football   like computers
read a lot of books   …

b) *Ask 4 friends the questions.*
Example: "Do you read a lot of books?"
           – "Yes, I do."
           "Do you play badminton?"
           – "No, I don't."

c) *What can you tell the class?*
"Comics are popular. But badminton isn't so popular. And computers aren't very popular."

92   *ninety-two*

Step C

In hospital

David is in hospital now, with a broken leg. Here are all his friends.

Jenny: Hello, David!
Sarah: How are you, David?
David: Oh, OK, thanks.
Robert: How's your leg?
David: Well, it hurts a bit. So please don't sit on it!
Becky: Poor David! I hope you're better soon.
David: Thanks, Becky. – It's good to see you all. The nurses are very nice, but it's a bit boring in hospital.
Robert: Hm. Have you got chocolate biscuits there on your cupboard?
David: Yes, Robert! Here you are. Don't eat them all.
Sarah: Can I write on your leg, David? Please!
David: Hm. OK. But only your name. No funny pictures, please.

1 What you can say to a friend in hospital

Make dialogues with a partner.

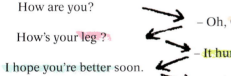

2 A word game: What's my job?

Look at exercise 3 on page 90 for more ideas and words.

You can't do a lot of things when you've got a broken leg – but you can play word games! *Write down the name of a job. Your partner must ask questions and find the job.*
Example: nurse

You: What's my job?
Partner: Do you sell things?
You: No, I don't.
Partner: Do you work in a school?
You: No, I don't.

Partner: Do you help people in hospital?
You: Yes, I do.
Partner: Oh, are you a nurse?
You: Yes, that's right.

3 Sound practice

[uː]
"Do you repair shoes?"
– "Yes, I do. Yes, I do."
"Can I have them back soon?"
– "Yes, at half past two."

[əʊ]
"Phone your mum and say hello."
– "Is she at home now?"
"I don't know."

Unit 8

ninety-three 93

Step C

4 A get well card

*Make a card for a friend in hospital.
Put or draw a picture on the card:*
a present, a girl/boy in hospital, a funny picture, … .
What can you write in your card?

> Get well soon.
>   This card is for you.
>   It isn't the same without you!
> …

5 Please don't!

Can you finish the sentences?
1. **Becky:** This card is a surprise for David, Simon, so please **don't tell** him.
2. **David:** You can have one or two of my biscuits, Robert, but please don't … .
3. **Robert:** The bus goes at 10 o'clock, Jenny, so please … .
4. **Mr Dixon:** You can have £5, Sarah, but … .
5. **Kim:** I like pop music, Sarah, but … .
6. **Mrs Penrose:** Mark is in bed, Jenny, so … .

be late.
make a noise.
play your 'Two'n'Two' CD.
ask for more money.
eat them all.
tell him. ✓

 ## 6 Listening practice: Radio requests

> Do you want a song on the radio?
> Then make a request!

Right or wrong? Please correct the wrong sentences.
a) 1. Anna Hunt's birthday is on April 9th.
   2. She is twelve years old today.
   3. The request comes from her sister.
b) 1. Michael Hilton goes to school by bike. 2. The request is from a girl on the number 19 bus.
   3. The girl has got brown eyes.
c) 1. The third request is for a boy in hospital. 2. David can go home today. 3. The request is from his parents.

 ## 7 Robert's photo

Make sentences about Robert's photo. Can you use all these words

in   on   under   behind   in front of

Example: David is lying **on** the bed
     or: There are books **in** the cupboard.

Unit 8

94 *ninety-four*

LOOKING AT THE UK:
Help!

an ambulance

Do you need help? The number is 999.

the fire brigade

the police

A fireman

B doctor

C ambulance driver

D police officer

1 Look at the pictures

You can call the fire brigade.
You can call an ... . *Go on.*

2 What's their job?

1. He takes people to hospital. He's an ... .
2. She helps people in hospital. She's a ... .
3. She wears a blue uniform. She's ... .
4. He's in the fire brigade... .

3 The UK and Germany

What is the same? What is different?

1. What number must you call in the UK? What about Germany?
2. What colour are police cars in the UK? Are German police cars the same colour?
3. What can you say about the colour of the uniforms? Are they the same in the UK and Germany?

ninety-five 95

Step D

 Fish fingers and ice cream

1. "Goodbye, Jenny. Grandma is on her way here. She can make tea for you and Mark today. OK?"
"Yes, OK, Uncle Colin. Goodbye. And please
5 give my love to David."
It is five past five on Tuesday afternoon.
Mr Penrose is usually at home with the children, but today he is going to the hospital.
Mrs Penrose works for a computer firm.
10 She is working late today.

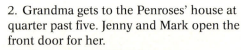

2. Grandma gets to the Penroses' house at quarter past five. Jenny and Mark open the front door for her.
"Hello, you two," Grandma says.
"Do you like fish fingers and ice cream?"
"Oh no, we don't," Jenny laughs.
"We do, we do!" Mark answers. "Don't listen to Jenny, Grandma!"
Grandma laughs, too. "Come on. Let's get the things from the car."

3. They go to the car. Grandma gives Jenny the ice cream. Then she gives Mark the fish fingers. But it is a windy day, and the front door closes behind them.
25 "Oh, come on. Let's go round to the back door," Jenny says.
But at the back door they get a surprise. They can't open the door. It is locked.

4. They can't get into the house.
Mark is hungry. "What can we do?" he asks.
"Must we wait for Mum or Dad?"
"Hm. The fish fingers and the ice cream don't like that idea," Grandma says.
But Jenny is looking at the house. "Aha!" she says. "The bathroom window is open. And there's a ladder in the garage ... ."

96 ninety-six

Step D

1 Tell the story

Can you find the right words? (Don't look at the text!)
1. Mr Penrose is going to the … . 2. And … is working late today. 3. But Grandma can make … for Jenny and Mark. 4. Grandma has got … and … in her car. 5. It is a … day, and the … closes. 6. And they can't … the back door – because it's … . 7. Now they can't get into the … . 8. But the … is open. 9. And there's a … in the garage.

2 Let's go on with the story

a) *Read the endings.*

A	B	C
Grandma climbs up the ladder. She gets into the house through the bathroom window. Then she opens the front door. Now she can make tea for the children.	A neighbour sees Grandma at the top of the ladder. "Who's that?" he thinks. "Maybe it's a burglar!" So he calls the police, and a police car comes.	Jenny climbs up the ladder. But she gets stuck in the bathroom window. Grandma goes to the neighbours' house, and they call the fire brigade.

b) *Talk about the endings.*
Example: I like ending B. It's an exciting ending.

I | like / don't like | ending … . It's a (an) | exciting good silly boring funny … | ending.

c) *Have you got an idea for another ending?*
d) *Now listen to this ending. Do you like it?*

3 Kim's Saturday job

a) Jenny asks Kim a lot of questions about her Saturday job.
What are her questions?
Example: 1. Do you work in a jeans shop?

1. you/work in a jeans shop?
2. the other assistants/work there every day?
3. your friends/buy their jeans from you?
4. you/sell sweatshirts in the shop, too?
5. shop assistants/get a lot of money?
6. you/save your money?
7. your parents/give you pocket money, too?

b) *Give answers for Kim (your ideas!), and make a dialogue. Start like this:*

Jenny: Do you work in a jeans shop, Kim?
Kim: Yes, I do. I work in 'Just Jeans' in the Victoria shopping centre.
Jenny: Do the …? *Go on.*

Step E

Let's check

1 Problems

Can you find all the jobs?
The problem:
1. You and your friend see a burglar.
2. There's a problem with a car.
3. You're in a shop. Your friend wants a red pullover.
4. A cat gets stuck at the top of a tree.
5. Your friend's arm hurts.

You say:
– We must tell that p… o… over there.
– Sorry, but I'm not a …!
– Can't you find a red pullover? Let's ask the s… a… .
– Maybe a f… can bring the cat down.
– You must go and see the d… .

2 Questions and answers

Make questions and answers with **do** **don't**
Example:
1. **Do** Mr and Mrs Burton sell clothes? – No, they **don't**.

1. Mr and Mrs Burton/sell clothes
2. the Crofts/come from London
3. Maxi and Mini/eat dog biscuits
4. Kim and Sarah/like the same music
5. David and Jenny/go to school by bus
6. the friends/wear jeans at school

3 Don't do that!

How can you say 'no' to your friends?
Example: 1. Hey, … look in my bag! *Go on.*

look in

draw on

play with

open

write with

4 What can you do with these things?

Look at the words in the box.
(Have you got more ideas?)
Example: 1. You can eat fish fingers.
(You can buy fish fingers, too.)

1. fish fingers 2. door 3. money
4. ladder 5. song 6. magazine

| to open | to climb up | to eat |
| to read | to save | to sing | … |

5 Just for fun

Please help us. Then we can help you!

A day at the seaside

Step A

On the train

Grandma Penrose, David, Mark, Simon, Becky and Maxi are getting on the train to Skegness.

Grandma: Come on, everyone! Get in, please!
Becky: Oh, look! There are five seats together there. Sorry, Maxi. You must sit on the floor.
Grandma: Oh no! Who has got the tickets?
David: It's OK, Grandma. I've got them.
Simon: Why isn't Jenny here?
David: She's at home. Her parents are coming to Nottingham today.
Becky: Oh, that's nice. Now they're all together again.
Mark: What can we do at Skegness? Can we eat ice creams?
Becky: Yes, of course. We can go to the beach and go swimming, too. Have you all got your swimming things?
David: No, I haven't. I can't go swimming with a broken leg.
Grandma: Never mind, David. We can go to the boating lake.
Mark: Oh, can I come, too, Grandma? I like boats and ice creams, too.
Grandma: It's OK, Mark. We can all have an ice cream at Skegness.

1 What can you do at Skegness?

a) *Look at the pictures. What can you say?*
Example: 1. You can eat ... . Go on, please.

b) *Now you are at the seaside with your friends. What can you do there? Please make dialogues.*
Example: "Let's go to the beach."
– " Oh no. Let's buy ice creams first. I'm hungry."
"OK. But then we can ... ." *Go on.*

2 A song: The sun has got his hat on   © West's Ltd. 138-40 Charing Cross Road, London

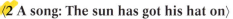

ninety-nine **99**

Step B

At Skegness

Now they are at Skegness station.
They are looking at the map.

Simon: Where's the beach?
Becky: Look at the map.
You go down the High Street.
Simon: Does that road go to the sea?
Becky: Yes, it does. Look – it says 'High Street'.
Grandma: Oh, but the beach is a dog-free zone.
We can't go there with Maxi.
Mark: Oh great, Maxi. You can come with David and me to the boating lake.
Becky: Does your leg hurt, David?
David: No, it doesn't, but I can't go swimming.
Grandma: OK, come on, then. Let's all meet at 3 o'clock on the beach. Then we can go to a snack bar.

Does he/ she/ it ...?
– Yes, he/ she/ it does.
– No, he/ she/ it doesn't.

1 Activities

Say what Becky, Simon and the others do and don't do. Example:
1. Becky: go to the drama group ✗
           go to a music group   ✓
Becky doesn't go to the drama group, but she goes to a music group.

2. Simon: play tennis   ✗
           play football   ✓
3. Sarah: take photos   ✗
           draw pictures   ✓
4. David: play cricket   ✗
           play the guitar ✓
5. Mark: go to school   ✗
           go to nursery school ✓
6. Robert: play the guitar ✗
           take photos   ✓

2 Does Simon like ice cream?

	Simon	Becky	David	Mark
ice cream	✓	✓	✓	✓
fish fingers	✓	✗	✗	✓
sausage and chips	✓	✗	✓	✓
cheese	✗	✓	✓	✗

Work with a partner. Make questions and answers.
Examples: "Does Simon like ice cream?"
– "Yes, he does."
"Does Becky like fish fingers?"
– "No, she doesn't. (But she likes ... .)"

Step B

At the boating lake

Grandma, David, Mark and Maxi are at the boating lake.

Grandma: Here we are. Do we want a boat for one hour?
David: Yes, we do! – Oh, does a boat really cost £5 for one hour?
Grandma: Yes, it does. It's a lot of money.
Mark: Have we got money for a boat *and* ice cream, Grandma?
Grandma: You and your ice creams, Mark. Yes, we have. It's OK. Now, do we buy the tickets over there?
David: Yes, we do. There's a little shop. Do we need a ticket for Maxi, too?
Grandma: I don't know. Does Maxi like boats?
Mark: Yes, she does! Of course she likes boats.

3 Questions at the boating lake

Example: Do they buy the tickets from the little shop? – Yes, they do.

Do Does	they buy the tickets from the little shop? a boat cost £4 for one hour? they need a ticket for Maxi? Maxi like boats? they want a boat for one hour? they take a big boat?	Yes, I/they do. No, I/ they don't. Yes, he/she/it does. No, he/she/it doesn't. I/they don't know.

4 Who am I?

You are a person in the book (Becky, David, ...).
Your friends must ask questions.
You can only answer with short answers. Example:

"Do you go to Haywood School?"
– "Yes, I do."
"Do you play the guitar?"
– "No, I don't."
"Does your mother work for a computer firm?"
– "No, she doesn't."
"Does your father work for a bank?"
– "Yes, he does."
"Then you must be ... ." *Please go on.*

Unit 9

Step B

On the beach

Becky and Simon are on the beach.
They are looking at crabs.

Simon: Where do crabs live?
Becky: Under rocks, I think. Look, there's a crab.
Simon: What do they eat? Bread, maybe. Here, crab. Do you like bread?
Becky: No, it doesn't eat bread.
Simon: Why do crabs live under rocks, Becky?
Becky: Because the water is nice and quiet there, I think.
Simon: I like the water, too.
Come on, let's go swimming.

5 What do crabs eat?

Put in the question words 'where', 'when', 'what', 'how', 'how much'.

1. *Grandma:* ... do we buy the tickets?
   David: At the shop over there.
2. *David:* ... do we meet the others?
   Grandma: At 3 o'clock.
3. *Simon:* ... do crabs eat?
   Becky: Fish, maybe.
4. *Simon:* ... does Mark like?
   David: He likes boats and ice creams.
5. *Simon:* ... do we get to the beach?
   Becky: We can take this road.
6. *Becky:* ... does the train to Nottingham go?
   Grandma: At 4.10.
7. *Grandma:* ... does a boat cost for one hour?
   David: £5.
8. *Mark:* ... do we eat?
   Grandma: We can eat at a snack bar.

6 Where do you live?

Where?	When?	How?	What?
live	have breakfast	go to school	do after school

Make dialogues with your partner.
Example: "Where do you live?" – "I live in .... ."

7 Sound practice

[ð] - [θ]

"It's **the** ten**th**," says Mo**th**er,
"**The** dogs need a ba**th**."
"OK," says my bro**th**er.
"Put **th**em all in **th**e ba**th**."

Then in get **th**e **th**ree.
"**Th**ere's no room for me!"
says my bro**th**er.
"Well, I **th**ink," says Mo**th**er,
"It's your turn next mon**th**!"

LOOKING AT THE UK:
At Skegness

1 Look at the pictures

What can you do at Skegness?
You can go swimming.
Please go on.

2 By train to Skegness

a) When does the first train to Skegness leave Nottingham?
When does the first train arrive in Skegness?
When does the second/third/next train …?

b) *You are at Nottingham station with your friends. Make dialogues.*
Example: "The first train to Skegness leaves at 5.54."
– "Oh no! That's too early."
"When does the next train leave?"
– "Er. At … ."

> Look at the timetable.
> The first train to Skegness leaves at 5.54.
> The first train arrives in Skegness at 8.18.

Unit 9

one hundred and three **103**

Step C

The sandcastle

Now Grandma and Mark are on the beach with Simon and Becky. David and Maxi are watching the friends from the promenade.

Mark: I want to make a sandcastle.
Simon: That's a good idea, Mark. Let's make a castle with water round it!
Becky: I want to get water for the castle. Can I have your bucket, please, Mark?
...
Grandma: Oh, it looks good now. That's a really big sandcastle.
Simon: Oh, look! It's Maxi. What's she doing here?
Mark: Ha, ha. She wants to make a sandcastle, too.
Becky: No, Maxi. This is a dog-free zone here.
Simon: Careful, Maxi. Our sandcastle!
Grandma: Too late! Now it's a very small castle.
Simon: Oh, Maxi! – I think a dog-free zone is a very good idea.

1 Beach activities

Make sentences with 'want to' or 'wants to'.
Example:
1. Mark – make a sandcastle.
Mark wants to make a sandcastle.
2. Simon and Becky – help Mark.
3. Becky – get water for the castle.
4. Maxi – make a sandcastle, too.
5. The friends – come to Skegness again.
6. Mark – eat more ice creams!

2 What can you say?

1. Your favourite group is on the radio. *You think*: I want to listen to the radio.
You ask your mother: Can I listen to the radio, please?
Your mother: Yes, of course./No, sorry. It's time for tea.
2. Your friend has got a new music magazine. *You think*: I want to... *Please go on*.
3. Your friends want to go to the seaside. You like the idea.
4. You and your friend see a chip shop. You're hungry.
5. You and your mother see a very nice blue sweatshirt. You like it.

104 one hundred and four

Step C

At a souvenir shop

David, Mark and Grandma are at a souvenir shop at Skegness.

David: Let's buy two postcards. I want to write to Sarah and Robert from the seaside. How much do the postcards cost?
Grandma: Look, you can get two for 50p. OK. Let's get two.
– What do you want, Mark?
Mark: Can I have that little red boat, please?
Grandma: Let's see, Mark.

3 In the shop

Make dialogues with a partner.

a picture book   two bars of chocolate
a comic

Let's get three postcards. → How much do they cost?
They cost 75 p.
                    OK. Let's get them.

does it   it   £1   It costs
                              80p

4 How much does it cost?   pint   bottle   pound   bar   packet

Example: 1. How much does a pound of apples cost? – A pound of apples costs … . *Go on.*

5 WORD POWER

This is David's postcard to Sarah from Skegness. Can you find the words?

6 My English folder

Find words about the seaside and write them in your folder.

Unit 9

one hundred and five **105**

Step D

Maxi's day at the seaside

1. Hello, everyone! I'm at the seaside today with my pets, Simon and Becky and their friends. Poor Mini is at home because her leg hurts. But it's good for me because I get all the sandwiches.

2. Why do people lie on the beach for hours in their swimming things? Aren't they silly! I don't understand them. The beach is a dog-free zone – so I'm with David. I'm glad because I can help him with his ice cream.
And then I can sleep.

3. I'm with David, Mark and Grandma in a boat on the lake now. What do those silly ducks want? The sandwiches are for me, not for the ducks. I must bark at them. Oh, look at those people in the other boat. They're throwing all their rubbish from their lunch in the water. That's terrible. I must bark at them, too. We need a people-free zone on the lake.

4. What's that over there? Oh – my pets are making a sandcastle. I must help them.

5. No more sandwiches! So I'm taking my pets home. I've got the tickets for everyone. I'm showing them the way to the station so they can't get lost.

Step D

1 Answer the questions

1. Where is Maxi?
2. Why isn't Mini there?
3. What do people do at the seaside?
4. Why does Maxi like the dog-free zone?
5. Why doesn't Maxi like the ducks?
6. What does Maxi do in the boat?
7. Why doesn't Maxi like the people in the other boat?
8. What are the friends doing on the beach?
9. Why does Maxi show her pets the way to the station?

2 Maxi's day

Mark is asking Becky questions about Maxi and Mini.
Can you finish the questions?

Example: 1. ... Maxi ... (get up)? – She gets up very early.
When does Maxi get up? – She gets up very early.
2. ... Maxi ... in the morning (do)? – She plays with Mini.
3. ... Maxi sometimes ... (bark)? – Because we sometimes get angry with her.
4. ... Maxi ... (sleep)? – She usually sleeps in the kitchen.
5. ... Mini ... (sleep)? – She sleeps in the kitchen, too.
6. ... Maxi ... (eat)? – She eats everything.

3 In your beach bag

*You are going to the seaside for the day.
What do you want to put in your beach bag?*

– "I want to put a ball in my beach bag."
– "I want to put a ball and a book in my beach bag."
– "I want to put a ball and a book and ... ."
Can you go on ? Play this game in class.

4 Listening practice: The 4.10 train

a) *Tell the story. Can you find sentences for the pictures?*

Example: 1. The children are in a snack bar at the station and they're hungry.
2. Grandma is ... . *Please go on.*

b) 1. What does David want to eat?
2. What does Mark want to eat? And Simon?
3. Why doesn't Becky want to eat?
4. Does David want to write a postcard to Jenny?
5. Why does Maxi go outside?
6. When does the train leave?
7. What does Mark want to do?
8. Where can Simon eat his chips?

one hundred and seven **107**

Step E

Let's check

1 Questions for Jenny

Mrs Croft is asking Jenny a lot of questions.
Put in 'do' or 'does'. Can you find the answers, too?

1. ... you come from Berlin?
2. ... you like Nottingham?
3. ... your mother speak English?
4. ... Mrs Penrose speak German?
5. ... David speak German?
6. ... you like Haywood School?
7. ... you often write to your friends in Berlin?

2 WORD POWER

You can make 'new' words from old words.
Can you find the 'new' words?

1. You buy it at the station.
2. You wear them in the water.
3. You play with it on the beach.
4. You can buy postcards here.
5. You can go in a boat here.

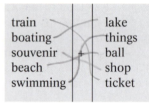

3 Your Saturday

Work with a partner.
Ask questions about your Saturdays.
Example:
"When do you get up on Saturdays?"
– "I get up at ... ." Go on, please.

do you get up on Saturdays?
do you often go on Saturdays?
do you often do on Saturdays?
do you get there?
do you go to bed on Saturdays?
do you do on Saturday evenings?

4 Maxi at home

Maxi can't speak, but you can understand her.
What does she want to do here?

go for a walk ✓   open the door   sleep
get into the car   eat   go outside

Example: 1. She wants to go for a walk. Please go on.

⟨The fun run[1]⟩

Characters[2]: *Tracey, Tommy, Mrs Jones, Mr Jones, Sally, Mr Simpson, Mrs Simpson, Sam, Barry, Helen, Mr Clark, Starter, children*

Scene 1. *It is Saturday morning. Tracey, her little brother Tommy and her father are having breakfast. Her mother comes in.*

Mrs Jones:	Hurry up[3], Tracey. We must go to the shops now.
Tracey:	*(eating her cornflakes)* Mmm. OK. Just a minute. *(Mum goes out.)* Mum, can Tommy come to our fun run this afternoon?
Mrs Jones:	Of course, dear. But come on, now.
Tracey:	OK. Let's go. Bye!
Tommy:	Bye. – Dad, what's a fun run?
Mr Jones:	*(eating his cornflakes)* A fun run? Ah – er – well. Tracey's tutor group needs money for their school trip[4] to Austria[5]. So they run[6] round the playing fields[7] at school. They look for sponsors[8]. A sponsor gives two pounds for one time[9] round. And they give extra money for a funny costume[10].
Tommy:	Are you a sponsor, Dad?
Mr Jones:	Yes, I'm always a sponsor. They have a fun run every year. I give them a lot of money! But you can watch Tracey and her friends this afternoon. It's great fun … . *(They go out.)*

Scene 2. *In the afternoon. Mr and Mrs Jones, Tracey and Tommy are on the way to Tracey's school. They meet Sally in her wheelchair[11] with her parents.*

Tommy:	What's your number for[12], Tracey?
Tracey:	*(as a clown[13] with a big number 3 on her back.[14])* That's my number for the fun run. Hey look, there's Sally! She's got a number, too.
Mrs Jones:	Hello Sally, are you in the run, too? Your wheelchair looks very nice today.
Sally:	Thank you. Yes, I like our fun runs.
Tracey:	But you can't go to Austria with us.
Sally:	No, I can't *(she looks sad[15])*, but I want to help you and get a lot of money for your trip.
Tommy:	Why can't Sally go to Austria?
Mrs Simpson:	Well, she wants to do everything like the other children. But she can't ski[16] … .
Mr Simpson:	And I haven't got a job now, so we haven't got much money.

Scene 3. *Starting point of the race[17]. The children and teachers are getting ready to run.*

Tracey:	Hi Sam. Where's your saxophone[18]? Aren't you playing it today?
Sam:	Of course I am. It's over there. I always play my saxophone. I get extra money for that!
Tracey:	Hey, hi Barry. What are you?
Barry:	I'm a vet, like my dad. Look, this is my dad's bag, and this is my frog and this is my snake. *(He gets a red frog and a blue snake out of his pockets.)*
Sally:	Who's that? *(A fireman is carrying[19] a ladder.)*
Barry:	The fireman? That's Mr Clark, our German teacher.
Tracey:	Hello, Mr Clark. Why are you carrying a ladder?
Mr Clark:	A good fireman always carries his ladder with him.

one hundred and nine **109**

Unit 9

(The children are laughing.)

Barry:	What a crazy teacher!
Starter:	Everyone ready? Right … go!

45 **Scene 4.** *At the start/finish[20].*

Mr Jones:	Look, Tommy, here's Tracey!
Tracey:	Oh, Dad. I'm so tired. I *can't* go round again.
Mr Jones:	Come on, Tracey. Look at Sally!
Sally:	Come on Tracey!
50 *Tracey:*	Oof! OK, here I come! *(Runs off[21] with Sally. Sam runs in with his saxophone.)*
Sam:	Hello, Mr Jones, hello Tommy. Do you like my saxophone?
Tommy:	Yes, I do. Play it, Sam.
Sam:	OK. *(Sam plays 'Oh when the saints[22] …' and goes out.*
55	*Tracey comes in again. She looks sad.)*
Mrs Jones:	It's the break[23] now. Do you feel OK, Tracey?
Tracey:	Oh yes. I'm just thinking about Sally. She really *wants* to go to Austria.
Mrs Jones:	But she can't ski.
Tracey:	Yes, but she can come with us on the plane[24]. And Austria is beautiful[25]! Sally
60	can look at the mountains[26], at the snow[27] and talk to the people.
Mrs Jones:	But the Simpsons haven't got much money just now … . *(They go out.)*

Scene 5. *After the run. The children come with lemonade.*

Barry:	This is great. We've got a lot of money now from our sponsors.
Tracey:	Hey, listen, everyone. *Sally* wants to go to Austria, too. What can we do?
65 *Sam:*	Mm. Let's put all the money together and pay for[28] her ticket.
Children:	Good idea./Oh yes, let's do that./I like Sally./Mm, I don't know.
Helen:	But then there's no money for us, for extra trips … .
Tracey:	Hey, that isn't fair[29]. We can collect[30] more money. We can wash cars for the neighbours or help in gardens … .
70 *Barry:*	Or we can go for walks with neighbours' dogs.
Helen:	OK, OK. You're right. Let's tell her then.
Tracey:	Here, she comes. Sally! You can come to Austria with us! We can pay for your ticket! Can you ask your parents?
Sally:	Really? Oh, that's great!
75	*(Cheers[31], Sam plays his song again, the children sing.)*
Children:	Oh when we go to Austr-i-a, oh when we go to Austr-i-a, Sally's one of our number, when we go to Austr-i-a.

Dieses kleine englische Theaterstück
könnt ihr gut aufführen, z. B. bei
einem Schulfest. Ihr könnt dabei auch
Ideen aus den Fächern Kunst oder Musik
einbauen.

Viel Spaß!

110 *one hundred and ten*

⟨Revision 3⟩

1 At Cleethorpes for the day

It is a Sunday morning in June. The Dixons are at Cleethorpes for the day.
Cleethorpes is their favourite seaside town.

Say what everyone in the picture is doing. Example: Sarah is making a big sandcastle.

2 Kim's postcard

It is Sunday afternoon Kim is writing a postcard to Debbie,
her friend from the 'Just Jeans' shop.
Please put in the verbs.

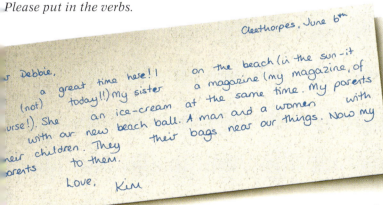

Cleethorpes, June 6th

Dear Debbie,
_____ a great time here!! I _____ on the beach (in the sun – it _____ (not) today!!) My sister _____ a magazine (my magazine, of course!). She _____ an ice-cream at the same time. My parents _____ with our new beach ball. A man and a woman _____ with their children. They _____ their bags near our things. Now my parents _____ to them.
Love, Kim

have	read
play	eat rain
lie	put
talk	come

⟨Revision 3⟩

3 Sundays

The Dixons are talking to their new neighbours on the beach.

Mr Dixon says, "We often ... to Cleethorpes on a Sunday, because we ... the beach. We always ... home early, so we ... a nice long day. Our girls, Sarah and Kim, sometimes ... with us."

come   like   leave   have   go

Mrs Dixon says, "Sarah always ... with us, but Kim doesn't always ... to come. She often ... with her friends at home on Sundays. Sometimes they ... badminton, or they ... to the cinema together."

come   go   play   go out   want

Kim says, "I ... the seaside, but it's nice in Nottingham, too! I ... in a jeans shop on Saturdays. So usually I ... late on Sundays!"

like   work   sleep

4 Different people – different things

Cleethorpes is the Dixons' favourite seaside town – but the Penroses like Skegness best. They often go there when the weather is nice. *Ask questions about*
— *what they like best,*
— *what they always take to Skegness.*

	what they like best	what they take to Skegness
Mr Penrose	the sea	a beach ball
Mrs Penrose	the promenade	a book
David	the boating lake	a camera
Mark	the beach	a bucket and spade

Examples: Does Mr Penrose like the boating lake best?
      – No, he doesn't. He likes the sea best.
      What does Mrs Penrose always take to Skegness?
      – She always takes a book.

5 On the way home

On the way home to Nottingham, Sarah and Kim often play games in the car. Now they are playing "What's my job?" It is Kim's turn, so she thinks of a job, and Sarah asks the questions.

Kim is an assistant at a sweet shop. What are her answers?

Sarah: Do you work with other people? – *Kim:* Yes, I do.
Sarah: Do you work for a big firm?   – *Kim:* No, I don't.

Go on. These are Sarah's next questions.

1. Do you work outside?
2. Do you work at a school?
3. Do you work in a hospital?
4. Do people come to you for something?
5. Ah! Do you work in a shop?
6. Does the shop sell clothes?
7. Does it sell things to eat?
8. Oh. Do you work in a supermarket then?
9. Hm. Do children often come to the shop?
10. Ah! Do you work in a sweet shop?

Play the game with your partner. Find other jobs.

112 *one hundred and twelve*

On a Yorkshire farm

Step A

Springfield Farm

Robert and Mrs Croft are in Yorkshire for five days. They are staying at Springfield Farm, with Mr and Mrs Richards. The farm is also a guest house. Jack Richards is fourteen. He is showing Robert the farm.

Robert: What a lot of sheep!
Jack: Yes, this is a sheep farm really. We've got three hundred and fifty sheep. And that's Sam over there – one of our sheepdogs.
Robert: Oh, lambs, too! They're nice.
Jack: Yes, it's lambing time now. – This is Lenny. He's my special friend. – We've got more animals on the farm: eight cows and six pigs. – But let's go and see the hens now. Grandpa is just feeding them and collecting the eggs. – Grandpa! This is Robert.

Grandpa: Hello, Robert! – Do you like nice big eggs for breakfast?
Robert: Yes, I do.
Grandpa: That's good. We've got twenty-eight hens here, and they all lay good Yorkshire eggs.
Jack: Oh, Grandpa – you always say that!

one sheep – two sheep

1 On the farm

feed   collect   wash up   make   play

What are they doing now? Look at the pictures and say what you can see.
1. Grandpa is feeding the pigs. 2. Mrs Richards ... . *Go on, please.*

2 WORD POWER

What animal is it? *Example:* It gives us milk. – It's a cow.
1. It gives us warm pullovers.   2. It has got a head and a long body – but it hasn't got legs.
3. It is at home in the water.   4. It is often black, and it has got feelers.   5. We get ham from this animal.

What can you say about these animals?

one hundred and thirteen **113**

Step B

Jack's special friend

Robert: Hello, Mrs Richards. What's Jack doing?
Mrs Richards: He's feeding Lenny. Lenny's mother has got three lambs. But she hasn't got enough milk for them all.
Jack: So I feed him with a bottle. I feed him every day.
Robert: Oh, can I feed him?
Jack: Yes, that's OK. Here you are. – It's OK, Lenny. Robert is your friend.
Robert: Hey, he's drinking. Look, Jack!
Jack: Yes, he always drinks all his milk. He's always hungry.
Mrs Richards: Like his friend Jack!

1 In the evening   drink   put ✓   feed   lie   listen

a) It is early evening.
Say what they are all doing.
1. Mrs Richards **is putting** … . *Go on.*

b) It's the same every evening!
1. At half past five Mrs Richards always **puts** … . 2. Jack is at home then, so he always … . 3. Lenny is always hungry, so he always … all … . 4. The cat always … at tea time. (She's hungry, too!) 5. And Grandpa … every evening.

2 Robert: at home and on the farm

walk home   do his homework   go to school
go to bed   listen to 'Tea and Talk'   have lunch

a) *Say what Robert usually does.*

1. At 8.30 in the morning Robert usually **goes** to school.
2. At 1 o'clock he usually … at school.
3. At 4.30 he … from school.
4. At 5 o'clock he … on the radio.
5. At 6.30 he … for school the next day.
6. At 9 o'clock he … .

b) But Robert is on the farm now. So everything is different. *What is he doing now?*

1. It's 8.30 now. Robert **isn't going** to school. He**'s lying** in bed.
2. It's … now. Robert isn't … . He … with the Richards in their kitchen. *Go on, please.*

114   one hundred and fourteen

Step B

3 Mr Richards

Jack's father works at the post office in Northallerton. He drives there every morning, and he comes home at half past five in the evening. So he can only work on the farm in his free time.
Put in the right forms.

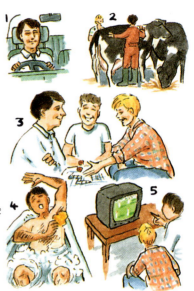

1. (*drive*) Mr Richards is in his car now. He **is driving** to Northallerton. He **drives** there every day.
2. (*help*) Mr Richards usually … his father on the farm after tea. But this evening he … Mrs Richards.
3. (*play*) Jack and his father often … a game in the evening. Now they … a word game with Robert.
4. (*sing*) Now Mr Richards … in the bath. He often … in the car, too!
5. (*watch*) He and Jack sometimes … football on TV. But now they … cricket.

4 Can you tell me?

a) *Ask questions, and your partner must give the answers.*
Examples: Does Mrs Dixon work on a farm? – No, she doesn't. She works for a vet.
    Does Mr Burton work in a shop? – Yes, he does. He works in a bike shop.
1. Mr Richards/in a shop? 2. Mrs Croft/for a doctor? 3. Mrs Penrose/in an office?
4. Mrs Dane/with children? 5. Mrs Burton/in a bank? 6. Mr Dixon/at home?

b) *Make more questions – about you and your friends and family.*
Examples: Do you live in Berlin? – Yes, we do./No, I don't. I live in Neustadt.
    Do your parents speak Italian? – No, they don't. But they speak Turkish.

you you and your friends you and your family your parents	live in Berlin/… play tennis listen to CDs speak Italian …

5 A song: Old MacDonald had a farm (trad.)

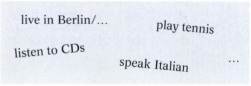

1. Old Mac Do-nald had a farm, E - I - E - I - O. And on his farm he had some chicks, E - I - E - I - O.

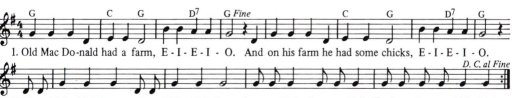

With a chick-chick here, and a chick-chick there, here a chick, there a chick, ev-ery-where a chick-chick.

2. … some ducks (quack-quack)   4. … a pig (oink-oink)
3. … some sheep (baa-baa)   5. … a cow (moo-moo)

Step B

The tractor

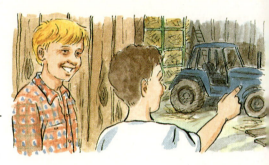

Robert: Hey, a tractor! Who drives that?
Jack: Grandpa usually drives it.
And my mum sometimes does.
I often drive it, too.
Robert: You? But you can't drive a tractor, Jack.
Jack: Who says I can't? It's OK on the farm.
But not on the roads. – And I must ask first, of course.
Robert: Who do you usually ask? Your mum?
Jack: No! I always ask Grandpa. Because he always says yes. – Come on, let's ask him now!

Who helps on the farm? – My dad helps.
Who does he help? – He helps Grandpa.

 6 Jobs on the farm

People Jobs →	feed/pigs	collect/eggs	drive/tractor	work with/sheep
Jack	never	often	often	sometimes
Mrs Richards	sometimes	usually	sometimes	not often
Grandpa	usually	sometimes	usually	often

Ask questions about the jobs. Your partner must give the answers.
Example: Who feeds the pigs?
– Grandpa usually feeds them./Grandpa usually does that job.
Mrs Richards sometimes feeds them, too. Jack never feeds them.

 7 Jobs at home

Ask a partner questions about jobs at home.
Examples: Who makes the breakfast? – My mum usually does that. I sometimes help her.
Who takes the dog for a walk? – We haven't got a dog.

work in the garden   feed the cat   make the beds   do the washing-up

8 Problems

Example: You see a fire! – Who do you call? – The fire brigade! *Go on, please.*

1. Your dog's leg is broken.
2. You don't feel very well.
3. You see burglars in the next house.
4. You don't know the way to the station.
5. You're at a post office and you want to phone your parents in Germany.
6. You can't find the cornflakes on the shelves at the supermarket.

the vet
the fire brigade ✔
the doctor   the police
a person in the street
a shop assistant
a clerk at the post office

116 one hundred and sixteen

Step C

The seasons

ⓐ Mrs Richards is showing Mrs Croft her photos.

"This is Springfield Farm in the spring. There are always a lot of lambs on the farm then."

"A lot of guests come here for their holidays in the summer."

"Look! Here you can see the farm in the autumn. It's often very windy in Yorkshire then."

"Here's the farm in the winter. We sometimes get a lot of snow in Yorkshire. The nights are often very cold here, too."

1 Through the year

Talk about your activities at different times of the year. Here are some ideas:

In the	spring summer autumn winter	I we	sometimes often usually always	play outside. go to the seaside. play in the snow. play tennis/… . go for walks. …

ⓑ In the summer, Jack sometimes makes milkshakes.

When you can't count things: How much?/not much.
When you can count things: How many?/not many.

Jack: "Mum! How much milk do we need?"
Mrs Richards: "Two pints of milk."
Jack: "And how many bananas do we need?"
Mrs Richards: "Four!"

2 Dialogues

Put in 'much' or 'many'.

1. *Jack:* How … sugar do we need for the milkshakes?
   Mrs Richards: We don't need … sugar. Only two or three spoons.
2. *Mrs Croft:* How … lambs does a mother sheep usually have?
   Mrs Richards: Two. Sometimes only one. You don't see … sheep with three lambs.
3. *Grandpa:* How … guests are there this week?
   Mrs Richards: Not … . Two from Monday to Wednesday, and four from Friday to Sunday.
4. *Mr Richards:* How … tea do we need from the supermarket?
   Mrs Richards: We don't need … this week. One big packet is enough.
   Mr Richards: And how … packets of cornflakes?
   Mrs Richards: Three, please.

Step D

Problems on the farm

1. "Mary! We've got a problem. One of the sheep is in trouble. She's waiting for her lambs – but they aren't coming. I think there must be two or three in her, but I'm not sure."
5 Grandpa comes into the kitchen, but he doesn't sit down.
"Let's phone the vet then," says Mrs Richards. "It's OK, Grandpa." She goes to the telephone.
10 "Don't go out again," she says to Grandpa. "You're tired. I can go to the lambing-shed now."
"Can Robert and I come, too?" asks Jack.
"Do you really want to come? You too,
15 Robert? Well, OK, we can wait there together."

2. There is a lot of noise in the lambing-shed. Noise from all the sheep and their new lambs. But one sheep is very quiet.
"There she is," says Mrs Richards.
"Let's hope Mr Smith comes soon."

3. "He's coming! That's his car now."
Mrs Richards goes out and calls the vet.
"Alan! We're in the shed here."
25 Mr Smith comes in and examines the sheep.
"How many lambs are there?" asks Mrs Richards.
"Two," says Mr Smith. "Sorry, Mary, but the lambs inside her are dead. – Well, we must
30 get them out and save the mother. – Jack, take your friend outside. This isn't a nice job."
But Robert wants to stay.

4. Soon the vet's work is finished. Robert is very quiet. He feels terrible.
35 "There's just one thing, Mary," says the vet. "This sheep doesn't feel very well yet. And she's got no lambs. Without lambs they sometimes die …"
"I know that, Alan," says Mrs Richards.
40 "But we've got no baby lambs without mothers now."

5. "Hey – what about Lenny?" says Robert. He feels a bit better now. "His mother can't feed him!"
"Lenny is too old," says Jack. "He's three weeks old now. You can't trick a mother sheep like that."
"Well, wait a minute," says Mrs Richards. "Let's ask Grandpa. Maybe he's got an idea … ."

118 *one hundred and eighteen*

Step D

1 Grandpa's idea

"Yes, I've got an idea," says Grandpa. "It's an old trick. – Jack, give me one of the dead lambs. Right – we just need the skin … . Now you and Robert can go and get Lenny."

Find the right texts for the pictures.
a) It is a surprise for Lenny – but he likes the milk. And his new mother likes him!
b) Grandpa puts the dead lamb's skin round Lenny.
c) Robert and Jack find Lenny in the kitchen. They take him to the shed.
d) Then Mr Smith shows the sheep her new lamb. "Here you are!" he says.

2 Can you get it right?

1. There is a problem with one of the sheep, so
2. Mrs Richards goes to the lambing-shed because
3. Jack and Robert go with her, and
4. Mr Smith examines the sheep, but
5. Robert stays in the shed because
6. The mother sheep needs a lamb, but
7. Lenny's mother doesn't want him, so
8. But Jack thinks there is a problem because

maybe the sheep can feed him.
he wants to watch the vet.
Lenny is three weeks old.
Grandpa is tired.
Mrs Richards phones the vet.
he can't save her lambs.
all the baby lambs have got mothers.
they wait for the vet together.

3 Tell the story again

Can you tell the story again? Finish the sentences. (Can you do it without the text?)

There is trouble on the farm. One of the sheep is waiting …, but … . Mrs Richards phones … . Grandpa doesn't go … because … . But Jack and Robert go with … to … . There they wait … . Mr Smith can't save …, but he can … . Jack doesn't take Robert … because Robert wants … . The sheep really needs …, because sheep without … sometimes … . Robert has got an idea now: maybe the sheep can have …, because … . But Jack thinks it is too late for that because … . But maybe they can trick … . Maybe Grandpa … .

4 Sound practice

[k] – [g]
We've **g**ot two ba**g**s of su**g**ar,
So what **c**an we ma**k**e?
We've **g**ot **c**hocolate and **e**ggs,
So let's ma**k**e a **c**ake!

[p] – [b]
Bo**bb**y is in trou**b**le
And his **p**ro**b**lems never sto**p**.
He's got a jo**b** at 'Su**p**erFish'
But no cra**b** in the sho**p**!

[t] – [d]
Davi**d**, Mar**k** an**d** Robert!
Don't eat all the brea**d**!
Tomatoes are much be**tt**er,
They're nice – an**d** goo**d** –
an**d** re**d**!

Step D

5 Dates and times

Can you answer these questions?

> Aren't you sure? Look at a calendar!

Example: When is the first day of spring this year?
– March the twentieth/The twentieth of March is the first day of spring this year.
– The first day of spring is on March the twentieth this year.

1. When is the first day of summer?
2. When is Mother's Day?
3. When do the next school holidays start?
4. When is the last day of the summer holidays?
5. When is your (your mother's/…'s) birthday?
6. What is the date next Saturday?

6 A new guest me you her him it us them

1. *Mrs Richards:* We've got a new guest this evening: Mrs Walker. We can put … in Room 4. But the bed isn't ready yet.
Mr Richards: I can make … .
Jack: I can help …, Dad.
Mr Richards: Thanks, Jack. But it's an easy job. I can do … without … really!
2. *Mrs Walker:* Hello! You must be Mrs Richards.
Mrs Richards: Yes – and this is Jack. Give … your bags, Mrs Walker. Jack! Take Mrs Walker's bags upstairs for …, and show … the room.
Jack: Right! Come with …, Mrs Walker.
3. *Mrs Walker:* What a nice room! – And I can see the sheep from here.
Jack: Yes. Sam the sheepdog is with … . Can you see …?

Mrs Walker: That big dog? Oh yes.
Jack: We have tea at six. Do you want to have … with … today?
Mrs Walker: Yes, please. And then maybe you can show … the farm.

7 Listening practice: Mrs Richards on the telephone

Can you get everything right?

1. The woman wants three rooms.
2. She wants the rooms for the last week in August.
3. The Greenwoods have got four children: a girl and three boys.
4. The Greenwoods' children are three, six and nine.
5. They have got three dogs. They want to bring them all.
6. Bed and breakfast costs £80. That's for one week.
7. The rooms are free for children.
8. Mrs Greenwood wants to take the rooms now.

120 *one hundred and twenty*

Step E

Let's check

1 WORD POWER

Find the pairs. (Maybe you can make sentences with them, too.)
Example: take – photo
– Let's take a photo of the farm.

take ✔ feed call
drive answer lay
close play

police question door
photo ✔ football
egg tractor animals

2 Sunday afternoon Put in the right forms.

1. It is Sunday afternoon. Jack and his father … (*play*) football. They often … (*do*) things together on Sundays. They sometimes … (*go*) to the cinema in Northallerton.

2. Becky usually … (*go*) out with the dogs on Sunday. Now she and Mrs Burton … (*take*) them to the park. It is a nice day, and the sun … (*shine*).

3. It is 4.30. Sarah and her father … (*make*) tea together. Kim usually … (*help*) in the kitchen. But today she … (*lie*) down. She doesn't feel well.

3 Role play: Mr Penrose's list

Mr Penrose can't go to the shops today. He gives David his list.

David: How much sugar do we need, Dad?
Mr Penrose: Get two packets of sugar, please.

sugar
lemonade
eggs
milk
chocolate
apples

two packets ✔
one pint   two bars
three big bottles
three pounds
two boxes

Go on, please. Ask questions with 'How much?' or 'How many?' Then find the right answers.

4 The people in this book

a) *What do you remember?*

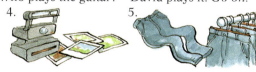

play ✔ read like sell take

1. Who plays the guitar? – David plays it. *Go on.*

b) 1. Mrs Richards – phone – about a sheep?
   Who does Mrs Richards phone about a sheep? – She phones the vet. *Go on, please.*
2. Grandma Penrose – take – to Skegness?
3. the friends – visit – in hospital?
4. Jenny and Robert – see – in a car near the 88 bus stop?
5. the Penroses – collect – at the airport?

A holiday[1] in Scotland[2]

It is a Saturday afternoon in July. The Burtons arrive at a holiday house near Inverness[3] in Scotland. A woman is waiting for them.
"Hello, I'm Mrs McNeil[4]. You must be the Burtons."
"That's right," says Mrs Burton. "This farmhouse[5] looks very nice! What a lovely[6] garden!"
"Yes," says Mrs McNeil, "it *is* a lovely garden. This is our old farmhouse, Tulloch House[7], but it's too big for us."
"And where do you live now?" Mr Burton asks. "We live in a new, small house," Mrs McNeil says.
"Well, Tulloch House is just right for us," says Mrs Burton. "We want a quiet holiday and a lot of long walks." "Woof!" says Mini.
"You can get milk from the Duncan[8] farm. Please be careful with your dogs – the Duncans have a lot of sheep on the hills."
"Oh, our dogs are very good!" Becky says.
"Good," says Mrs McNeil. "Here are the keys[9] and here is our telephone number. Have a nice holiday."
"Thank you, Mrs McNeil. Goodbye."

They all look at the house and are very happy. Tulloch House is a big old farmhouse with apple trees and a stream[10] in the garden. A big tree stands near the back door. The hills are behind the house. Simon is running[11] round near the back door; Becky is climbing an apple tree. Mr and Mrs Burton go into the house with the bags.

The dogs are excited[12]. They are sniffing[13] all round outside the house.
"Come and look at the house, children," calls Mrs Burton. "Bring the dogs."
Mini and Maxi don't want to go into the house. They run round the garden and bark.
"Silly dogs!" says Mr Burton. "Simon, Becky, take them for a walk."

They go for a walk on the hills. The dogs are happy. Then they all run back to the house. Maxi sniffs round the apple trees, Mini goes to the stream.
"Mini, Maxi, come in," says Simon and the dogs go into the kitchen. "Why are you sitting near the door?" Simon asks.
"Maybe they don't like it here," he says to Becky.
"Don't be silly," says Becky. "They want to go into the garden again. They are excited. They can sleep[14] in my room."

In the night Becky wakes up[15]. Maxi and Mini are barking. Mrs Burton comes into Becky's room and asks, "What's all this noise?"
"There's a noise at my window," says Becky. Mrs Burton listens. "It must be the tree outside. It's very windy."
In the morning the children go to the Duncans' farm with Maxi and Mini for milk and eggs.
Mrs Duncan comes to the door.
"Are you staying at Tulloch House?" she asks. "Do you like it?"

122 *one hundred and twenty-two*

"Yes, we do," says Simon.

"Do your dogs like it?"

Simon starts to speak, but Becky says, "Yes, they do." What a funny question, she thinks. In the afternoon the family goes for a long walk over the hills. The dogs are running about[16]. They are happy.

"What a great holiday," Mr Burton says. "The dogs must sleep in the kitchen tonight[17]," says Mrs Burton after tea. "I don't want to wake up in the night again."

But that night Becky wakes up. Everything is quiet. Maybe it is the tree again, she thinks, and soon goes to sleep[18] again.

The next day the Burtons go to Loch Ness[19]. Simon wants to see the Loch Ness monster[20]. They look at the lake all day, but they don't see a monster.

"I don't think there is a monster," says Becky. "But there are a lot of monsters – and ghosts[21] in Scotland," says Simon.

"Don't be silly, Simon," Mrs Burton says. They all laugh. That evening they go to the farm again.

"Are you having a good holiday?" asks Mrs Duncan.

"Yes, thank you," says Simon.

"People don't usually stay long at Tulloch House," Mrs Duncan tells them. "They think there's a ghost, but that's silly. It's just windy here at night."

"Yes, that's silly," says Simon.

But that night Simon wakes up, too. The dogs are barking in the kitchen. There is a crash outside. Simon goes downstairs. He opens the front door, looks outside and finds a broken flowerpot.

"It's OK," he says to Becky and his parents, "just an accident."

Mrs Burton looks worried, but she says nothing.

In the morning Mr Burton asks, "Can you get two pints of milk from the farm, Becky?"

But Becky doesn't want to go. "Mrs Duncan always asks funny questions," she says.

"Oh, she just wants to speak to someone[22]," says Mrs Burton. "There aren't many people here."

"I can go," says Simon.

He goes to the farm with the dogs. The door is open and he can see Mrs Duncan.

"Ah, the boy from Tulloch House," she says. "A storm[23] is coming. You must look after[24] your dogs tonight."

The night is very windy and nobody can sleep. At four o'clock in the morning there is a funny noise again. Maxi and Mini bark and the Burtons all run downstairs. The dogs are barking at the door. Mr Burton opens the door and they all look out. They see a big black shape[25]. It jumps[26] into the stream and then runs away. The dogs want to run after it, but nobody can see the shape now. They look round outside, but everything is quiet. It is not windy now.

"Ooh, it must be a ghost," says Simon.

Mr and Mrs Burton look worried.

"What is it?" Mrs Burton asks.

They all go back to bed, but nobody can go to sleep again.

The next morning Mrs Burton phones Mrs McNeil and tells her about the black shape. "Maybe someone doesn't like tourists? Someone with sheep on the hills?" Mrs Burton asks. "The children think it's a ghost, and the dogs are always so excited … ."

Mrs McNeil laughs, "Oh, I'm sorry, listen. We've got a big black sheepdog. Sometimes he gets out and runs back to the old house. He likes the big garden. He's here now but he's very wet and dirty."

Mrs Burton laughs now, too. "Oh dear[27]," she says, "I'm so glad it's your dog!"

"Come and see us and bring the dogs. Maybe they want to play with him," says Mrs McNeil.

"I must tell the children," Mrs Burton says. "Thank you, Mrs McNeil. We can come and see you this afternoon."

one hundred and twenty-three **123**

Grammar

Hallo,
genauso wie im Straßenverkehr gibt es auch für jede Sprache Regeln. Diese Sprachregeln nennt man **Grammatik**. Die Regeln der englischen Sprache unterscheiden sich in manchen Punkten von den deutschen Regeln. Dieser Grammatikteil fasst die Sprachregeln zusammen, die du aus dem Unterricht kennst. Hier kannst du also nachschauen:
- wenn du Hausaufgaben machst,
- wenn du bei einer Aufgabe unsicher bist,
- wenn du etwas vergessen hast und es nochmals auffrischen möchtest,
- wenn du dich auf eine Klassenarbeit oder einen Test vorbereitest.

Ich will dir die Arbeit natürlich möglichst leicht machen. Deshalb habe ich mir einen Wegweiser für dich ausgedacht:

 Wo die Taschenlampe leuchtet, musst du besonders aufpassen!

Auf einen Blick Hier siehst du auf einen Blick, was zusammengehört. Diese Zusammenfassungen helfen dir auch, wenn du später etwas nachschlagen willst. Gut, nicht wahr?
Wenn du bestimmte Regeln finden möchtest, dann schlage einfach die Seite 143 auf. Dort ist die Grammatikliste.

Let's start

1 Nottingham / 2 Hello

1 "I'm ...."

I'm Sarah.
I'm from Nottingham.

I'm Robert.
I'm from London.

Mit *I'm* kannst du dich selbst vorstellen.

2 "He's ...", "She's ...."

That's Sarah.
She's from Nottingham.

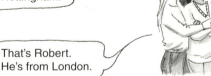

That's Robert.
He's from London.

Mit *he's* und *she's* kannst du eine dritte Person vorstellen und etwas über sie sagen. Für eine weibliche Person (z. B. Sarah) steht *she*, für eine männliche Person (z. B. Robert) steht *he*. Deshalb heißen *he* und *she* persönliche Fürwörter (Personalpronomen).

Let's start

He **is** in my class.
He **'s** in my class.

She **is** from Nottingham.
She **'s** from Nottingham.

Beim Sprechen lässt man das *i* von *is* meistens weg. Wenn du diese **Kurzform** schreiben willst, dann markierst du das ausgelassene *i* mit einem Auslassungszeichen. Dieses nennt man auch Apostroph.

3 "Is she …?" "Is he …?"

Mit *Is she …?* und *Is he …?* kannst du Fragen über eine dritte Person stellen.
Bei diesen Fragen steht das Verb (hier: *is*) am Anfang, genauso wie im Deutschen.
Im Englischen braucht man immer die **Langform**, um diese Fragen zu bilden.
Mehr über die Kurzformen und Langformen findest du bei Punkt 11.

3 School!

4 "Am I …?"

Wie bei Fragen mit *is* (vergleiche Punkt 3) braucht man hier die Langform *(am)*, um Fragen zu bilden.
Das Wort *I* wird immer groß geschrieben.

5 "You're … ."

You're my friend, Sarah.

Wenn du einer anderen Person etwas über sie sagen willst, kannst du *you're* benutzen.
You're ist die Kurzform von *you are*.
Hier wird das *a* in *are* weggelassen.

6 "Are you …?"

Mit *Are you …?* kannst du eine andere Person etwas über sie fragen. Du brauchst die Langform *are*, um Fragen zu bilden.

one hundred and twenty-five **125**

Let's start

4 Tutor group 7MD

7 'My', 'your', 'his', 'her'

I'm twelve.	**My** friend David is eleven.
You're in class ten.	**Your** teacher is Mr Cooper.
He's from London.	**His** name is Robert.
She's a tutor.	**Her** group is 7 MD.

Die Wörter *my*, *your*, *his* und *her* zeigen, wer etwas besitzt oder zu wem etwas gehört. Sie heißen deshalb besitzanzeigende Fürwörter (Possessivpronomen).

You're klingt sehr ähnlich wie *your*:

You're ten. (*Du* bist zehn.)
Your comic is nice. (*Dein* Comic ist nett.)

8 "We're ...", "You're ...", "They're ...."

I'm Robert. That's Sarah. We're friends.

Becky and Sarah, you're late.

That's Mr Cooper and that's Mrs Dane. They're OK.

We, *you* und *they* stehen für mehrere Personen (= Mehrzahl).
You kann *du* heißen (Einzahl), oder *ihr* (Mehrzahl), oder *Sie* (höfliche Anrede).

Beispiele: *David, you're late.* (du)
Sarah and Robert, you're my friends. (ihr)
Mr Cooper, you're my new teacher. (Sie)

9 "Are we ...?", "Are you ...?", "Are they ...?"

We're in 7 MD.   Becky and Sarah, you're in 7 MD, too.   They're our teachers.

Are we in 7 MD?   Becky and Sarah, are you in 7 MD, too?   Are they our teachers?

Wie bei Punkt 6 werden hier die Fragen gebildet, indem man *are* an den Anfang stellt.

10 "It's ...."

David: Where's my pencil?   And my folder?   And my book?

Robert: It's on the desk.   It's under the desk.   It's in your bag.

Wenn du über Sachen reden willst, gebrauchst du *it*. *It* steht für Sachen und kann sowohl *er* als auch *sie* und *es* heißen. Man benutzt *it* außerdem für unbekannte Tiere. Wenn ein Tier einen Namen hat, wird es mit *he* oder *she* bezeichnet.

Beispiele: *That's a dog. It's nice.*   Aber: *That's my dog Mini. She's funny.*

Let's start

5 Haywood School

11 'To be': Kurzformen und Langformen

Jetzt hast du alle Formen des Verbs *to be* kennengelernt. *To be* ist die Grundform (der Infinitiv) und entspricht dem deutschen Wort *sein*. Der Infinitiv wird in bestimmten Fällen mit *to* und in anderen Fällen ohne *to* gebraucht. Bei Überschriften und in Vokabellisten wird er mit *to* angegeben.

f einen Blick

	Langformen (long forms)	Kurzformen (short forms)
Einzahl (Singular)	**I am** from London. **You are** nice. **He is** in my tutor group. **She is** late. **It is** my bag.	**I'm** from London. **You're** nice. **He's** in my tutor group. **She's** late. **It's** my bag.
Mehrzahl (Plural)	**We are** from Nottingham. **You are** my friends. **They are** English.	**We're** from Nottingham. **You're** my friends. **They're** English.

Die Langformen verwendet man:
– beim Schreiben,
  z. B. bei Aufsätzen
– bei Briefen an Fremde.

Die Kurzformen verwendet man:
– beim Sprechen
– wenn man Gespräche aufschreibt
– bei Briefen an Freunde.

Beim Sprechen lässt man oft Buchstaben weg, z. B. hier das *a* von *am* und *are* und das *i* von *is*. Beim Aufschreiben der Kurzformen markiert man diese Stelle immer mit einem Apostroph (Auslassungszeichen).

12 Aussagen und Fragen mit dem Verb 'to be'

f einen Blick

	Aussagesatz	Fragesatz
Einzahl (Singular)	**I'm** late. **You're** my friend. **He's** from London. **She's** nice. **It's** a new ball.	**Am I** late? **Are you** my friend? **Is he** from London? **Is she** nice? **Is it** a new ball?
Mehrzahl (Plural)	**We're** late. **You're** English. **They're** at Haywood School.	**Are we** late? **Are you** English? **Are they** at Haywood School?

Die Frage wird gebildet, indem man die Langformen des Verbes *to be* an den Anfang stellt. Diese Langformen sind *am*, *are* und *is*. Schau auch nach bei den Punkten 3, 4, 6 und 9.

one hundred and twenty-seven

Let's start / Unit 1

Grammar

13 Die Verneinung von 'to be'

Auf einen Blick

I'm not	English.
You aren't	late.
He isn't	German.
She isn't	at Haywood school.
It isn't	on your desk.
We aren't	in tutor group 7 MD.
You aren't	the teacher.
They aren't	in London.

I'm not crazy.

Nur bei *I am* wird *not* in ungekürzter Form verwendet. Ansonsten wird *not* verkürzt (*n't*) und an die Form von *be* angehängt (*isn't, aren't*).

Unit 1

Unit 1   Step A

14 Die Pluralform der Substantive (regelmäßige Formen)
The plural of nouns (regular forms)

one book   four book**s**   a girl   two girl**s**

Um über mehrere Dinge oder Personen zu sprechen, verwenden wir die Pluralform des Substantives (= Mehrzahlform des Hauptwortes). Diese Form ist im Englischen ganz einfach zu bilden: Man hängt ein *-s* an das Hauptwort.

one box   three box**es** [ɪz]   one pencil case   two pencil case**s** [ɪz]

Bei einem Wort wie *box*, das schon auf einen *s*-Laut endet [bɒks], hängen wir ein *-es* an. Wenn ein Wort schon auf *-e* endet, genügt das einfache *-s*, z.B. *pencil case – pencil cases*.

Ist doch ganz einfach, nicht wahr? Hauptwort + *-s/es*.

Die Aussprache des Mehrzahl-*s*/-*es*

book – book**s** [s]	dog – dog**s** [z]	box – box**es** [ɪz]
comic – comic**s** [s]	girl – girl**s** [z]	case – case**s** [ɪz]
group – group**s** [s]	boy – boy**s** [z]	

Bei der Aussprache des Mehrzahl-*s* musst du aufpassen. Nach hart gesprochenen Mitlauten wie 'p' und 'k' wird das Mehrzahl-*s* scharf ausgesprochen: [s].
Nach weich gesprochenen Mitlauten wie 'g' und 'l' und nach den Vokalen 'a, e, i, o, u' und deren Verbindungen mit -y, z.B. *boy*, wird das Mehrzahl-*s* weich ausgesprochen: [z].
-es wird immer als [ɪz] ausgesprochen.

Unit 1 Step B

15 Die Possessivpronomen 'our', 'your', 'their'
The possessive determiners 'our', 'your', 'their'

Mit *our, your, their* kannst du ausdrücken, was zu mehreren Personen gehört oder was diese besitzen. Deshalb heißen sie besitzanzeigende Fürwörter oder Possessivpronomen. Für die Einzahl kennst du schon *my, your, his* und *her* (siehe Punkt 7).

Weißt du's noch? *You* kann *du, ihr* oder *Sie* heißen! (Siehe Punkt 8.) Mit *your* ist es genau so: es kann *dein, euer* oder *Ihr* bedeuten. Das ist doch eigentlich ganz praktisch.

Mrs Dane: Becky, that's your book. *(dein)*
Mrs Dane: Becky and Sarah, Robert is in your tutor group. *(euer)*
Becky: Mrs Dane, here's your book. *(Ihr)*

16 Die Possessivpronomen The possessive determiners

f einen Blick

Einzahl (Singular)	Here's **my** school. Here's **your** pencil case. That's **his** bike. That's **her** computer.	I → my you → your he → his she → her	Wenn man sagt, zu wem etwas gehört oder wer etwas besitzt, verwendet man besitzanzeigende Fürwörter (Possessivpronomen).
Mehrzahl (Plural)	Here's **our** school. Here's **your** teacher. That's **their** tutor group.	we → our you → your they → their	

17 'has got'

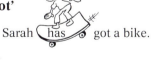
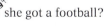

Wenn man sagen will, dass jemand etwas hat, benutzt man *she has got* oder *he has got*. Bei *has got* gibt es genau wie bei *is* und *are* eine Langform und eine Kurzform.

she has got → she's got

he has got → he's got

Hier brauchst du wieder einen Apostroph.

Wenn du wissen willst, wann man Lang- oder Kurzform verwendet, sieh bei Punkt 11 nach.

one hundred and twenty-nine **129**

Unit 1

Die Frage, ob jemand etwas hat, drückt man durch *Has he got ...?/Has she got ...?* aus. Dafür brauchst du immer die Langform. *Has* wird an den Anfang der Frage gestellt. Das *got* dagegen bleibt hinter dem Personalpronomen *she* oder *he*.

Mit *she hasn't got/he hasn't got* kann man sagen, dass jemand etwas nicht hat. Hier wird die Kurzform genauso gebildet wie bei *isn't* und *aren't* (siehe Punkt 13). *Has not* wird zu *hasn't* zusammengezogen. Dabei wird das *not* zu *n't*.

18 'have got'

Wie du bei Punkt 17 gesehen hast, verwendet man *has got* nur bei *he* und *she* (und *it*). Bei allen anderen Personen gebraucht man *have got*. Die Kurzformen von *have got* lauten: *I've got, you've got, we've got, you've got, they've got*.

Die Fragen bildet man genauso wie bei *has got* (Punkt 17).

Die verneinte Form von *have got* ist *haven't got*.

19 'have got'/'has got'
Auf einen Blick

	Aussage (statement)	Frage (question)	Verneinung (negation)
Einzahl (Singular)	I've got you've got he's got she's got	have I got? have you got? has he got? has she got?	I haven't got you haven't got he hasn't got she hasn't got
Mehrzahl (Plural)	we've got you've got they've got	have we got? have you got? have they got?	we haven't got you haven't got they haven't got

So kannst du dir die Formen einprägen:
He has got a dog.
And she has got a frog.
But I and you, we, you and they have got, have got, have got
– a dog and a frog.

Unit 1   Step C

20 Der unbestimmte Artikel   The indefinite article

a [ə]	an [ən]
Is this **a b**all? Yes, that's **a g**ood idea. That's **a c**razy example. Our English teacher has got **a G**erman car.	Have you got **an a**pple? Oh, that's **an o**ld dog biscuit. This is **an e**asy example. The Burtons have got **an E**nglish car.

130   *one hundred and thirty*

Der unbestimmte Artikel (deutsch: ein oder eine) heißt im Englischen *a* oder *an*.
Beispiel: *Have you got an apple?* – Hast du einen Apfel?
Vor einem Konsonanten (**b**all, **g**ood, **c**razy, **G**erman) verwendet man *a* [ə].
Vor einem Vokal (**a**pple, **o**ld, **e**asy, **E**nglish) verwendet man *an* [ən].

21 'This' und 'that'

This weist auf etwas hin, was in der Nähe ist, *that* dagegen auf etwas, das weiter entfernt ist. Deshalb heißen *this* und *that* hinweisende Fürwörter (Demonstrativpronomen). *This* wird oft zusammen mit *here* verwendet, *that* mit *over there*. Nach *this* wird die Langform *is* gebraucht, nach *that* meistens die Kurzform *'s*.

Unit 2

Unit 2 Step A

22 Die Pluralform der Substantive (unregelmäßige Formen)
The plural of nouns (irregular forms)

    a man – four men
one woman – three women
  a child – five children

Einige Substantive haben eine unregelmäßige Form im Plural. Da es nur wenige sind, kann man sich diese Formen leicht merken.

Unit 2 Step B

23 Die Pluralform der Substantive (Besonderheiten)
The plural of nouns (special forms)

one knife [f] – two knives [vz]
  a shelf [f] – shelves [vz]

Auch bei einigen Mehrzahlformen mit *-s* ändert sich die Aussprache – und die Schreibweise. Substantive mit der Endung *-f* oder *-fe* haben im Plural oft die Endung *-ves*.

  family – families
    boy – boys

Substantive, die auf einen Mitlaut (=Konsonanten) und *-y* enden, haben im Plural die Endung *-ies*. Endet ein Substantiv auf einen Selbstlaut (=Vokal) und *-y*, hängt man ein *-s* an. Das *y* bleibt.

Unit 2

24 Das Possessivpronomen 'its' — The possessive determiner 'its'

The CD is in its box.
(... in ihrer Hülle.)

Mit *its* kann man angeben, was zu einer Sache oder zu einem Tier gehört. *Its* ist ein besitzanzeigendes Fürwort (Possessivpronomen), wie z.B. *my, your, her, him* (siehe Punkt 7). *Its* kann sowohl *sein* als auch *ihr* bedeuten.

The frog is in its pond.
(... in seinem Teich.)

Its klingt genauso wie *it's* (=it is). Du darfst die beiden Wörter beim Schreiben nicht verwechseln.

25 Kurzantworten auf Fragen mit 'to be' — Short answers with 'to be'
Auf einen Blick

	YES, ...	NO, ...
Are you Robert Croft?	Yes, I am.	No, I'm not.
Am I in your tutor group?	Yes, you are.	No, you aren't.
Is Mr Dixon a bank clerk?	Yes, he is.	No, he isn't.
Is Sarah in her room?	Yes, she is.	No, she isn't.
Is my pump in the garage?	Yes, it is.	No, it isn't.
Are you from London?	Yes, we are.	No, we aren't.
Are we late?	Yes, you are.	No, you aren't.
Are they in the kitchen?	Yes, they are.	No, they aren't.

Anstatt nur mit *Yes* oder *No* zu antworten, benutzt man im Englischen oft eine *Kurzantwort* mit einem Verb. Kurzantworten klingen höflicher als nur *Yes* oder *No*. Sie setzen sich aus einem Personalpronomen (z.B. *she*) und einem Verb (z.B. *is*) zusammen.

26 Kurzantworten auf Fragen mit 'have got' — Short answers with 'have got'
Auf einen Blick

	YES, ...	NO, ...
Have you got a cat?	Yes, I have.	No, I haven't.
Have I got my lunch box?	Yes, you have.	No, you haven't.
Has he got a knife?	Yes, he has.	No, he hasn't.
Has she got a red bike?	Yes, she has.	No, she hasn't.
Has it got a pump?	Yes, it has.	No, it hasn't.
Have you got our telephone number?	Yes, we have.	No, we haven't.
Have we got the bag?	Yes, you have.	No, you haven't.
Have they got a car?	Yes, they have.	No, they haven't.

Wie bei den Kurzantworten mit *to be* (Punkt 25) sind diese Kurzantworten mit *have got* höflicher als nur *Yes* oder *No*. Du kannst auch hier das Verb aus der Frage für die Kurzantwort übernehmen. *Got* fällt in der Antwort weg.

Unit 2   Step C

27 'These' und 'those'

> Hey! These are my biscuits here, Maxi. Those are your biscuits over there, Maxi. Look!

These ist der Plural von *this,* und *those* ist der Plural von *that* (vergleiche mit Punkt 21).
Mit *these* kannst du auf Sachen oder Personen, die in deiner Nähe sind, hinweisen.
Mit *those* weist du auf Sachen oder Personen hin, die weiter entfernt sind.
Deshalb nennt man *these* und *those* hinweisende Fürwörter (Demonstrativpronomen).

Unit 3

Unit 3   Step A

28 "There is ...", "There are ..."

| There is a girl from Berlin in our tutor group. | In unserer Klasse ist ein Mädchen aus Berlin. |
| There are two big airports in Berlin. | In Berlin gibt es zwei große Flughäfen. |

Mit *there is/there's* oder *there are* kannst du Sätze einleiten, um auf Dinge oder Personen hinzuweisen (ähnlich wie mit *es gibt, es ist, es sind* im Deutschen).
Wenn es sich um *eine* Person oder *einen* Gegenstand handelt, wird *there is* (short form: *there's*) verwendet. Bei *mehreren* Personen oder Dingen steht *there are*. Um Fragen zu bilden, stellst du wieder um: *Is there ...?, Are there ...?*

Unit 3   Step B

> Vergleiche:
> *She can speak English.*
> = Sie kann Englisch.

29 Das Hilfsverb 'can' (Aussage und Verneinung)
The modal auxiliary 'can' (statement and negation)

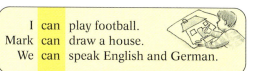

I	can	play football.
Mark	can	draw a house.
We	can	speak English and German.

Mit *can* drückst du aus, dass jemand etwas kann – also eine Fähigkeit. Das Hilfsverb *can* ist in allen Personen gleich. Direkt nach *can* steht das Verb (z. B. *play, draw, speak*) in der Grundform (dem Infinitiv) ohne *to*.

I	can't	do this exercise.
She	can't	draw people.
We	can't	see my Dad in the picture.

Die verneinte Form von *can* [kæn] heißt *can't* [kɑːnt]. Die Langform heißt *cannot* [ˈkænɔt] und wird in einem Wort geschrieben. Auch die Formen *can't* und *cannot* sind in allen Personen gleich.

Unit 3

30 Das Hilfsverb 'can' (Frage und Kurzantwort)
The modal auxiliary 'can' (question and short answer)

Um Fragen mit *can* zu bilden, stellst du das Hilfsverb *can* an den Anfang des Satzes.

Frage	Kurzantwort	
Can you draw a cat?	Yes, I can.	No, I can't.
Can Becky play football?	Yes, she can.	No, she can't.
Can they speak Turkish?	Yes, they can.	No, they can't.
Can you help me with my homework?	Yes, I can.	Sorry, I can't.

Zu den Kurzantworten vergleiche Punkt 25 und 26. Das Verb im Infinitiv fällt bei den Kurzantworten weg.

31 Die Fragewörter 'who', 'what', 'where', 'how'
The question words 'who', 'what', 'where', 'how'

Who's	in the living-room?	Mark.
What's	in your bag?	My books and my folder.
Where's	my English book?	On the table in the kitchen.
How old	is Robert?	He's eleven.

Mit *who* fragt man nach Personen, mit *where* fragt man nach einem Ort.

32 Der s-Genitiv   The s-genitive

Becky's mother has got a green bike.	Beckys Mutter ...
The girl's bike is red.	Das Fahrrad des Mädchens ...
The Penroses' house is in Arndale Road.	Das Haus der Penroses ...
The boys' room is untidy.	Das Zimmer der Jungen ...

Um auszudrücken, dass etwas oder jemand zu einer Person gehört, benutzt man den s-Genitiv. Im Singular hängt man zuerst einen Apostroph (') und dann ein s an das Substantiv. Bei regelmäßigen Pluralformen mit der Endung -s hängt man im Genitiv Plural nur einen Apostroph (') an. Die Aussprache ändert sich nicht.

the girl's room – das Zimmer des Mädchens
the girls' room – das Zimmer der Mädchen

Bei Hauptwörtern mit unregelmäßigen Pluralformen (Punkt 22) wird 's angehängt; z.B. *the children's teacher, the men's folders, the women's cars.*
Vergleiche die unterschiedliche Schreibung im Deutschen:
Mr Dixon's car is green. = Herrn Dixons Auto ist grün.

Unit 3 / Unit 4

33 Die Objektform der Personalpronomen: 'me', 'him', 'her'
The object form of the personal pronouns: 'me', 'him', 'her'

Subjektform	Objektform			
I	Please tell	**me**	about your school.	(mir)
	You can speak to	**me**	in English.	(mit mir)
	You can phone	**me**	at my aunt's house.	(mich)
he	Give	**him**	this pencil, please.	(ihm)
	Let's talk to	**him**.		(mit ihm)
	Can you see	**him**?		(ihn)
she	You can help	**her**	in the garage.	(ihr)
	Let's play with	**her**.		(mit ihr)
	Can you see	**her**?		(sie)

Im Deutschen haben die Personalpronomen *ich*, *er* und *sie* **zwei** Objektformen, nämlich *mir/mich*; *ihm/ihn* und *ihr/sie*. Im Englischen gibt es dagegen für die Objektform von *I*, *he* und *she* nur je *eine* Form: *me*, *him* und *her*.

34 Das Hilfsverb 'must'   The modal auxiliary 'must'

I **must** do my homework now.
She **must** be in the picture, Robert.
We **must** work in the garden this afternoon.

Mit *must* drückst du eine Notwendigkeit oder eine Verpflichtung aus. Das Hilfsverb *must* ist in allen Personen gleich. Direkt nach *must* steht das Verb im Infinitiv ohne *to*.

Unit 4

Unit 4   Step B

35 Die Verlaufsform des Präsens
The present progressive

David is reading a comic. Mark is playing a game. And Becky and Sarah are playing a game, too.

Wenn du ausdrücken willst, was jemand gerade macht, verwendest du die Verlaufsform des Präsens (Gegenwart). Die Verlaufsform (present progressive) wird so gebildet:

Form von 'to be'	Grundform (Infinitiv) eines Verbes	ing-Endung
is		
are	**play**	**ing**

one hundred and thirty-five **135**

Unit 4

Im Deutschen gibt es die Verlaufsform nicht.
Die Bedeutung dieser Form wird deshalb oft mit
gerade, im Augenblick oder *jetzt* ausgedrückt.
Beispiel: *She's doing her homework.*
 = Sie macht gerade ihre Hausaufgaben.
Um Fragen mit der Verlaufsform zu bilden,
stellst du die Form von *to be* (hier: *is*)
an den Satzanfang.

David is reading a comic.

Is David reading a comic?

36 Die Verlaufsform des Präsens (Aussage und Verneinung)
The present progressive (statement and negation)

Auf einen Blick

I'm repairing	my bike.	I'm not reading	a comic.
You're playing	with my game.	You aren't doing	your homework.
He's working	in the garage.	He isn't watching	TV.
She's reading	a book.	She isn't listening	to music.
It's raining.		It isn't raining.	
We're watching	TV.	We aren't helping	Mum.
You're playing	with my computer.	You aren't watching	TV.
They're working	in the garden.	They aren't working	in the kitchen.

37 Die Verlaufsform des Präsens (Frage und Kurzantwort)
The present progressive (question and short answer)

Are you doing	your homework, Simon?	– Yes, I am.	
Are you working	together?	– Yes, we are.	
Is David playing	a game?	– Yes, he is.	
Are you reading	a comic, Becky?	– No, I'm not.	I'm reading a book.
Are you doing	your homework, boys?	– No, we aren't.	We're playing a game.
Is she listening	to the radio?	– No, she isn't.	She's watching TV.
Are they playing	football?	– No, they aren't.	They're playing tennis.

Bei den Antworten verwendet man meist die Kurzantworten mit *to be*.

38 Die Objektform der Personalpronomen   The personal pronouns (object form)
Auf einen Blick

You can phone	me.		I → me
This biscuit is for	you.		you → you
Can we play with	him?		he → him
Can you see	her?		she → her
The frog is in the garden. Can you see	it?		it → it
In this photo, you can see	us	in the kitchen.	we → us
These biscuits aren't for	you,	Maxi and Mini.	you → you
Where are the children? I can't find	them.		they → them

136 *one hundred and thirty-six*

Unit 5

Unit 5 Step B

39 Die Verlaufsform des Präsens (unregelmäßige Formen)
The present progressive (irregular forms)

Die Verlaufsform des Präsens hast du schon unter Punkt 35 kennengelernt.
Hier geht es um einige unregelmäßige Formen.

Sarah	is making	a poster. → mak~~e~~ + ing
Jenny	is writing	a letter. → writ~~e~~ + ing
Robert	is getting	the tea ready. → get + t + ing
Mini	is sitting	under the bed. → sit + t + ing
Mark	is lying	on the floor. → l~~ie~~ + y + ing

Um die Verlaufsform bestimmter Verben zu bilden, fällt das stumme *-e* am Ende des Verbes weg. Verben mit einem kurzen, betonten Vokal vor dem Endkonsonanten verdoppeln den Endkonsonanten; *ie* am Ende eines Verbes wird zu *y*.

40 Die Ordnungszahlen 1.–100.   The ordinal numbers

first	1st	eleventh	11th	twenty-first	21st	tenth	10th
second	2nd	twelfth	12th	twenty-second	22nd	twentieth	20th
third	3rd	thirteenth	13th	twenty-third	23rd	thirtieth	30th
fourth	4th	fourteenth	14th	twenty-fourth	24th	fortieth	40th
fifth	5th	fifteenth	15th	twenty-fifth	25th	fiftieth	50th
sixth	6th	sixteenth	16th	twenty-sixth	26th	sixtieth	60th
seventh	7th	seventeenth	17th	twenty-seventh	27th	seventieth	70th
eighth	8th	eighteenth	18th	twenty-eighth	28th	eightieth	80th
ninth	9th	nineteenth	19th	twenty-ninth	29th	ninetieth	90th
tenth	10th	twentieth	20th	thirtieth	30th	one hundredth	100th

Erster, zweiter, dritter usw. sind Ordnungszahlen. Im Deutschen bildest du sie, indem du *-ter* an die Zahl anhängst (z. B. *vierter, fünfter, sechster*).
Im Englischen hängt man in der Regel *-th* an (z. B. *fourth, fifth, sixth*). Dabei ändert sich in einigen Fällen die Schreibweise der Zahl.
First, second und *third* haben andere Endungen, die auch für zusammengesetzte Zahlen gelten (*thirty-first, forty-second, fifty-third*).

41 Das Datum   The date

Man schreibt:

31st December
oder
December 31st

Man spricht:

"The thirty-first of December"
oder
"December the thirty-first"

Unit 5

Unit 5 Step C

42 Die Uhrzeit   The time

It's 5 o'clock – time for tea! (fünf Uhr)
It's half past 8. Jenny is going to school. (halb neun)
It's 3 minutes to 9. Mr Dixon is late. (drei Minuten vor neun)

quarter past

quarter to

Im Englischen benutzt man *past* bei Zeitangaben für die ersten 30 Minuten nach der vollen Stunde, z. B.:
5.05 = *five past five*
5.10 = *ten past five*
5.15 = *quarter past five*
5.30 = *half past five* (halb sechs)

Nach *half past* zählt man zur nächsten Stunde hin:

5.35 = *twenty-five to six*
5.45 = *quarter to six*
5.55 = *five to six*

o'clock wird nur bei vollen Stunden verwendet: *5 o'clock, 8 o'clock* etc.

Bei Fünferzahlen (5, 10, 15 usw.) fehlt gewöhnlich das Wort *minutes*. Bei anderen Minutenangaben musst du *minutes* hinzufügen, z. B.:
5.16 = *sixteen minutes past five*
5.48 = *twelve minutes to six*

43 Der bestimmte Artikel
The definite article

Während es im Deutschen **der, die** und **das** gibt, wird im Englischen immer *the* verwendet (also für männliche und weibliche Personen und für Sachen im Singular und im Plural).

the [ðə]	the [ði:]
the banana	the apple
the tidy room	the untidy room
the unit	
the uniform	

The kann man [ðə] oder [ði:] aussprechen.
Die Aussprache von *the* richtet sich nach der Aussprache des Anfangslauts des folgenden Wortes. Das Wort *uniform* beginnt zwar mit einem Vokal, wird aber [ˈjuːnɪfɔːm] ausgesprochen.
In diesem Fall wird *the* als [ðə] ausgesprochen.
Vor allen anderen Vokalen wird es zu [ði:].

Das Gleiche gilt auch für *a* und *an* (s. Punkt 20). Es heißt **an u**ncle [ən ˈʌŋkl], aber **a u**nit [ə ˈjuːnɪt].

Let's start

Unit 6

Unit 6 Step B

44 Der of-Genitiv The of-genitive

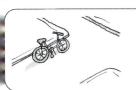 There is a bike at the **end of the road.** It is **Robert's** bike.	 Monday is the first **day of the week.** **Jenny's** birthday is on Monday.

Der of-Genitiv gibt an, welcher *Sache* etwas zugeordnet ist. Der s-Genitiv gibt an, welcher *Person* oder welchen *Personen* etwas gehört oder zugeordnet ist (siehe auch Punkt 32).

Unit 7

Unit 7 Step B

45 Die einfache Form des Präsens The simple present

f einen Blick

I	play	football.
You	play	badminton.
He	play**s**	tennis.
She	play**s**	tennis, too.
The dog	play**s**	with the balloon.
We	play	cricket at school.
You	play	football.
They	play	in a team.

He, she, it, **s** muss mit.

Bei *I, you, we* und *they* hat die einfache Form des Präsens die gleiche Form wie der Infinitiv (ohne *to*).

Bei *he, she, it* wird ein -s angehängt.

Die Aussprache und Schreibung der Verben nach *he, she, it* (3. Person Singular) folgen den gleichen Regeln wie die Pluralform der Substantive (vergleiche mit Punkt 14).

Es gibt aber Besonderheiten:

 I go [gəʊ] – she goes [gəʊz]

I do [duː] – he does [dʌz]

I say [seɪ] – she says [sez]

Bei der Aussprache von *does, goes* und *says* musst du aufpassen.

Unit 7

Das *simple present* benutzt man, um über Gewohnheiten zu sprechen.
Außerdem wird es verwendet, um Geschichten zu erzählen, in denen eine Sache nach der anderen passiert.

Beispiel: It is Saturday morning.
First, Simon **goes** into the kitchen. Then he **comes** into the living-room with his cornflakes. After that he **reads** his comic. Then he **goes** to bed again.

46 Die Wortstellung in Aussagesätzen — Word order in statements

Subjekt	Verb	Objekt
David	plays	the guitar.
Becky	has got	a computer.
We	are making	a cake.
They	can repair	the bike.

Die Wortstellung im englischen Aussagesatz lautet:

Subjekt – Verb – Objekt (**S – V – O**).

Im Gegensatz zum Deutschen kann man diese Reihenfolge nicht umstellen.

Auch Zeitangaben wie zum Beispiel *every morning, every day* ändern die Reihenfolge nicht. Sie stehen am Anfang oder am Ende des Satzes. Beispiel:

	S	V	O	
	Simon	plays	football	every week.
Every week	Simon	plays	football.	

Vergleiche mit dem Deutschen:
Simon spielt jede Woche Fußball.
Jede Woche spielt Simon Fußball.

47 Adverbien der Häufigkeit
Adverbs of frequency

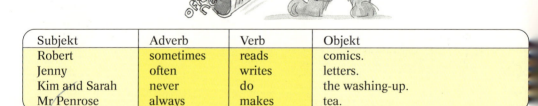

Subjekt	Adverb	Verb	Objekt
Robert	sometimes	reads	comics.
Jenny	often	writes	letters.
Kim and Sarah	never	do	the washing-up.
Mr Penrose	always	makes	tea.

Beim *simple present* stellst du die Adverbien der Häufigkeit (zum Beispiel *sometimes, often, never, always*) meistens zwischen Subjekt und Verb. Verb und Objekt bilden nämlich eine feste Einheit, und man darf keine anderen Satzteile dazwischenstellen.

Vergleiche mit dem Deutschen: Mr Penrose always makes the breakfast.
Mr Penrose macht immer das Frühstück.

Unit 7 Step C

48 Mengenangaben mit 'of' Expressions of quantity with 'of'

a	bottle	of	lemonade	eine Flasche Limonade
two	bars	of	chocolate	zwei Tafeln Schokolade
a	pound	of	bananas	ein Pfund Bananen
one	packet	of	cornflakes	eine Packung Cornflakes

Mengenangaben werden im Englischen mit Hilfe des Wortes *of* gemacht.

Unit 8

Unit 8 Step B

49 Verneinte Sätze mit 'do' Negative sentences with 'do'

	Hilfsverb	Vollverb		Hilfsverb	Vollverb	
I	can	speak	German, but I	can't	speak	Turkish.
I		like	ice cream, but I	don't	like	milk.

Wenn du etwas verneinen willst, brauchst du dafür meistens ein Hilfsverb (z. B. *can*) und ein Vollverb (z. B. *speak*) im Infinitiv. Gibt es im Aussagesatz kein Hilfsverb (zum Beispiel *I like ice cream*), so musst du bei der Verneinung *don't* (= *do* + *not*, verkürzt zu *n't*) verwenden.

50 Fragen und Kurzantworten mit 'do'
Questions and short answers with 'do'

Achte auf die Aussprache: do [duː], aber don't [dəʊnt].

You can play the guitar.
Can you play the guitar?

They read comics.
Do they read comics?

Wenn du eine Frage bilden willst und kein Hilfsverb im Aussagesatz hast, setzt du das Hilfsverb *do* ein. Kurzantworten auf Fragen mit *do* sind *Yes, I do.* oder *No, I don't*.

Beispiel: *Do you like ice cream? – Yes, I do./No, I don't.*

Do und *don't* benutzt du bei den Personalpronomen *I, you, we, they*.

Unit 8 / Unit 9

Unit 8   Step C

51   Der verneinte Imperativ   The negative imperative

Wenn du jemandem sagen willst, dass er oder sie etwas nicht machen soll, benutzt du
don't + Vollverb im Infinitiv (= verneinte Befehlsform oder verneinter Imperativ).

Don't make a noise.	Mach/Macht/Machen Sie keinen Lärm.
Don't go in.	Geh/Geht/Gehen Sie nicht hinein.

Die Form des verneinten Imperativs ist im Englischen immer dieselbe, ganz gleich, ob eine
oder mehrere Personen angesprochen werden.

Unit 9

Unit 9   Step B

52   Verneinte Sätze mit 'doesn't'   Negative sentences with 'doesn't'

	Hilfsverb	Vollverb	
Mrs Penrose		works	for a computer firm.
Mr Penrose	doesn't	work	for a computer firm. He works at home.

Du kennst die Verneinung mit dem Hilfsverb *do* schon aus Unit 8, z. B. *I don't like ice cream.*
Sie setzt sich zusammen aus *don't* + Vollverb im Infinitiv.
In der dritten Person Singular (bei *he, she, it*) heißt die Form von *do: does.*
Für die Verneinung musst du also *does not = doesn't* [dʌznt] verwenden.

She works.
↓
She doesn't work.

53   Fragen und Kurzantworten mit 'does'   Questions and short answers with 'does'

Hilfsverb	Subjekt	Vollverb	
Does	Mark	like	ice cream? Yes, he does.
Does	Maxi	like	chocolate? No, she doesn't.

Fragen und Kurzantworten in der dritten Person Singular bildest du genauso wie für die
anderen Personen (z. B. *Do you like chocolate?* Siehe Punkt 50). Du musst aber die Form
does statt *do* nehmen.

Fragen im Englischen sind
doch nicht schwer, oder?

142   *one hundred and forty-two*

54 Fragen mit Fragewörtern und 'do'/'does'
Questions with question words and 'do'/'does'

Fragewort	Hilfsverb	Subjekt	Vollverb	
What	does	Mrs Penrose	do?	She works for a computer firm.
Where	do	the Penroses	live?	In Arndale Road.
When	do	the Penroses	get up?	At half past seven.
How	does	Mark	get to nursery school?	He walks with his father.
Why	does	Mr Penrose	walk with him?	Because Mark is only four.

Du stellst das Fragewort an den Anfang der Frage.
Die anderen Wörter stehen in derselben Reihenfolge wie bei den Fragen unter Punkt 53.

55 'do'/'does' in Fragen, Kurzantworten und verneinten Sätzen
'do'/'does' in questions, short answers and negative sentences

Auf einen Blick

Do you like fish?	Yes, I do, but I don't like fish fingers.
Does Mark go to school?	No, he doesn't, but he goes to nursery school.
Do the Dixons live in Arndale Road?	No, they don't. They live in Larwood Grove.
Where does Jenny live?	She lives in Nottingham now.
What do the dogs eat?	They eat dog biscuits.

Unit 10

Unit 10   Step B

56 Gegenüberstellung: Present Progressive – Simple Present
contrast: present progressive – simple present

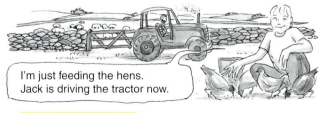

I'm just feeding the hens.
Jack is driving the tractor now.

Mrs Richards feeds the hens every day. Jack often drives the tractor.

= present progressive   = simple present

Das Präsens wird im Englischen durch zwei verschiedene Formen ausgedrückt:
present progressive und *simple present*.

Unit 10

Wenn du sagen willst, was jemand gerade macht, benutzt du das *present progressive*. Dabei kommen oft Signalwörter wie zum Beispiel *just, now* vor.
Wenn du über Gewohnheiten sprechen willst, benutzt du das *simple present,* oft mit Signalwörtern wie *always, sometimes, often, never, every day, every morning* usw.
Außerdem kann man das *simple present* verwenden, um Geschichten zu erzählen.
Auch hier gibt es typische Signalwörter wie *first, then, after that.* Vergleiche mit den Punkten 35, 39 und 45.

57 Das Fragewort 'who' als Subjekt und Objekt
The question word 'who' as subject and object

Mit *who* kann man nach dem Subjekt oder nach dem Objekt im Satz fragen.

Objekt	Hilfsverb	Subjekt	Vollverb	Objekt	
		David	asks	Grandpa.	
		Who	asks	Grandpa?	– David.
Who	does	David	ask?		– He asks Grandpa.

Wenn du mit *who* nach dem Subjekt fragst, kommt das Verb direkt nach *who.*
Wenn du mit *who* nach dem Objekt fragst, musst du ein Hilfsverb (zum Beispiel *does*) verwenden. Nach dem Hilfsverb stehen Subjekt und Vollverb.

Auf einen Blick

Objekt	Hilfsverb	Subjekt	Hilfsverb	Vollverb	Objekt	
		Who		asks	Mrs Croft?	Wer fragt Mrs Croft?
		Who	can	phone	the vet?	Wer kann den Tierarzt anrufen?
		Who	must	call	the police?	Wer muss die Polizei rufen?
Who	does	she		ask?		Wen fragt sie?
Who	must	the boys		phone?		Wen müssen die Jungen anrufen?
Who	can	the police		help?		Wem kann die Polizei helfen?

Unit 10   Step C

58 Mengenangaben mit 'How much', 'How many' und 'not much', 'not many'
Expressions of quantity with 'How much', 'How many', and 'not much', 'not many'

How much milk do you want?	How many biscuits do you want?
– Not much.	– Not many. Only two or three.

Bei Mengenangaben verwendet man *how much* oder *how many* in Fragen, *not much* oder *not many* in negativen Sätzen. Dabei werden *how much* und *not much* für nicht zählbare Mengen verwendet. *How many* und *not many* dagegen werden für zählbare Mengen verwendet.

144 *one hundred and forty-four*

⟨Grammar list⟩

Deutsch/Lateinisch	Englisch	Englisches Beispiel	Punkt in der Grammatik
Adverb	adverb		
Adverb der Häufigkeit	adverb of frequency	sometimes, often, etc.	**47**
Apostroph	apostrophe	That's Sarah.	**2**
(Auslassungszeichen)			
Artikel	article		
bestimmter Artikel	definite article	the [ðə, ði:]	**43**
unbestimmter Artikel	indefinite article	a, an	**20**
Aussagesatz	statement	Robert is from London.	**12**
Befehlsform (Imperativ)	imperative	Sit down.	
verneinte Befehlsform	negative imperative	Don't eat that.	**51**
Datum	date	1st April	**41**
Einzahl (Singular)	singular	one house	**14**
Fragen und Kurz-	questions and		
antworten	short answers		
mit 'to be'	with 'to be'	Are you ...? Yes, I am.	**25**
mit 'can'	with 'can'	Can she ...? Yes, she can.	**30**
mit 'do'	with 'do'	Do you ...? Yes, I do.	**50, 53**
mit 'have/has got'	with 'have/has got'	Have you ...? No, I haven't.	**26**
mit der Verlaufsform	with the present	Are you reading?	
des Präsens	progressive	No, I'm not.	**37**
Fragesatz → Gegenwart	question		
Fragewort	question word	Where? What? Who? etc.	**31**
Fürwort	pronoun		
besitzanzeigendes Fürwort	possessive determiner	my, your, his, her, etc.	**7, 15, 16**
hinweisendes Fürwort	demonstrative pronoun	this, that, these, those	**21, 27**
persönliches Fürwort	personal pronoun	I, you, she, he, etc.	**11**
Gegenwart (Präsens)	present tense		
einfache Form	simple present	I go to the shops.	**45**
einfache Form (Frage	simple present (question	Do you play tennis?	**50**
und Verneinung)	and negation)	She doesn't play tennis.	**52**
Verlaufsform	present progressive	I'm going to the shops.	**35, 39**
Genitiv	genitive		
of-Genitiv	of-genitive	the end of the road	**44**
s-Genitiv	s-genitive	Sarah's bike	**32**
Grundform (Infinitiv)	infinitive	to be	**11**

one hundred and forty-five **145**

Grammar list

Deutsch/Lateinisch	Englisch	Englisches Beispiel	Punkt in der Grammatik
Hauptwort (Substantiv)	noun	cat, man, school, etc.	14
Hilfsverb	modal auxiliary	can, must	29, 34
Kurzantwort	short answer	Yes, I am.	25
Kurzform	short form	he's, she's, etc.	11
Langform	long form	he is, she is, etc.	11
Mehrzahl (Plural)	plural	four houses	14
Mitlaut (Konsonant)	consonant	b, k, l, p, etc.	14
Mengenangaben Mengenangaben mit 'How much', 'How many' Mengenangaben mit 'of'	expressions of quantity	How much sugar do you want? a packet of biscuits	58 48
Objektform	object form	me, him, her, etc.	38
Ordnungszahl	ordinal number	first, second, third, etc.	40
Person dritte Person	person third person	he, she, it; they	2
Plural → Mehrzahl			
Präposition (Verhältniswort)	preposition	in, on, under, etc.	10
Präsens → Gegenwart			
Pronomen → Fürwort			
Satz	sentence	He reads his comic.	46
Selbstlaut (Vokal)	vowel	a, e, i, o, u	14
Singular → Einzahl			
Subjektform (der Personalpronomen)	subject form	I, you, he, she, etc.	11
Uhrzeit	time	It's half past four.	42
Verb (Tätigkeitswort)	verb	to go, to play	46
Verneinung	negation	It isn't on your desk.	13
Wortstellung	word order	He often plays tennis.	46

Vocabulary

a) Aufbau des Vokabulars

Im Unterricht erklärt dir deine Lehrerin oder dein Lehrer die neuen Wörter. Du musst sie aber auch lernen. Dabei hilft dir diese Liste der neuen Vokabeln.

In der linken Spalte findest du die englischen Wörter in der Reihenfolge, in der sie in der Unit vorkommen. Dahinter steht die Lautschrift in eckigen Klammern. Sie zeigt, wie das Wort ausgesprochen wird und wie es betont wird. Wie du die Lautschrift lesen musst, steht unten auf dieser Seite.

In der mittleren Spalte stehen Beispielsätze oder kleine Zeichnungen sowie wichtige Hinweise, die dir beim Lernen helfen.

In der rechten Spalte findest du eine deutsche Übersetzung des englischen Wortes. Oft lassen sich aber Wörter aus einer Sprache nicht einfach in die andere übersetzen. Deshalb stehen manchmal mehrere Wörter in der rechten Spalte, die dir zeigen, wie das englische Wort benutzt wird.

Tipps zum Vokabellernen findest du in den Kästchen vor jeder Unit.

b) Abkürzungen und Zeichen

(pl)	Plural, Mehrzahl	=	ist gleich
(sg)	Singular, Einzahl	⟷	ist das Gegenteil von

c) Lautschrift

Wie die englischen Wörter ausgesprochen werden, lernst du im Unterricht. Die Lautschrift im Vokabular hilft dir, die Aussprache und Betonung eines Wortes nachzusehen. Sie benutzt einige normale Buchstaben und einige besondere Zeichen. Die Aussprache der einzelnen Zeichen kannst du dir anhand eines einfachen Wortes merken. Die Betonung eines Wortes wird durch einen Betonungsstrich **vor** der betonten Silbe gezeigt: ['] zeigt den Hauptakzent des Wortes, [,] den Nebenakzent. Der Bindebogen [‿] zeigt, dass zwei Wörter in der Aussprache miteinander verbunden werden.

Konsonanten		Vokale		Doppellaute	
[ŋ]	morni**ng**	[ɑː]	f**a**ther	[aɪ]	**I, my**
[r]	**r**ed	[ʌ]	b**u**t, **u**nder	[aʊ]	n**ow**, h**ou**se
[s]	cla**ss**	[e]	p**e**n	[eə]	th**ere**, p**air**
[z]	**is**	[ə]	**a** sist**er**	[eɪ]	n**a**me, th**ey**
[ʒ]	televi**si**on	[ɜː]	g**ir**l	[ɪə]	h**ere**, **i**dea
[dʒ]	**G**ermany, pa**ge**	[æ]	**a**pple	[ɔɪ]	b**oy**
[ʃ]	**sh**e	[ɪ]	**i**t	[əʊ]	**o**ld, hell**o**
[tʃ]	**ch**air, lun**ch**	[iː]	**ea**sy, sh**e**	[ʊə]	**you're**
[ð]	**th**e	[ɒ]	g**o**t, **o**n		
[θ]	**th**anks	[ɔː]	b**a**ll	Alle anderen Zeichen werden genauso ausgesprochen, wie sie im Deutschen geschrieben werden [j, k, ...].	
[v]	**v**ideo, ha**ve**	[ʊ]	b**oo**k		
[w]	**w**ord, **o**ne	[uː]	t**oo**, tw**o**		

one hundred and forty-seven **147**

Let's start

Let's start

Mit dem Lernen fängst du an, indem du das Wort, das Beispiel und die deutsche Entsprechung liest. Danach kannst du z.B. die mittlere und die rechte Spalte abdecken und ausprobieren, ob du noch die deutsche Übersetzung zum englischen Wort weißt.
Das geht natürlich auch umgekehrt, indem du versuchst, vom deutschen Begriff aus, dich an das englische Wort zu erinnern.
Auch das Aufschreiben und das laute Vorsagen der englischen Wörter können dir beim Lernen helfen. Mehr darüber steht in den Lerntipps, die vor jeder Unit im Vokabelverzeichnis zu finden sind.

Let's start. [ˌlets ˈstɑːt] Lasst uns anfangen.

1 In Nottingham

in [ɪn] in
Nottingham [ˈnɒtɪŋəm] Stadt in Mittelengland
Hello. [həˈləʊ] Hallo., Guten Tag.
I'm (= I am) [aɪm] ich bin
I [aɪ] ich
Sarah [ˈseərə] weiblicher Vorname
Robert [ˈrɒbət] männlicher Vorname

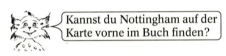

2 Hello

(a) **Becky** [ˈbekɪ] weiblicher Vorname
My name is … [ˈmaɪ neɪm ɪz] Ich heiße …
my [maɪ] mein/meine

name [neɪm] Name
is [ɪz] ist
Burton [ˈbɜːtn] Familienname
Croft [krɒft] Familienname
new [njuː] neu
yes [jes] ja
from [frɒm] aus, von
London [ˈlʌndən] Hauptstadt von Großbritannien

Im Englischen werden innerhalb eines Satzes nur Namen und das kurze Wort *I* groß geschrieben.

Robert is from *London*.

(b) **Woof!** [wʊf] Wau! *(Hundebellen)*
oh [əʊ] oh
dog [dɒɡ] Hund

 Woof, woof.

148 *one hundred and forty-eight*

Let's start

What's your name? [ˌwɒts jɔː ˈneɪm]	Man kann nicht immer einfach Wort für Wort übersetzen. Vergleiche: *What's your name?* – Wie heißt du? my ⟷ your	Wie heißt du?/Wie heißen Sie?
what's (= what is) [wɒts]		was ist …
your [jɔː]		dein/deine, Ihr/Ihre
Maxi [ˈmæksɪ]		*Hundename*
and [ænd]		und
that's (= that is) [ðæts]		das ist
Mini [ˈmɪnɪ]		*Hundename*
Your turn. [ˈjɔː tɜːn]		Du bist an der Reihe.
Monny [ˈmɒnɪ]		*Name eines Maskottchens*
a [ə]		ein/eine
song [sɒŋ]		Lied
Dixon [ˈdɪksn]		*Familienname*
I'm at Haywood School. [ˈaɪm ət ˈheɪwʊd ˈskuːl]	*at* wird [æt] ausgesprochen, wenn es betont wird. Unbetont spricht man es [ət] aus.	Ich bin an der Haywood-Schule.
at [æt], [ət]		an
Haywood School [ˈheɪwʊd ˈskuːl]		*Name einer Gesamtschule in Nottingham*
school [skuːl]		Schule
Is she …? [ˈɪz ˈʃiː]	Is she at Haywood School? Yes, she's in my tutor group.	Ist sie …?
she's (= she is) [ʃiːz]		sie ist
she [ʃiː]		sie
tutor group [ˈtjuːtə ˌgruːp]		Klasse (*in einer englischen Schule*)
tutor [ˈtjuːtə]		Klassenlehrer/in, Betreuungslehrer/in
group [gruːp]		Gruppe
Look. [lʊk]		Sieh mal./Seht mal.
to look [lʊk]	Am vorangestellten Wörtchen *to* kann man erkennen, dass es sich um eine Grundform (Infinitiv) handelt.	sehen, anschauen
David [ˈdeɪvɪd]		*männlicher Vorname*
Penrose [ˈpenrəʊz]		*Familienname*
he's (= he is) [hiːz]		er ist
he [hiː]		er
too [tuː]	David is in my tutor group, *too*.	auch
Is he …? [ˈɪz ˈhiː]		Ist er …?
nice [naɪs]		nett, schön
a [ə]		ein/eine
friend [frend]	Becky is my *friend* and David is my *friend*, too.	Freund/in
Please, look at page … [ˈpliːz ˌlʊk ət peɪdʒ]		Bitte schau/schaut auf Seite …
please [pliːz]		bitte
to look at [ˈlʊk ət]		anschauen
page [peɪdʒ]		Seite
class [klɑːs]	My new *class* is nice.	Klasse (*in einer deutschen Schule*)
poster [ˈpəʊstə]		Poster, Plakat
Make a poster. [meɪk ə ˈpəʊstə]		Mach/Macht ein Poster.
to make [meɪk]		machen

Let's start

Vocabulary

3 School!

(a) here [hɪə]
Am I ... ? ['æm_aɪ]
late [leɪt]
Goodbye. [gʊd'baɪ]

I'm *here*.
Am I late?

Hello. ⟷ Goodbye.

hier
Bin ich ... ?
spät, zu spät
Auf Wiedersehen, Tschüs.

no [nəʊ]
you [juː]
crazy ['kreɪzɪ]
bag [bæg]

yes ⟷ *no*
I ⟷ *you*

nein
du, Sie
verrückt
Tasche

1 here's (= here is) [hɪəz]
pen [pen]
Thank you. ['θæŋk_ju]
Please go on. [ˌpliːz gəʊ_'ɒn]

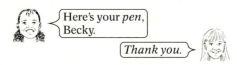

Here's your *pen*, Becky.
Thank you.

hier ist
Füller
Danke schön.
Bitte mach/macht weiter.

to go on [gəʊ_'ɒn]
book [bʊk]
folder ['fəʊldə]
pencil case ['pensl keɪs]
pencil ['pensl]
case [keɪs]
comic ['kɒmɪk]
ball [bɔːl]
lunch box ['lʌntʃ bɒks]

weitermachen
Buch
Mappe, Hefter
Federmäppchen
Bleistift
Etui, Hülle
Comic
Ball
Dose für belegte Brote zum Mittagessen

lunch [lʌntʃ]
box [bɒks]
2 teacher ['tiːtʃə]
What's that in English?
[ˌwɒts ðæt_ɪn_'ɪŋglɪʃ]
English ['ɪŋglɪʃ]
biro ['baɪrəʊ]
4 sound practice
['saʊnd ˌpræktɪs]

That's my *teacher*. She's my tutor, too.

Wörter für Staatsangehörigkeit werden immer groß geschrieben.

Mittagessen
Schachtel, Kiste, Dose
Lehrer/in
Wie heißt das auf Englisch?
englisch, Englisch
Kugelschreiber
Aussprachübung

practice ['præktɪs]
Listen. ['lɪsn]
to listen ['lɪsn]
Say. [seɪ]
to say [seɪ]

Listen!

Übung, Training
Hör/Hört zu.
zuhören
Sag/Sagt es.
sagen

(b) twelve [twelv]
Are you ... ? [ɑː juː]

12
Are you twelve? – No, I'm eleven.

zwölf
Bist du ... ?/Sind Sie ... ?

eleven [ɪ'levn]
How old are you?
[haʊ_'əʊld_ɑː juː]
how [haʊ]
old [əʊld]
not [nɒt]
Sorry! ['sɒrɪ]

11
How old are you? – I'm twelve.

elf
Wie alt bist du?

wie
alt
nicht
Entschuldigung./Tut mir Leid.

you're (= you are) [jʊə]
ten [ten]
girl [ɡɜːl]

10

du bist/Sie sind
zehn
Mädchen

150 *one hundred and fifty*

Tutor group 7MD

Das Vokabellernen geht einfacher, wenn du dir eine Vokabelkartei machst. Dazu brauchst du einen Karton und viele Kärtchen aus dünner Pappe oder dickem Papier. Den Karton unterteilst du mit einer Pappwand quer in zwei Fächer.
Wenn ihr Vokabeln zum Lernen aufhabt, schreibst du das englische Wort auf die eine Seite der Karteikarte und die deutsche Übersetzung auf die Rückseite.
Dann stellst du die Karten in den vorderen Teil deines Kartons. Später überprüfst du beim Durchblättern der Karten, ob du die Übersetzung des Wortes noch weißt und zwar deutsch – englisch und englisch – deutsch. Zwischendurch solltest du die Reihenfolge der Karten neu mischen. Wenn du ganz sicher bist, dass du ein Wort kannst, stellst du die Karte in das hintere Fach.

Du kannst auch einen Schuhkarton zum Basteln nehmen!

seven [sevn]	7	sieben
7MD [ˌsevn emˈdiː]		*Name der Klasse mit den Anfangsbuchstaben ihrer Lehrerin Margaret Dane*
your *(pl)* [jɔː]		euer/eure; Ihr/Ihre
her [hɜː]	That's my teacher. I'm in *her* tutor group.	ihr/ihre
Mrs [ˈmɪsɪz]		Frau *(Anrede für verheiratete Frauen)*
Dane [deɪn]		*Familienname*
Good morning. [ɡʊd ˈmɔːnɪŋ]		Guten Morgen.
good [ɡʊd]		gut
morning [ˈmɔːnɪŋ]		Morgen
the [ðə]		der/die/das
boy [bɔɪ]	Robert is new. I'm *his* friend.	Junge
his [hɪz]		sein/seine
you're (= you are) *(pl)* [jʊə]	Sarah, Becky, *you're* eleven.	ihr seid/Sie sind
you [juː]	Yes. We're eleven.	ihr/Sie
right [raɪt]		richtig
we're (= we are) [wɪə]		wir sind
we [wiː]		wir
teachers *(pl)* [ˈtiːtʃəz]	Was heißt nur diese Abkürzung *pl*? Ach ja, das steht auf Seite 147.	Lehrer/innen
OK [əʊˈkeɪ]		OK, in Ordnung
they're (= they are) [ðeə]		sie sind
they [ðeɪ]		sie *(Pl)*
Mr [ˈmɪstə]		Herr *(Anrede für Männer)*
Cooper [ˈkuːpə]		*Familienname*
girls and boys [ˌɡɜːlz n ˈbɔɪz]		Mädchen und Jungen
German [ˈdʒɜːmən]	Mr Cooper is a *German* teacher.	deutsch, Deutsch

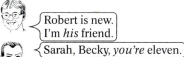

Let's start

Vocabulary

2 **answer** [ˈɑːnsə] — Antwort
3 **questions** *(pl)* [ˈkwestʃənz] — Fragen
  Greenwood [ˈgriːnwʊd] — *Name einer Schule*

(c) **Hey!** [heɪ] — He!
  where [weə] — wo
  on [ɒn] — auf
  desk [desk] — Schreibtisch, Pult
  under [ˈʌndə] — unter
  chair [tʃeə] — Stuhl
  Aaah! [ɑː] — Oh! Huch!
  it's (= it is) [ɪts] — es ist, er ist, sie ist
  it [ɪt] — es/er/sie
  Sneaky Snake [ˈsniːkɪ ˌsneɪk] — *Name eines Spielzeugs*
  snake [sneɪk] — Schlange
4 **where's** (= where is) [weəz] — wo ist
5 **game** [geɪm] — Spiel
  to play [pleɪ] — spielen
  Is it … ? [ɪz ɪt] — Ist es … ?

on ⟷ under

Where's Robert? He's here.

5 Haywood School

Du behältst die neuen Wörter besser, wenn du sie dir nur 5 Minuten anschaust, aber dafür nach einer halben Stunde wiederholst und am Ende deiner Hausaufgaben noch einmal 5 Minuten überprüfst.

3 mal 5 Minuten ist mehr als eine halbe Stunde!

(a) **picture** [ˈpɪktʃə] — Bild
  year [jɪə] — Jahr, Jahrgang
  or [ɔː] — oder
  in the morning [ɪn ðə ˈmɔːnɪŋ] — morgens, am Vormittag
  in the afternoon [ɪn ðiː ˌɑːftəˈnuːn] — nachmittags, am Nachmittag
  the [ðiː] — der/die/das
  afternoon [ɑːftəˈnuːn] — Nachmittag

Is it Mini *or* Maxi in the picture? It's Maxi.

morning ⟷ afternoon

1 **sentences** *(pl)* [ˈsentənsɪz] — Sätze
3 **Let's learn words.** [ˌlets lɜːn ˈwɜːdz] — Lasst uns Wörter lernen.
  Let's [lets] — Lasst uns
  to learn [lɜːn] — lernen
  word [wɜːd] — Wort
  easy [ˈiːzɪ] — einfach, leicht
  pair [peə] — Paar
  Write the pairs in your folder. [raɪt ðə ˈpeəz ɪn jɔː ˈfəʊldə] — Schreibt die Paare in eure Mappe.
  to write [raɪt] — schreiben
  question [ˈkwestʃən] — Frage

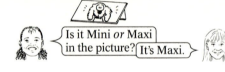

Let's learn words: dog, school, boy, is

Maxi and Mini are a crazy *pair*!

answer ⟷ question

152 *one hundred and fifty-two*

Let's start

I'm not sure. [aɪm nɒt 'ʃɔ:]	Is Robert eleven? / *I'm not sure.*	Ich bin mir nicht sicher.
sure [ʃɔ:]		sicher
she isn't (= she is not) [ʃiː ‿'ɪznt]	she is ⟷ *she isn't*	sie ist nicht
they aren't (= they are not) [ðeɪ ‿'ɑːnt]	they are ⟷ *they aren't*	sie sind nicht
playground ['pleɪɡraʊnd]		Schulhof, Spielplatz
Hmm.		Hm./Tja.
chocolate ['tʃɒklət]		Schokolade
to **find** [faɪnd]		finden
listening practice ['lɪsnɪŋ ˌpræktɪs]		Hörverstehensübung

The lesson

lesson [lesn]	My English *lesson* is in the morning.	Unterrichtsstunde
classroom ['klɑːsrʊm]		Klassenzimmer
Dixon ['dɪksn]		*Familienname*
funny ['fʌnɪ]		lustig, komisch
Sit down. [sɪt 'daʊn]		Setz dich./Setzt euch.
to **sit down** [sɪt 'daʊn]		sich hinsetzen
now [naʊ]		jetzt, nun
homework ['həʊmwɜːk]		Hausaufgaben
to **bring** [brɪŋ]		bringen
quiet ['kwaɪət]	! Please *be quiet*!	still, ruhig
Good afternoon. [ɡʊd ˌɑːftə'nuːn]	Good morning. ⟷ *Good afternoon.*	Guten Tag. (*Anrede am Nachmittag*)
wrong [rɒŋ]	right ⟷ *wrong*	falsch
to **correct** [kə'rekt]		korrigieren, verbessern

Let's check

to **check** [tʃek]		überprüfen, kontrollieren

School:			
assembly (U 7)	*Versammlung*	lunch box	*Dose für belegte Brote*
bag	*Tasche*	number (U 1)	*Nummer, Zahl*
biro	*Kugelschreiber*	page	*Seite*
book	*Buch*	pen	*Füller*
chair	*Stuhl*	pencil	*Bleistift*
class	*dt. Klasse*	pencil case	*Federmäppchen*
classroom	*Klassenzimmer*	playground	*Schulhof, Spielplatz*
computer (U 1)	*Computer*	school bag (U 2)	*Schultasche*
crayon (U 2)	*Buntstift*	school Uniform (U 3)	*Schuluniform*
desk	*Schreibtisch, Pult*	teacher	*Lehrer/in*
English teacher	*Englischlehrer/in*	tutor group	*engl. Klasse*
exercise (U 4)	*Übung, Aufgabe*	to be late	*zu spät kommen*
folder	*Mappe, Hefter*	to correct	*korrigieren, verbessern*
German teacher	*Deutschlehrer/in*		
head teacher (U 7)	*Schuldirektor/in*	at the top of the page (U 5)	*oben (auf der Seite)* ⟷
homework	*Hausaufgaben*	⟷ at the bottom of … (U 6)	*unten (auf der Seite)*
lesson	*Unterrichtsstunde*	right ⟷ wrong	*richtig ⟷ falsch*

Unit 1

Unit 1 At home with the Burtons

Vocabulary

> Auch die „alten" Wörter solltest du dir noch mal vornehmen.

> Hast du schon eine Vokabelkartei angelegt? Dann sind die Karten bestimmt schon alle im hinteren Fach.
> Aber denk daran: Alle paar Wochen solltest du auch diese Karten einmal durchschauen. Wenn du ein Wort nicht mehr kannst, wandert die Karte wieder ins vordere Fach zurück und wird mit den neuen Wörtern wiederholt.
> (Auf S. 164 in Unit 5 findest du einen Vorschlag für ein Spiel mit diesen Karteikärtchen.)

unit ['ju:nɪt] — Lektion, Kapitel
At home with the Burtons. [ət 'həʊm wɪð ðə ˌbɜ:tnz] — Zu Hause bei den Burtons.
at home [ət 'həʊm] — zu Hause
with [wɪð] — bei, mit

Step A Superdogs

(a) **step** [step] — Schritt, Stufe
superdogs (pl) ['su:pədɒgz] — Superhunde
brother ['brʌðə] — Bruder
one [wʌn] — ein/eine/eins
Simon ['saɪmən] — männl. Vorname
clever ['klevə] — intelligent, klug
two [tu:] — zwei
Wow! [waʊ] — Ausruf

> That's Becky and her brother *Simon*.

one [wʌn] eins	**five** [faɪv] fünf	**nine** [naɪn] neun
two [tu:] zwei	**six** [sɪks] sechs	**ten** [ten] zehn
three [θri:] drei	**seven** ['sevn] sieben	**eleven** [ɪ'levn] elf
four [fɔ:] vier	**eight** [eɪt] acht	**twelve** [twelv] zwölf

1 **example** [ɪg'zɑ:mpl] — Beispiel
2 **for Superkids** [fə 'su:pəkɪdz] — für Superkinder
for [fɔ:], [fə] — für

> Weißt du noch? Kurze Wörter wie *at* und *for* werden [ət], [fə] ausgesprochen, wenn sie unbetont sind.

(b) **biscuit** ['bɪskɪt] — Keks
car [kɑ:] — Auto
but [bʌt] — aber
bed [bed] — Bett

The *biscuits* are for Becky.

Step B The Burtons

kitchen ['kɪtʃɪn] — Küche
their [ðeə] — ihr/ihre (Pl)
mother ['mʌðə] — Mutter
father ['fɑ:ðə] — Vater

Becky and Simon are in the *kitchen*.

Their *mother* is in the garden.
mother ⟷ *father*

154 *one hundred and fifty-four*

Unit 1

hungry [ˈhʌŋgrɪ]	I'm *hungry*. Where are *our* biscuits? *Thanks*. Here's a biscuit, Simon.	hungrig
our [ˈaʊə]		unser/unsere
Thanks! [θæŋks]		Danke!
dog biscuit [ˈdɒg ˌbɪskɪt]		Hundekuchen
Dad [dæd]	 *Dad* wird nur groß geschrieben, wenn das Wort als Name verwendet wird.	Vati, Papa

Say it to the beat.
 [ˌseɪ ɪt tə ðə ˈbiːt]   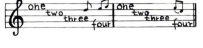   Sag/t es im Rhythmus.
Clap your hands.
 [ˌklæp jɔː ˈhændz]   Klatsch/t mit den
   Händen.
to clap [klæp]   klatschen
hand [hænd]   Hand
Stamp your feet.   Stampf/t mit deinen/
 [ˌstæmp jɔː ˈfiːt]   euren Füßen.
to stamp [stæmp]   stampfen
feet *(pl)* [fiːt]   Füße
together [təˈgeðə]   zusammen
all the way [ˌɔːl ðə ˈweɪ]   *hier:* den ganzen Weg

Step B Two rooms

room [ruːm]	Raum, Zimmer
Simon has got … [ˈsaɪmən hæz gɒt]	Simon hat …
football [ˈfʊtbɔːl]	Fußball
skateboard [ˈskeɪtbɔːd]	Skateboard
radio [ˈreɪdɪəʊ]	Radio
CD player [siː ˈdiː pleɪə]	CD-Spieler
CD [siː ˈdiː]	CD
computer [kəmˈpjuːtə]	Computer
she hasn't got … [ʃiː ˈhæznt gɒt]	sie hat nicht/kein …

she has got …   she hasn't got …

Step B Good idea!

idea [aɪˈdɪə]		Idee
I haven't got … [aɪ ˈhævnt gɒt]		ich habe nicht/kein …
Have you got … ? [ˈhæv juː gɒt]	*Have you got* an idea? –	Hast du … ?
I've got … [aɪv gɒt]	Yes, *I've got* a good idea.	Ich habe …
Oops! [uːps]		Hoppla!
garden [ˈgɑːdən]	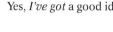	Garten
sister [ˈsɪstə]	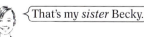 That's my *sister* Becky.	Schwester
to work [wɜːk]		arbeiten
partner [ˈpɑːtnə]		Partner/in

one hundred and fifty-five **155**

Unit 1

Vocabulary

(b) big [bɪg] — groß
tree [triː] — Baum
bad [bæd] — schlimm, schlecht
hole [həʊl] — Loch
pond [pɒnd] — Teich

to ask [ɑːsk] — fragen

Have you got my comic, Becky? — *No, ask Simon.*

Mum [mʌm] — Mama, Mutti

Dad ⟷ Mum

Looking at the UK: Nottingham

Looking at the UK [ˌlʊkɪŋ ət ðə juː ˈkeɪ] — Ein Blick auf das Vereinigte Königreich!
the UK (= the United Kingdom) [juː ˈkeɪ], [juːˈnaɪtɪd ˈkɪŋdəm] — Vereinigtes Königreich von Großbritannien und Nordirland
this [ðɪs] — dies/dieser/diese/dieses
England [ˈɪŋglənd] — England
Germany [ˈdʒɜːmənɪ] — Deutschland
Berlin [bɜːˈlɪn] — Berlin
Sherwood [ˈʃɜːwʊd] — *Bezirk in Nottingham*
Arndale Road [ˈɑːndeɪl ˈrəʊd] — *Straße in Nottingham*
road (= Rd.) [rəʊd] — Straße
1 house [haʊs] — Haus
2 home [həʊm] — Heim, Zuhause
flat [flæt] — Wohnung

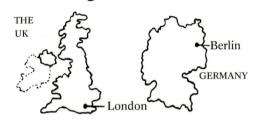

The teacher has got three rooms in her *flat*.

Step C Look!

(a) there [ðeə] — da, dort
an [ən] — ein/eine
apple [ˈæpl] — Apfel
egg [eg] — Ei
broken [ˈbrəʊkən] — kaputt, zerbrochen

Becky is in the garden. Simon is *there*, too.

2 Word power [ˈwɜːd ˌpaʊə] — Die Kraft der Wörter

That's your book over there.

(b) over there [ˌəʊvə ˈðeə] — da drüben, dort
4 role play [ˈrəʊl pleɪ] — Rollenspiel
together [təˈgeðə] — zusammen
6 What is it? [wɒt ˈɪz ɪt] — Was gibt's?
7 telephone [ˈtelɪfəʊn] — Telefon
number [ˈnʌmbə] — Nummer, Zahl
o [əʊ] — *hier:* null *(bei Telefonnummern)*

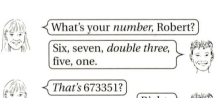

What's your number, Robert?
Six, seven, double three, five, one.
That's 673351?
Right.

double three [ˈdʌbl θriː] — *hier:* zweimal die 3
8 that's [ðæts] — *hier:* also *(wenn man etwas zum besseren Verständnis wiederholt)*

Margaret [ˈmɑːgrɪt] — *weibl. Vorname*
Tim [tɪm] — *männl. Vorname*

Unit 1 / Unit 2

Vocabulary

Step D **The frog**

frog [frɒg]		Frosch
bike [baɪk]		Fahrrad
Arnot Hill Park		_Park in Nottingham_
[ˌɑːnət hɪl ˈpɑːk]		
park [pɑːk]		Park
Hi! [haɪ]		Hallo!
table [ˈteɪbl]		Tisch
ready [ˈredɪ]		fertig, bereit
not … yet [nɒt … jet]	The pond is_n't_ ready _yet_.	noch nicht
poor [pɔː]		arm
more [mɔː]	An apple. – Here are _more_ apples.	mehr, weitere
At the door. [ət ðə ˈdɔː]		An der Tür.
door [dɔː]		Tür
to come in [kʌmˈɪn]		hereinkommen
thing [θɪŋ]	_things:_ ball dog bag girl bike frog	Ding, Sache

Step E **Let's check**

to **put in** [ˈpʊtˈɪn]		einsetzen, hineintun

Unit 2 The Dixons

Wörter lernen sich einfacher und schneller, wenn man sie sich päckchenweise vornimmt. Am besten lernt man nur 10–15 Wörter in einem Päckchen.

Vorsicht!
Nimm dir nicht zu viel auf einmal vor!
Schwere Pakete kannst du auch nicht heben.

Step A **Sarah and her family**

family [ˈfæməlɪ]	The Dixons are a _family_.	Familie
man [mæn]	Mr Burton is a _man_. Simon is a boy.	Mann
men _(pl)_ [men]		Männer
Eddy [ˈedɪ]		_männl. Vorname_
bank clerk [ˈbæŋkˈklɑːk]		Bankangestellte/r
bank [bæŋk]		Bank
clerk [klɑːk]		Büroangestellte/r
woman [ˈwʊmən]	man ⟷ _woman_	Frau
women _(pl)_ [ˈwɪmɪn]		Frauen
Janet [ˈdʒænɪt]		_weibl. Vorname_

one hundred and fifty-seven **157**

Unit 2

vet's assistant ['vets ə'sɪstənt]		Tierarzthelfer/in
vet [vet]		Tierarzt/Tierärztin
assistant [ə'sɪstənt]		Helfer/in, Assistent/in
cat [kæt]		Katze
Tabby ['tæbɪ]		*Name einer Katze*
Kim [kɪm]		*weibl. Vorname*
child [tʃaɪld]		Kind
children *(pl)* ['tʃɪldrən]	Becky and Simon are *children*.	Kinder

(b) red [red] — rot
black [blæk] — schwarz
green [griːn] — grün
yellow ['jeləʊ] — gelb
blue [bluː] — blau
brown [braʊn] — braun
crayon ['kreɪən] — Buntstift
colour ['kʌlə] — Farbe
Here you are. ['hɪə juˌɑː] — Hier, bitte schön.

3 to draw [drɔː]   Let's *draw* frogs with our green crayons.   zeichnen

Step B What a crazy family!

(a) What a … ['wɒt ə] — Was für ein/e …
knife [naɪf] — Messer *(Sg)*
knives *(pl)* [naɪvz] — Messer *(Pl)*
spoon [spuːn] — Löffel
today [tə'deɪ]   We've got English *today*.   heute
shelf [ʃelf] — Regal
shelves *(pl)* [ʃelvz] — Regale
families *(pl)* ['fæmɪlɪz]   The Dixons and the Burtons are *families*.   Familien

2 Wood [wʊd] — *Familienname*
Miller ['mɪlə] — *Familienname*
That's great! [ˌðæts 'greɪt] — Das ist toll/großartig!

(b) parents *(pl)* ['peərənts]   Your mother and father are your *parents*.   Eltern
very ['verɪ] — sehr
untidy [ʌn'taɪdɪ] — unordentlich
its [ɪts] — sein, seine/ihr, ihre

Step B In the garage

garage ['gærɑːdʒ] — Garage
flat tyre [ˌflæt 'taɪə] — platter Reifen, Platten
flat [flæt] — flach, platt
tyre ['taɪə] — Reifen
pump [pʌmp] — Luftpumpe
to go [gəʊ] — gehen, fahren

a *pump*
a *tyre*
a *flat tyre*

158 *one hundred and fifty-eight*

Unit 2

dice *(sg + pl)* [daɪs]	It's your turn. *Throw* the dice.	Würfel
to **throw** [θrəʊ]		werfen

Step B In Larwood Grove

Larwood Grove [ˈlɑːwʊd ˈɡrəʊv]		*Straße in Nottingham*
shop [ʃɒp]	a book *shop*, a bike *shop*, a computer *shop*	Geschäft, Laden
other [ˈʌðə]		andere, weitere
Nosy [ˈnəʊzi]		*hier: Familienname*
nosy [ˈnəʊzi]	Mrs A and Mr B are *neighbours*.	neugierig
neighbour [ˈneɪbə]		Nachbar/in

Step C Is that my new CD, Sarah?

little [lɪtl]	big ⟷ *little*	klein
those [ðəʊz]	*These* are my books.	die da drüben
these [ðiːz]	*Those* are your books.	diese hier
to **act** [ækt]		spielen, nachspielen
dialogue [ˈdaɪəlɒɡ]	Let's *talk about* school.	Dialog, Gespräch
to **talk about** [ˈtɔːk_ə‿baʊt]	No, let's *talk about* cars.	reden über, sprechen über

Step D The ring

ring [rɪŋ]		Ring
living-room [ˈlɪvɪŋruːm]		Wohnzimmer
to **see** [siː]		sehen
Be careful! [bɪ ˈkeəfʊl]		Pass auf! Vorsicht!
again [əˈɡen]		wieder, noch einmal
silly [ˈsɪli]		dumm, albern
Come on! [kəm_ˈɒn]	*Come on*, Becky, we're late.	Komm schon!/Kommt schon!
to **get** [ɡet]		*hier:* holen
outside [ˌaʊtˈsaɪd]		draußen
at the top of [ət ðə ˈtɒp_əv]		ganz oben
to **put** [pʊt]		setzen, stellen, legen
What's all this noise? [ˌwɒts_ɔːl ðɪs ˈnɔɪz]	Woof, woof woof!	Was soll der Lärm?
noise [nɔɪz]	What's all this noise?	Lärm, Krach, Geräusch
nothing [ˈnʌθɪŋ]		nichts
everything [ˈevrɪθɪŋ]		alles
on the hillside [ˌɒn ðə ˈhɪlsaɪd]		am Hang
ticky tacky [ˈtɪki ˈtæki]		*hier:* billiges Material

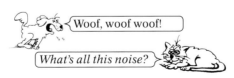

Unit 2 / Unit 3

Vocabulary

all the same [ˌɔːl ðə ˈseɪm]		alle gleich
there's [ˈðeəz]		es gibt, es ist
a green one [ə ˈgriːn wʌn]		eine grüne
pink [pɪŋk]		rosa
made out of [ˌmeɪd ˈaʊt_əv]		gemacht aus, hergestellt aus
to look [lʊk]		*hier:* aussehen
just the same [ˌdʒʌst ðə ˈseɪm]		*hier:* genau gleich

Unit 3 The new girl from Germany

Lernen ist Gewohnheitssache!

Lerne Vokabeln in Ruhe zu Hause, möglichst immer am gleichen Arbeitsplatz. Versuche einen Arbeitsplatz zu finden, an dem du immer ohne Störung arbeiten kannst.
Wenn du mit Musik lernen kannst, dann versuche, zum Lernen eine ruhige Musik zu finden.
An deinem Arbeitsplatz solltest du auch zu Beginn der Arbeit alles zur Hand haben: Schreibzeug, Hefte, Bücher, Karteikasten usw.

Step A At the airport

(a) **airport** [ˈeəpɔːt] — Flughafen
people *(pl)* [ˈpiːpl] — The Burtons are nice *people*. — Leute
Heathrow [ˌhiːˈθrəʊ] — Name eines Londoner Flughafens

there are [ðeər_ˈɑː] — *There are* three airports in Berlin. — es gibt, es sind
there is [ðeər_ˈɪz] — *There is* a very big airport in Frankfurt. — es gibt, es ist
(b) **Jenny** [ˈdʒenɪ] — weibl. Vorname
Her father is German. [hɜː ˌfɑːðər_ɪz ˈdʒɜːmən] — Ihr Vater ist Deutscher.
British [ˈbrɪtɪʃ] — britisch
aunt [ɑːnt] — Tante
uncle [ˈʌŋkl] — Onkel
cousin [ˈkʌzn] — Cousin/e
Mark [mɑːk] — männl. Vorname
Welcome to … [ˈwelkəm tʊ] — Willkommen in …
to help [help] — helfen

Mrs Penrose is my *aunt*, Mr Penrose is my *uncle* and David and Mark are my *cousins*.

2 **Italian** [ɪˈtæljən] — italienisch, Italienisch
Spanish [ˈspænɪʃ] — spanisch, Spanisch
Greek [griːk] — griechisch, Griechisch
Turkish [ˈtɜːkɪʃ] — türkisch, Türkisch
Poland [ˈpəʊlənd] — Polen
to start [stɑːt] — anfangen, beginnen
to ask for [ˈɑːsk fɔː] — bitten um

Poland und andere Länder findest du auf der Karte hinten im Buch.

Unit 3

Step B In the car

You're lucky. [jɔ: 'lʌkɪ] Du hast Glück.
to be **lucky** [bɪ 'lʌkɪ] Glück haben
can [kæn] können
to **speak** [spi:k] sprechen
can't [kɑ:nt] nicht können
to **do** [du:] tun, machen
What about … ? [wɒt ə'baʊt] Was ist mit … ?
who [hu:] wer

quiz [kwɪz] Quiz, Ratespiel
to **tell** [tel] erzählen

Step B At home in Sherwood

Aunty ['ɑ:ntɪ] *Anrede für eine Tante*
so [səʊ] also
present ['prezənt] A *present* for Becky. Geschenk

Pat [pæt] *weibl. Vorname*
Colin ['kɒlɪn] *männl. Vorname*

Edward's Lane *Straße in Nottingham*
  ['edwədz ˌleɪn]
Mansfield Road *Straße in Nottingham*
  ['mænsfi:ld 'rəʊd]
form [fɔ:m] Form
houses *(pl)* ['haʊzɪz] Häuser

Vorsicht bei der Aussprache:
hou*s*e [haʊs], houses ['haʊzɪz]

Step B Let's say hello

her [hɜ:] ihr/sie
to **give** [gɪv] geben
me [mi:] mir/mich

him [hɪm] ihm/ihn
to [tu:] *hier:* mit, zu
terrible ['terəbl] schrecklich, furchtbar
maybe ['meɪbi:] vielleicht
to **phone** [fəʊn] anrufen

on the telephone am Telefon
  [ɒn ðə 'telɪfəʊn]

this afternoon heute Nachmittag
  [ðɪs ˌɑ:ftə'nu:n]
must [mʌst] müssen
to **go to the shops** einkaufen gehen
  [gəʊ tə ðə 'ʃɒps]
uniform ['ju:nɪfɔ:m] Uniform

Unit 3

Looking at the UK: How can you get there?

How can you get there?
[ˌhaʊ kən jʊ ˈget ðeə]
to **get there** [ˈget ðeə]
by [baɪ]
plane [pleɪn]
ferry [ˈferɪ]
hovercraft [ˈhɒvəkrɑːft]
train [treɪn]
through [θruː]
Channel Tunnel [ˈtʃænl ˈtʌnl]

The Channel [ðə ˈtʃænl]
tunnel [ˈtʌnl]
2 **map** [mæp]
from ... to [frəm ... tə]
Belgium [ˈbeldʒəm]
the Netherlands
[ðə ˈneðələndz]
France [frɑːns]
North Sea [nɔːθ ˈsiː]
sea [siː]
3 **photo** [ˈfəʊtəʊ]

Wie kannst du/kann man
  dort hinkommen?
hinkommen
hier: mit
Flugzeug
Fähre
Luftkissenboot
Zug
durch
Tunnel unter dem
  Ärmelkanal
Ärmelkanal
Tunnel
Landkarte
hier: von ... nach
Belgien
die Niederlande

Frankreich
Nordsee
Meer
Foto

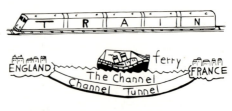

Diese Länder findest du auch auf der Karte hinten im Buch.

Step C Tea

tea [tiː]

ham [hæm]
cheese [tʃiːz]

2 **What's for tea?** [wɒts fə ˈtiː]

salad [ˈsæləd]
bread [bred]
butter [ˈbʌtə]
milk [mɪlk]
tea [tiː]
sugar [ˈʃʊgə]
3 to **pass** [pɑːs]
to **have** [hæv]
of [ɒv], [əv]

hier: Mahlzeit am
  frühen Abend
gekochter Schinken
Käse

Was gibt es zum Abend-
  brot?
gemischter Salat
Brot
Butter
Milch
Tee
Zucker
reichen, weitergeben
haben
von

Can I have the milk, please?
Can you pass me the sugar, please?

Step D The photo

camera [ˈkæmərə]
right away [ˈraɪt əˈweɪ]
to **take a photo of**
  [teɪk əˈfəʊtəʊ ɒv]
all [ɔːl]
cannot [ˈkænɒt], [kɑːnt]
only [ˈəʊnlɪ]
leg [leg]

Fotoapparat, Kamera
sofort
ein Foto machen von

alle/alles
nicht können
nur, erst
Bein

Cannot wird in einem Wort geschrieben.

story [ˈstɔːrɪ]	Mark can tell the *story* about the frog.	Geschichte, Erzählung
like [laɪk]		(so) wie

Step E Let's check

different [ˈdɪfrənt]	unterschiedlich, anders

⟨Christmas¹ in the UK⟩

¹Christmas [ˈkrɪsməs] *Weihnachten* – ²Christmas eve [ˈkrɪsməs ˈiːv] *Heiligabend* – ³stocking [ˈstɒkɪŋ] *Strumpf* – ⁴Father Christmas [ˌfɑðə ˈkrɪsməs] *Weihnachtsmann* – ⁵mince pie [ˌmɪns ˈpaɪ] *gefülltes Weihnachtsgebäck* – ⁶a long way [ə ˈlɒŋ weɪ] *langer Weg* – ⁷December [dɪˈsembə] *Dezember* – ⁸Christmas Day [ˌkrɪsməs ˈdeɪ] *Erster Weihnachtsfeiertag* – ⁹dinner [ˈdɪnə] *Essen, Hauptmahlzeit* – ¹⁰turkey [ˈtɜːkɪ] *Truthahn* – ¹¹Christmas pudding [ˌkrɪsməs ˈpʊdɪŋ] *kuchenartige Weihnachtssüßspeise* – ¹²cracker [ˈkrækə] *Knallbonbon* – ¹³to pull [pʊl] *ziehen* – ¹⁴to wait [weɪt] *warten* – ¹⁵till [tɪl] *bis zum/zur* – ¹⁶hat [hæt] *Hut* – ¹⁷Boxing Day [ˈbɒksɪŋ ˌdeɪ] *Zweiter Weihnachtsfeiertag* – ¹⁸ticket [ˈtɪkɪt] *Eintrittskarte* – ¹⁹pantomime [ˈpæntəmaɪm] *Weihnachtsmärchen* – ²⁰Aladdin [əˈlædɪn] *Aladin* – ²¹play [pleɪ] *Schauspiel* – ²²song [sɒŋ] *Lied* – ²³It's great fun [ɪts ˌgreɪt ˈfʌn] *Es macht viel Spaß* – ²⁴to wish [wɪʃ] *wünschen* – ²⁵merry [ˈmerɪ] *fröhlich* – ²⁶happy [ˈhæpɪ] *glücklich*

⟨Revision 1⟩

revision [rɪˈvɪʒn]	Wiederholung

Unit 4 Free time

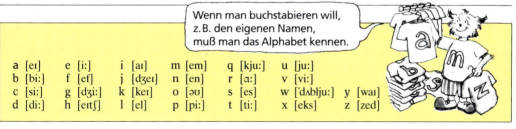

free [friː]	frei
time [taɪm]	Zeit

Step A The alphabet

alphabet [ˈælfəbət]		Alphabet
ABC book [eɪbiːˈsiː ˌbʊk]		ABC-Fibel
letter [ˈletə]	The alphabet has got 26 *letters*.	Buchstabe
rhyme [raɪm]		Reim
then [ðen]		dann
to count [kaʊnt]		zählen
of course [əv ˈkɔːs]		natürlich, selbstverständlich

Unit 4

Vocabulary

shoe [ʃuː]		Schuh
last [lɑːst]	Z is the *last* letter in the alphabet.	letzter/letzte/letztes
It's time for … [ɪts‿ˈtaɪm fə]	Now *it's time for* a rhyme.	Es ist Zeit für …
to **watch** [wɒtʃ]		(zu)schauen, gucken
TV [ˈtiːˈviː]		Fernsehen
boring [ˈbɔːrɪŋ]	Can I *read* your comic, please? Yes, of course.	langweilig
to **read** [riːd]		lesen
kite [kaɪt]		Drachen
well [wel]		gut, nun, na ja
to **repair** [rɪˈpeə]		reparieren

2
to **spell** [spel]	Can you *spell* your name? M-A-R-K.	buchstabieren
to **think** [θɪŋk]		denken, glauben

Step B **In the living-room**

to **be on** [bɪ‿ˈɒn]	Listen! The radio *is on*.	eingeschaltet sein
nobody [ˈnəʊbədɪ]		niemand, keiner

2
in the evening [ɪnði‿ˈiːvnɪŋ]	in the morning ⟷ *in the evening*	abends, am Abend
evening [ˈiːvnɪŋ]		Abend

Step B **Mrs Croft**

to **come** [kʌm]		kommen
In a minute. [ɪn‿ə ˈmɪnɪt]		Augenblick noch! Warte/ mal einen Moment.
minute [ˈmɪnɪt]		Minute
just [dʒʌst]	I'm *just* repairing my kite. Can you help me? – Yes, *in a minute*.	eben, gerade, nur
to **wash up** [wɒʃ‿ˈʌp]		abwaschen, (Geschirr) spülen
Ugh! [ɜːh]		*Ausruf des Abscheus*
to **work late** [ˈwɜːk leɪt]		länger arbeiten
on (the radio) [ɒn]		*hier:* im (Rundfunk)
job [dʒɒb]	What's Mr Dixon's *job*? He's a bank clerk.	Beruf, Arbeit
exciting [ɪkˈsaɪtɪŋ]		aufregend, spannend

4
to **think of** [ˈθɪŋk‿əv]		ausdenken
activity [ækˈtɪvɪtɪ]		Tätigkeit
to **find out** [faɪnd‿ˈaʊt]		herausfinden

Step B **The idea**

them [ðem]	The boys are working in the garden. Let's help *them*.	sie/ihnen
stone [stəʊn]		Stein
round [raʊnd]		um … herum
it [ɪt]		ihn/sie/es; ihm/ihr
to **get** [get]		bekommen
out [aʊt]	in ⟷ *out*	draußen, heraus
us [ʌs]	We are in the garden. Can you see *us*?	uns

164 *one hundred and sixty-four*

Unit 4

Vocabulary

you [juː]   dich/euch/Sie; dir/euch/Ihnen

spade [speɪd]   Spaten

Looking at the UK: Free time

This ball is for *tennis*.

tennis ['tenɪs]   Tennis

It isn't for *cricket*.

cricket ['krɪkɪt]   *englischer Rasensport*
pop music ['pɒp 'mjuːzɪk]   Popmusik
music ['mjuːzɪk]   Musik

same [seɪm]   gleich
T-shirt ['tiːʃɜːt]   T-Shirt
sweatshirt ['swetʃɜːt]   Sweatshirt
badminton ['bædmɪntən]   Federballspiel

Step C What's the weather like?

What's ... like?   Wie ist ... ?
    [wɒts ... laɪk]
weather ['weðə]   Wetter
warm [wɔːm]   warm
sunny ['sʌnɪ]   sonnig
windy ['wɪndɪ]   windig
to go for a walk   spazieren gehen
    [ˌgəʊ fər_ə 'wɔːk]
walk [wɔːk]   Spaziergang
to rain [reɪn]   regnen
cold [kəʊld]   kalt
wet [wet]   nass

to sit [sɪt]   sitzen
to sail [seɪl]   segeln
cross [krɒs]   über
stormy ['stɔːmɪ]   stürmisch
waters *(pl)* ['wɔːtəz]   Gewässer
near [nɪə]   nahe

Step D The flowerpot

flowerpot ['flaʊəpɒt]   Blumentopf
Saturday ['sætədɪ]   Samstag, Sonnabend
no [nəʊ]   kein/keine
team [tiːm]   Mannschaft
door [dɔː]   *hier:* (Garagen-)Tor
goal [gəʊl]   Tor *(beim Sport)*
to be good at ... [bɪ 'gʊd_ət] Sarah *is good at* football.   gut sein in ...
to kick [kɪk]   treten, mit dem Fuß stoßen

Crash! [kræʃ]   Rums!
floor [flɔː]   Boden

one hundred and sixty-five **165**

Unit 4

Audrey [ˈɔːdrɪ]   weibl. Vorname
to **laugh** [lɑːf]   lachen
angry [ˈæŋgrɪ]   böse, verärgert

Monny is *laughing*.

3   **exercise** [ˈeksəsaɪz]   Übung, Aufgabe

Step E **Let's check**

2   **opposite** [ˈɒpəzɪt]   Yes ⟷ No, little ⟷ big are *opposites*.   Gegenteil

Hobbies:		tennis	Tennis
ball	Ball	TV	Fernsehen
bike	Fahrrad	video (U 5)	Video
boat (U 9)	Boot		
camcorder (U 5)	Videokamera	to dance (U 5)	tanzen
CD player	CD-Spieler	to draw	zeichnen
cinema (U 6)	Kino	to go for a walk	spazieren gehen
comic	Comic	to go swimming (U 9)	schwimmen gehen
computer	Computer	to listen	zuhören
cricket	engl. Rasensport	to make a cake (U 5)	einen Kuchen backen
drama group (U 7)	Theatergruppe	to play	spielen
football	Fußball	to phone	anrufen
game	Spiel	to read	lesen
guitar (U 5)	Gitarre	to repair	reparieren
kite	Drachen	to sing (U 5)	singen
pop music	Popmusik	to take a photo of	ein Foto machen von
radio	Radio	to watch	(zu)schauen, gucken
skateboard	Skateboard	to work in the garden	im Garten arbeiten

Unit 5 Jenny's birthday

Vokabellernen kannst du auch spielend, allein oder mit Freunden aus deiner Klasse.

„Remember"

Schreib die englischen Wörter, die du lernen willst, auf kleine Zettel. Auf die Rückseite jedes Zettels schreibst du in einer anderen Farbe die deutsche Bedeutung. (Wenn du eine Kartei führst, kannst du auch die Karteikarten nehmen.)
Breite die Karten mit der deutschen Bedeutung nach oben aus. Wenn du den englischen Begriff nennen kannst, darfst du die Karte einsammeln. Wenn du beim Überprüfen feststellst, dass deine Antwort nicht richtig war, musst du die Karte wieder hinlegen.
Das Spiel geht natürlich auch umgekehrt.

Step A A surprise party

Surprise, surprise!

birthday [ˈbɜːθdeɪ]		Geburtstag
surprise [səˈpraɪz]		Überraschung
party [ˈpɑːtɪ]		Party, Feier
in … days [ɪn … deɪz]		in … Tagen
day [deɪ]		Tag
invitation [ˌɪnvɪˈteɪʃn]		Einladung
to invite [ɪnˈvaɪt]		einladen
cake [keɪk]		Kuchen, Torte
problem [ˈprɒbləm]		Problem
guitar [gɪˈtɑː]	David can play the *guitar.*	Gitarre
to sing [sɪŋ]		singen
to dance [dɑːns]		tanzen

ten [ten]	zehn	**twenty** [ˈtwentɪ]	zwanzig
eleven [ɪˈlevn]	elf	**twenty-one** [ˌtwentɪˈwʌn]	einundzwanzig
twelve [twelv]	zwölf	**thirty** [ˈθɜːtɪ]	dreißig
thirteen [ˌθɜːˈtiːn]	dreizehn	**forty** [ˈfɔːtɪ]	vierzig
fourteen [ˌfɔːˈtiːn]	vierzehn	**fifty** [ˈfɪftɪ]	fünfzig
fifteen [ˌfɪfˈtiːn]	fünfzehn	**sixty** [ˈsɪkstɪ]	sechzig
sixteen [ˌsɪksˈtiːn]	sechzehn	**seventy** [ˈsevntɪ]	siebzig
seventeen [ˌsevnˈtiːn]	siebzehn	**eighty** [ˈeɪtɪ]	achtzig
eighteen [ˌeɪˈtiːn]	achtzehn	**ninety** [ˈnaɪntɪ]	neunzig
nineteen [ˌnaɪnˈtiːn]	neunzehn	**a hundred** [əˈhʌndrəd]	hundert

over [ˈəʊvə]   under ⟷ *over*   über

Unit 5

Step A Jenny's letter

letter ['letə]   a letter   Brief
dear [dɪə]   liebe/lieber/liebes
How are you? [haʊ‿'ɑː juː]   3 letters   Wie geht es dir/euch/Ihnen?

I'm fine. [aɪm 'faɪn]   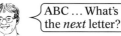   Mir geht's gut.
next [nekst]   nächste/nächster/nächstes

month [mʌnθ]   There are 12 *months* in a year.   Monat
first [fɜːst]   erste/erster/erstes
without [wɪð'aʊt]   You can't write *without* a pen.   ohne
February ['februəri]   Februar
That's all for now.   Das wär's für heute.
  [ðæts 'ɔːl fə ˌnaʊ]
love [lʌv]   *hier:* alles Liebe *(als Briefschluss)*

January ['dʒænjʊəri]	Januar	**July** [dʒʊ'laɪ]	Juli
February ['februəri]	Februar	**August** ['ɔːgəst]	August
March [mɑːtʃ]	März	**September** [sep'tembə]	September
April ['eɪprɪl]	April	**October** [ɒk'təʊbə]	Oktober
May [meɪ]	Mai	**November** [nəʊ'vembə]	November
June [dʒuːn]	Juni	**December** [dɪ'sembə]	Dezember

---

3 to **remember** [rɪ'membə]   behalten, sich merken, sich erinnern

Step B Everyone is very busy

everyone ['evrɪwʌn]   *Everyone* is here.   jede/jeder, alle
busy ['bɪzi]   The children are very *busy*.   beschäftigt
to get ready [get 'redi] They are *getting ready* for school. (sich) vorbereiten
shopping list ['ʃɒpɪŋ lɪst]   Einkaufsliste
list [lɪst]   Here's a *list* of the children in 7MD. Liste
to lie [laɪ]   liegen
she is lying [ʃiːz 'laɪɪŋ]   sie liegt im Augenblick
balloon [bə'luːn]   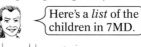   Luftballon

Step B What is the date?

date [deɪt]   Datum
on the seventh of   am siebten
  [ɒn ðə 'sevnθ‿əv]
at ... o'clock [ət ... ə'klɒk]   um ... Uhr
3 when [wen]   wann

Unit 5

first [fɜːst]	erste/r/s	**sixteenth** [ˌsɪksˈtiːnθ]	sechzehnte/r/s
second [ˈsekənd]	zweite/r/s	**seventeenth** [ˌsevnˈtiːnθ]	siebzehnte/r/s
third [θɜːd]	dritte/r/s	**eighteenth** [ˌeɪˈtiːnθ]	achtzehnte/r/s
fourth [fɔːθ]	vierte/r/s	**nineteenth** [ˌnaɪnˈtiːnθ]	neunzehnte/r/s
fifth [fɪfθ]	fünfte/r/s	**twentieth** [ˈtwentɪəθ]	zwanzigste/r/s
sixth [sɪksθ]	sechste/r/s	**twenty-first** [ˈtwentɪfɜːst]	einundzwanzigste/r/s
seventh [ˈsevnθ]	siebte/r/s		
eighth [eɪtθ]	achte/r/s	**thirtieth** [ˈθɜːtɪəθ]	dreißigste/r/s
ninth [naɪnθ]	neunte/r/s	**fortieth** [ˈfɔːtɪəθ]	vierzigste/r/s
tenth [tenθ]	zehnte/r/s	**fiftieth** [ˈfɪftɪəθ]	fünfzigste/r/s
eleventh [ɪˈlevnθ]	elfte/r/s	**sixtieth** [ˈsɪkstɪəθ]	sechzigste/r/s
twelfth [twelfθ]	zwölfte/r/s	**seventieth** [ˈsevntɪəθ]	siebzigste/r/s
thirteenth [ˌθɜːˈtiːnθ]	dreizehnte/r/s	**eightieth** [ˈeɪtɪəθ]	achtzigste/r/s
fourteenth [ˌfɔːˈtiːnθ]	vierzehnte/r/s	**ninetieth** [ˈnaɪntɪəθ]	neunzigste/r/s
fifteenth [ˌfɪfˈtiːnθ]	fünfzehnte/r/s	**hundredth** [ˈhʌndrətθ]	hundertste/r/s

Step C What time is it?

What time is it? [ˌwɒt ˈtaɪm ɪz ɪt] — Wie spät ist es? Wie viel Uhr ist es?
quarter [ˈkwɔːtə] — Viertel
past [pɑːst] — nach *(bei Uhrzeiten)*

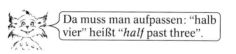

Da muss man aufpassen: "halb vier" heißt "half past three".

half [hɑːf] — halb; Hälfte
to [tʊ], [tə] — *hier:* vor
to tell the time [ˈtel ðə ˈtaɪm] — die Uhrzeit angeben
tomorrow [təˈmɒrəʊ] — morgen

Looking at the UK: A British house

upstairs [ˌʌpˈsteəz] — oben (im Gebäude)
bedroom [ˈbedrʊm] — Schlafzimmer
bathroom [ˈbɑːθrʊm] — Badezimmer
toilet [ˈtɔɪlɪt] — Toilette
downstairs [ˌdaʊnˈsteəz] — unten (im Gebäude)
hall [hɔːl] — Diele, Flur
bath [bɑːθ] — Bad, Badewanne
to have a bath [hæv ə ˈbɑːθ] — baden
breakfast [ˈbrekfəst] — Frühstück
plan [plæn] — Plan

Step D A great birthday

candle [ˈkændl] — Kerze
another [əˈnʌðə] — noch einen/eine/eins
happy [ˈhæpɪ] — fröhlich, glücklich
Happy birthday! [ˌhæpɪ ˈbɜːθdeɪ] — Herzlichen Glückwunsch zum Geburtstag!
video [ˈvɪdɪəʊ] — Video
Helen [ˈhelɪn] — *weibl. Vorname*

Unit 5 / ⟨Revision 2⟩ / Unit 6

Vocabulary

House:
backdoor ↔ front door (U8)	Hintertür ↔ Haustür	living-room	Wohnzimmer
bathroom	Badezimmer	parents' bedroom	Elternschlafzimmer
bed	Bett	room	Raum, Zimmer, Platz
chair	Stuhl	shelf (shelves)	Regal/e
children's bedroom	Kinderschlafzimmer	spoon	Löffel
flat	Wohnung	table	Tisch
floor	Boden, Stockwerk	telephone	Telefon
fork (neu)	Gabel	toilet	Toilette
garage	Garage	window (U 8)	Fenster
garden	Garten		
hall	Diele, Flur	to be locked (U 8)	abgeschlossen sein
kitchen	Küche	at home	zu Hause
knife (knives)	Messer	upstairs ↔ downstairs	unten ↔ oben
ladder (U 8)	Leiter		

⟨Patrick's first day⟩

¹Oh dear! [əʊ 'dɪə] *Oh je!* – ²to open ['əʊpən] *öffnen*

⟨Nottingham: what can you do there?⟩

¹leaflet ['liːflɪt] *Prospekt* – ²to finish ['fɪnɪʃ] *beenden, aufhören* – ³to buy [baɪ] *kaufen* – ⁴clothes ['kləʊðz] *Kleidung* – ⁵museum [mjuː'zɪəm] *Museum* – ⁶fan [fæn] *Fan* – ⁷game [geɪm] *Spiel*

⟨Revision 2⟩

camcorder ['kæmkɔːdə]   Videokamera
scene [siːn]   Szene

Unit 6 In town

> Es führt kein Weg daran vorbei:
> Die Schreibweise der Wörter
> prägt sich am besten durch Schreiben ein.

Das Aufschreiben der Wörter für deine Lernkartei
oder in dein Vokabelheft hilft dir schon, die Schreibweise zu behalten.
Besonders schwierige Wörter kannst du auf einen Haftzettel schreiben,
dabei die Buchstaben, die du sonst immer falsch schreibst, in einer stärkeren
Farbe hervorheben. Diese Zettel heftest du z.B. in der Nähe deines Arbeits-
platzes oder am Bett an. So prägen sie sich gut ein.

Step A In Nottingham

town [taʊn]   Stadt
Robin Hood ['rɒbɪn 'hʊd]   Figur einer englischen
    Sage

170 *one hundred and seventy*

Unit 6

Vocabulary

statue ['stætʃu:]		Statue, Denkmal
in front of [ɪn 'frʌnt əv]		vor
castle ['kɑ:sl]	Neuschwanstein is a *castle* in Germany.	Burg
Old Market Square [əʊld 'mɑ:kɪt 'skweə]		*Platz in Nottingham*
market ['mɑ:kɪt]		Markt
square ['skweə]		Platz
centre ['sentə]		Mitte, Zentrum
city ['sɪtɪ]		(Groß-)Stadt
shopping centre ['ʃɒpɪŋ ˌsentə]		Einkaufszentrum
Victoria [vɪk'tɔ:rɪə]		*weibl. Vorname*
a lot of [ə'lɒt əv]	 *a lot of* boxes	viel/viele, eine Menge
restaurant ['restərɒnt]	I'm hungry. Let's go to that *restaurant*.	Restaurant
street [stri:t]		Straße
St Peter's Church [snt ˌpi:təz 'tʃɜ:tʃ]		Sankt-Peter-Kirche
church [tʃɜ:tʃ]		Kirche
near [nɪə]	The Crofts' house is *near* the Dixons' house in Larwood Grove.	in der Nähe von

Step B Days of the week

week [wi:k]	There are seven days in a *week*.	Woche
Friday ['fraɪdeɪ]		Freitag
Saturday ['sætədeɪ]		Samstag
into ['ɪntʊ]		in, hinein
cinema ['sɪnɪmə]		Kino
too [tu:]	*Why* can't Mark get the biscuits from the shelf?	allzu, zu
why [waɪ]		warum
because [bɪ'kɒz]	*Because* he's too little.	weil
to get the bus [ˌget ðə 'bʌs]		den Bus nehmen
bus [bʌs]	Vorsicht bei der Pluralform: *buses*!	Bus
end [end]		Ende
double decker ['dʌbl 'dekə]		Doppeldecker
at the bottom of [ət ðə 'bɒtəm əv]	at the top of ⟷ at the bottom of	unten, am unteren Ende
to walk [wɔ:k]		(zu Fuß) gehen
bus stop ['bʌs stɒp]		Bushaltestelle

Monday ['mʌndeɪ]	Montag	**Friday** ['fraɪdeɪ]	Freitag
Tuesday ['tju:zdeɪ]	Dienstag	**Saturday** ['sætədeɪ]	Samstag
Wednesday ['wenzdeɪ]	Mittwoch	**Sunday** ['sʌndeɪ]	Sonntag
Thursday ['θɜ:zdeɪ]	Donnerstag		

---

best [best]	Mrs Dane is the *best* English teacher at our school. She's my *favourite* teacher, too.	beste/bester/bestes
favourite ['feɪvərɪt]		Lieblings-
calendar ['kælɪndə]		Kalender

one hundred and seventy-one **171**

Unit 6

Vocabulary

Step C At the Victoria shopping centre

to **try** on [traɪ_ˈɒn]	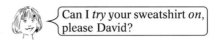 Can I *try* your sweatshirt *on*, please David?	anprobieren
clothes *(pl)* [ˈkləʊðz]		Kleider
jeans *(pl)* [dʒiːnz]	These *jeans* are red. They're nice.	Jeans
pullover [ˈpʊlˌəʊvə]		Pullover
to **wear** [weə]	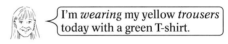 I'm *wearing* my yellow *trousers* today with a green T-shirt.	tragen, anhaben
trousers *(pl)* [ˈtraʊzəz]		Hose/Hosen
anorak [ˈænəræk]		Anorak
shirt [ʃɜːt]		Hemd(bluse)

3 to **answer** [ˈɑːnsə]   Please *answer* the question. Give me an answer please.   (be)antworten

Step C Excuse me, please

Excuse me, please. [ɪkˈskjuːz mɪ pliːz]		Entschuldigung. Entschuldigen Sie bitte.
to **tell** [tel]		sagen, mitteilen
way [weɪ]		Weg
down [daʊn]	up ⟷ *down*	herunter, hinunter
Friar Lane [ˈfraɪə ˈleɪn]		Straßenname
straight on [streɪt_ˈɒn]	Don't *turn* left. Go *straight on*.	geradeaus
to **turn** [tɜːn]		abbiegen
left [left]		(nach) links
Maid Marian Way [ˌmeɪd ˈmærɪən ˈweɪ]		Straßenname
right [raɪt]	left ⟷ *right*	(nach) rechts
Castle Gate [ˈkɑːsl ˈgeɪt]		Straßenname
on the left/right [ɒn ðə ˈleft], [ɒn ðə ˈraɪt]	 That's Becky, *on the right*.	links/rechts, auf der linken/rechten Seite
Angel Row [ˈeɪndʒəl ˈrəʊ]		Straßenname
Mount Street [ˈmaʊnt ˌstriːt]		Straßenname
Beastmarket Hill [ˈbiːstmɑːkɪt ˈhɪl]		Straßenname
hill [hɪl]		Hügel
Parliament Street [ˈpɑːləmənt ˌstriːt]		Straßenname
South Parade [ˈsaʊθ pəˈreɪd]		Straßenname
Exchange Walk [ɪksˈtʃeɪndʒ ˈwɔːk]		Straßenname

6 **behind** [bɪˈhaɪnd]   in front ⟷ *behind*   hinter

Step C David's grandma

grandma [ˈgrænmɑː]	Oma
Twinning Office [ˈtwɪnɪŋ ˌɒfɪs]	Städtepartnerschaftsbüro
office [ˈɒfɪs]	Büro, Amt

172 *one hundred and seventy-two*

Unit 6

to **eat** [iːt]		essen
hot [hɒt]	cold ⟷ hot	heiß
potato, *(pl)* potatoes [pəˈteɪtəʊ]		Kartoffel
special [ˈspeʃəl]		besondere/r/s; *hier:* Spezialität des Hauses
tomato, *(pl)* tomatoes [təˈmɑːtəʊ]		Tomate
person [ˈpɜːsn]	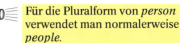 Für die Pluralform von *person* verwendet man normalerweise *people*.	Person
twin town [ˈtwɪn ˈtaʊn]		Partnerstadt
twin [twɪn]		Zwilling

Step D Robert and Jenny in town

Beeston [ˈbiːstən]		Bezirk von Nottingham
driver [ˈdraɪvə]		Fahrer/in
Bestwood [ˈbestwʊd]		Bezirk von Nottingham
long [lɒŋ]		lang
back [bæk]		zurück
worried [ˈwʌrɪd]	w⊙rried	besorgt, beunruhigt
to **stand** [stænd]		stehen
to **stop** [stɒp]	start ⟷ stop	anhalten
to **give ... a lift** [lɪft]		... im Auto mitnehmen

Clothes:		skirt *(neu)*		Rock	
anorak	*Anorak*	trousers		*Hose, Hosen*	
colour	*Farbe*	T-shirt		*T-Shirt*	
jacket *(neu)*	*Jacke*	uniform		*Uniform*	
jeans	*Jeans*				
pair	*Paar*	to buy (U 7) ⟷ to sell (U 8)		*kaufen ⟷ verkaufen*	
pocket (U 8)	*Tasche*	to wear clothes		*Kleidung tragen, anhaben*	
pullover	*Pullover*	to go to the shops		*einkaufen gehen*	
sweatshirt	*Sweatshirt*				
shirt	*Hemd(bluse)*	big ⟷ small		*groß ⟷ klein*	
shoe	*Schuh*	different ⟷ same		*unterschiedlich ⟷ gleich*	
shop	*Geschäft, Laden*	favourite		*Lieblings-*	
shopping-centre	*Einkaufszentrum*	short (U 9) ⟷ long		*kurz ⟷ lang*	
size (U 7)	*Größe*	warm ⟷ cold		*warm ⟷ kalt*	

Unit 7

Unit 7 School days

Die neuen Vokabeln kann man immer. Aber Wörter, die länger zurückliegen, fallen einem nicht mehr ein.

Dass man nicht alles behält, ist doch normal.
Dagegen hilft Wiederholung.
Nimm dir zusammen mit Freunden Vokabeln aus einer früheren Unit vor.
Ihr könnt sie euch gegenseitig ganz durcheinander abfragen oder
das Remember-Spiel damit machen.

Step A Lunch time

(a) **competition** [kɒmpəˈtɪʃn] — Wettbewerb, Preisausschreiben
healthy living [ˈhelθɪ ˈlɪvɪŋ] — gesunde Lebensweise
prize [praɪz] — The first *prize* in the competition is a bike. — Preis, Gewinn
to lend [lend] — leihen, verleihen
p [piː] — *Abkürzung für* penny, pence *(kleinste britische Münze)*

sausage [ˈsɒsɪdʒ] — Würstchen, Wurst
chips *(pl)* [tʃɪps] — Pommes frites
How much? [haʊ ˈmʌtʃ] — *How much* are the chips? – They're 60p. — Wie viel?
£1 [wʌn ˈpaʊnd] — £1 = 100p — britisches Geld
to buy [baɪ] — kaufen
packet [ˈpækɪt] — A packet of *crisps*. — Päckchen
crisps *(pl)* [krɪsps] — Kartoffelchips

(b) **money** [ˈmʌnɪ] — Geld
pence *(pl)* [pens] — Say "sixty p" or "sixty *pence*". — Pfennige *(britisches Geld)*
pound (= £) [paʊnd] — £1.20: say "one *pound* twenty". — Pfund *(britisches Geld)*
reduced in size [rɪˌdjuːst ɪn ˈsaɪz] — verkleinert
size [saɪz] — Größe

1 **White** [waɪt] — *Familienname*
white [waɪt] — weiß

Step B Jenny's day

to get up [getˈʌp] — aufstehen
every [ˈevrɪ] — jede/jeder/jedes
to finish [ˈfɪnɪʃ] — beenden, aufhören
to come home [kʌm ˈhəʊm] — nach Hause kommen

1 **after** [ˈɑːftə] — nach
to go to bed [gəʊ tə ˈbed] — to get up ⟷ to go to bed — ins Bett gehen, schlafen gehen

174 *one hundred and seventy-four*

Unit 7

Vocabulary

Step B **Mark's day**

early [ˈɜːlɪ]	late ⟷ *early*	früh
cornflakes *(pl)* [ˈkɔːnfleɪks]		Cornflakes
nursery school [ˈnɜːsərɪ ˌskuːl]	Mark is only 4. He goes to *nursery school*.	Kindergarten
to **collect** [kəˈlekt]		abholen
irregular [ɪˈregjʊlə]		unregelmäßig

Step B **A busy day**

sometimes [ˈsʌmtaɪmz]		manchmal
never [ˈnevə]		nie
often [ˈɒfn]		oft
always [ˈɔːlweɪz]	never ⟷ *always*	immer
to **take home** [teɪk ˈhəʊm]		nach Hause bringen
word order [ˈwɜːd ˌɔːdə]		Satzstellung
to **do the washing-up** [ˈduː ðə ˌwɒʃɪŋˈʌp]		spülen, abwaschen
washing-up [ˌwɒʃɪŋˈʌp]		Abwasch
Oh dear! [əʊ ˈdɪə]		Oh je!
mess [mes]		Unordnung
to **tidy up** [ˈtaɪdɪ ˌʌp]		aufräumen
tidy [ˈtaɪdɪ]	untidy ⟷ *tidy*	ordentlich, aufgeräumt
door [dɔː]		Tür
Well done! [wel ˈdʌn]		Gut gemacht! Bravo!
housework [ˈhaʊswɜːk]		Hausarbeit

Looking at the UK: Haywood School

assembly [əˈsemblɪ]		Versammlung
pupil [ˈpjuːpl]	There are 630 *pupils* at Haywood School.	Schüler/in
drama group [ˈdrɑːmə gruːp]		Theatergruppe
hockey [ˈhɒkɪ]		Rasenhockey

Step C **The poster**

Get out! [get ˈaʊt]	Hinaus mit dir!/Hinaus mit euch!
dirty [ˈdɜːtɪ]	schmutzig, dreckig
head [hed]	Kopf
arm [ɑːm]	Arm
hand [hænd]	Hand
eye [aɪ]	Auge
mouth [maʊθ]	Mund
beetle [ˈbiːtl]	Käfer
body [ˈbɒdɪ]	Körper
exercise book [ˈeksəsaɪz ˌbʊk]	Heft

one hundred and seventy-five **175**

Unit 7

winner ['wɪnə]   Gewinner/in
feeler ['fi:lə]   Fühler
⟨3⟩ shoulder ['ʃəʊldə]   Schulter
knee [ni:]   Knie
toe [təʊ]   Zeh
ear [ɪə]   Ohr
nose [nəʊz]   Nase

Step C At the shops

ⓐ **pound** [paʊnd]   Pfund *(Gewicht)*
banana [bə'nɑ:nə]   Banane
Anything else? ['enɪθɪŋ 'els]   Sonst noch etwas? ✳
pint [paɪnt]   *etwa 0,5l*
ⓑ **bottle** ['bɒtl]   Flasche ✳
lemonade [lemə'neɪd]   Limonade
bar [bɑ:]   Tafel ✳

4 to **go together** [gəʊ tə'geðə]   zusammenpassen
lb = pound [paʊnd]   *Abkürzung für* pound
           (Gewicht)

6 **supermarket** ['su:pəˌmɑ:kɪt]   Supermarkt

Step D The healthy living prize

Benson ['bensn]   *Familienname*
headteacher [ˌhed'ti:tʃə]   Schuldirektor/in
to **take** [teɪk]   nehmen
lucky ['lʌkɪ]   glücklich, Glücks-
Peter ['pi:tə]   *männl. Vorname*
Wall [wɔ:l]   *Familienname*
Annabel ['ænəbel]   *weibl. Vorname*
Barker ['bɑ:kə]   *Familienname*
Suvina [sə'vi:nə]   *weibl. Vorname*
Adib [ə'dɪb]   *Familienname*
extra ['ekstrə]   zusätzlich
soap [səʊp]   Seife
bubble bath ['bʌbl ˌbɑ:θ]   Schaumbad
to **trip** ['trɪp]   stolpern
to **fall over** [fɔ:l‿'əʊvə]   hinfallen
all over ['ɔ:l‿əʊvə]   überall auf
3 **verb** [vɜ:b]   Verb

Step E Let's check

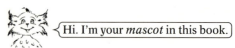

5 **mascot** ['mæskət]   Maskottchen

176 *one hundred and seventy-six*

Food:		milk	Milch
apple	Apfel	milkshake (U 10)	Milchmixgetränk
banana	Banane	potato, potatoes	Kartoffel/n
biscuit	Keks	salad	Salat
bread	Brot	sausage	Würstchen, Wurst
butter	Butter	sugar	Zucker
cake	Kuchen, Torte	sweet (U 8)	Bonbon, süß
chocolate	Schokolade	tea	Tee (Mahlzeit am frühen Abend)
cheese	Käse		
chips	Pommes frites	tomato, tomatoes	Tomate/n
cornflakes	Cornflakes	water (U 9)	Wasser
crisps	Kartoffelchips		
egg	Ei	to eat	essen
fish (U 8)	Fisch	to drink (U 10)	trinken
fish finger (U 8)	Fischstäbchen		
ham	gekochter Schinken	hungry	hungrig
ice cream (U 8)	Eiskrem	healthy ↔ unhealthy	gesund ↔ ungesund
lemonade	Limonade		

⟨ **Nottingham castle caves**[1] ⟩

[1] cave [keɪv] *Höhle* – [2] to meet [mi:t] *treffen, sich treffen* – [3] torch [tɔ:tʃ] *Taschenlampe* – [4] to explore [ɪkˈsplɔ:] *erforschen, erkunden* – [5] ticket [ˈtɪkɪt] *Eintrittskarte* – [6] tour [tʊə] *Führung* – [7] half an hour [ˈhɑ:f ən ˈaʊə] *eine halbe Stunde* – [8] guide [gaɪd] *Führer* – [9] to keep together [ˌki:p təˈgeðə] *zusammenbleiben* – [10] step [step] *Stufe* – [11] to forget [fəˈget] *vergessen* – [12] corner [ˈkɔ:nə] *Ecke* – [13] at the back of [ət ðə ˈbæk əv] *hinten* – [14] treasure [ˈtreʒə] *Schatz* – [15] suddenly [ˈsʌdənlɪ] *plötzlich* – [16] something [ˈsʌmθɪŋ] *etwas* – [17] bracelet [ˈbreɪslɪt] *Armband* – [18] dark [dɑ:k] *dunkel* – [19] to drop [drɒp] *fallen lassen* – [20] at last [ət ˈlɑ:st] *endlich* – [21] to look for [ˈlʊk fɔ:] *suchen*

Unit 8 The accident

Wörter alphabetisch ordnen – kein Problem!

Manchmal hilft es beim Wiederholen, Wörter in eine ganz neue Reihenfolge zu bringen. Du könntest z.B. die Wörter deines Lernpäckchens in alphabetischer Reihenfolge oder nach Wortgruppen zusammenstellen. Wenn du einen Karteikasten angelegt hast, kannst du die Wörter aus dem hinteren Fach jetzt alphabetisch ordnen. Dazu musst du nicht nur auf den ersten, sondern auch auf die folgenden Buchstaben achten. Beispiel: Unter „s" kommt das Wort *shop* vor *soap*, weil das „h" im Alphabet vor dem „o" kommt.

accident [ˈæksɪdənt]   Unfall

Step A Money and jobs

pocket money [ˈpɒkɪt ˌmʌnɪ]   Taschengeld
pocket [ˈpɒkɪt]   Tasche (*bei Kleidung*)
sweet [swi:t]   Bonbon
magazine [ˌmægəˈzi:n]   Zeitschrift
to save [seɪv]   sparen

Unit 8

Vocabulary

(b) to **sell** [sel] — verkaufen
to **like** [laɪk] — mögen, gern haben
to **want** [wɒnt] — (haben) wollen
to **need** [niːd] — brauchen, benötigen
shop assistant [ˈʃɒpəˌsɪstənt] — Verkäufer/in
to **know** [nəʊ] — wissen, kennen
mechanic [mɪˈkænɪk] — Mechaniker/in

 Wie bei *knife* wird das *k* nicht gesprochen, so dass *know* genau wie *no* klingt.

Step B Saturday morning

song [sɒŋ] — Lied
'**n**' [n] — und (*kurze gesprochene Form von* and)
"Happy Birthday to you" is a song.
Two 'n' Two = Two and Two

I don't like … [aɪ dəʊnt ˈlaɪk] — ich mag nicht …
Bye. [baɪ] — Tschüs! (*kurze gesprochene Form von* Goodbye.)

Achtung bei der Aussprache von *don't* [dəʊnt]!

Step B In Edward's Lane

popular [ˈpɒpjʊlə] — beliebt
to **go home** [gəʊ ˈhəʊm] — nach Hause gehen

Step C In hospital

hospital [ˈhɒspɪtl] — Krankenhaus
It's good to see you. [ɪts ˌgʊd tə ˈsiː jʊ] — Schön, dich/euch zu sehen.
to **hurt** [hɜːt] — weh tun, schmerzen
a bit [əˈbɪt] — etwas, ein bisschen
I hope you're better soon. [aɪ ˈhəʊp jʊə ˌbetə ˈsuːn] — Ich hoffe, es geht dir bald besser.
to **hope** [həʊp] — hoffen
soon [suːn] — bald
nurse [nɜːs] — Krankenschwester/ Krankenpfleger
A *nurse*. She works in a hospital.

cupboard [ˈkʌbəd] — Schrank

4 **card** [kɑːd] — Karte
Let's buy a nice *card* for David's birthday.

Get well soon! [ˈget wel ˈsuːn] — Gute Besserung!
Get well soon = I hope you're better soon.

6 **request** [rɪˈkwest] — Bitte, Wunsch
Anna [ˈænə] — *weibl. Vorname*
Hunt [ˈhʌnt] — *Familienname*
Michael [ˈmaɪkəl] — *männl. Vorname*
Hilton [ˈhɪltən] — *Familienname*

7 to **use** [juːz] — benutzen
My pen's broken. I can't *use* it.

178 *one hundred and seventy-eight*

Unit 8

Vocabulary

Looking at the UK: Help!

Help! [help]	Hilfe!
to call [kɔːl]	rufen, anrufen
fire brigade [ˈfaɪə brɪˌɡeɪd]	Feuerwehr
ambulance [ˈæmbjʊləns]	Krankenwagen
police [pəˈliːs]	Polizei
to take [teɪk]	*hier:* bringen
fireman [ˈfaɪəmən]	Feuerwehrmann
police officer [pəˈliːs ˌɒfɪsə]	Polizist/in
doctor [ˈdɒktə]	Arzt/Ärztin

Step D **Fish fingers and ice cream**

fish finger [fɪʃ ˈfɪŋɡə]		Fischstäbchen
fish [fɪʃ]	one *fish* – three *fish*	Fisch
ice cream [ˌaɪs ˈkriːm]		Eiskrem
give my love to … [ˌɡɪv maɪ ˈlʌv tə]		grüß/grüßt … recht herzlich
usually [ˈjuːʒʊəlɪ]		gewöhnlich, normaler-weise
firm [fɜːm]		Firma
to open [ˈəʊpən]		öffnen, aufmachen
front door [ˈfrʌnt ˈdɔː]		Haustür
to close [kləʊz]	to open – *to close*	schließen, zumachen
back door [ˈbæk ˈdɔː]		Hintertür
locked [lɒkt]		abgeschlossen
to wait for [ˈweɪt fɔː]		warten auf
window [ˈwɪndəʊ]		Fenster
open [ˈəʊpən]		offen, geöffnet
ladder [ˈlædə]		Leiter
text [tekst]		Text
ending [ˈendɪŋ]		Ende, Schluss *(bei Ge-schichten)*
to climb up [ˌklaɪm ˈʌp]	Achtung: das *b* in *climb* wird nicht gesprochen.	hochklettern, erklettern
burglar [ˈbɜːɡlə]		Einbrecher/in
to get stuck [ɡet ˈstʌk]		stecken bleiben

Step E **Let's check**

fun [fʌn]	Spaß

Body:		ear	*Ohr*	foot *(neu)*	*Fuß*	leg	*Bein*
arm	*Arm*	eye	*Auge*	hand	*Hand*	mouth	*Mund*
body	*Körper*	feet	*Füße*	head	*Kopf*	nose	*Nase*

one hundred and seventy-nine **179**

Unit 9

Unit 9 A day at the seaside

Du behältst Vokabeln besonders gut, wenn du sie zusätzlich vor dem Einschlafen noch einmal ansiehst.

Vokabeln lernen im Schlaf?

at the seaside [ət ðə ˈsiːsaɪd] — am Meer, an der See

Step A On the train

Skegness [skegˈnes] — englischer Seebadeort
seat [siːt] — There are four *seats* there, let's sit down. — Sitz, Sitzplatz
ticket [ˈtɪkɪt] — Fahrkarte
beach [biːtʃ] — Strand
to **go swimming** [gəʊ ˈswɪmɪŋ] — schwimmen gehen
Never mind. [ˈnevə ˌmaɪnd] — Mach dir nichts daraus./ Macht euch nichts daraus.

boating lake [ˈbəʊtɪŋ leɪk] — Bootsteich
lake [leɪk] — (der) See, Teich
boat [bəʊt] — Boot

⟨2⟩ **sun** [sʌn] — Sonne
to **have on** [hæv ˈɒn] — anhaben, tragen
hat [hæt] — Hut
hip, hip, hurray [hɪp hɪp hʊˈreɪ] — hipp, hipp, hurra!
everybody [ˈevrɪbɒdɪ] — = everyone — jede/jeder
gay [geɪ] — fröhlich
holiday [ˈhɒlədɪ] — Urlaub(stag)

Step B At Skegness

station [ˈsteɪʃn] — Look, the train is coming into the *station*. — Bahnhof
the High Street [ˈhaɪ striːt] — Bei diesem Straßennamen verwendet man ausnahmsweise *the*. — Straßenname, etwa "Hauptstraße"
dog-free zone [ˈdɒgfriː ˈzəʊn] — hundefreie Zone
to **meet** [miːt] — Let's *meet* after school and do our homework together. — (sich) treffen
snack bar [ˈsnæk bɑː] — Imbissstube

180 *one hundred and eighty*

Unit 9

Step B At the boating lake

hour ['aʊə]   60 minutes = 1 hour   Stunde
really ['rɪəlɪ]   wirklich
to cost [kɒst]   The apples *cost* 60p.   kosten

short [ʃɔːt]   long ⟷ *short*   kurz

Step B On the beach

crab [kræb]   Krebs
to live [lɪv]   The Burtons *live* in Sherwood.   leben, wohnen
rock [rɒk]   Fels
water ['wɔːtə]   Wasser

room [ruːm]   *hier:* Platz

Looking at the UK: At Skegness

timetable ['taɪmteɪbl]   Fahrplan
to leave [liːv]   *hier:* abfahren
to arrive [ə'raɪv]   to leave ⟷ *to arrive*   ankommen

Step C The sandcastle

sandcastle ['sændkɑːsl]   Sandburg
promenade [ˌprɒmə'nɑːd]   Promenade
bucket ['bʌkɪt]   Eimer
to look [lʊk]   aussehen
small [smɔːl]   klein
bookshop ['bʊkʃɒp]   Buchhandlung

Step C At a souvenir shop

souvenir [ˌsuːvə'nɪə]   Souvenir, Andenken, Mitbringsel
postcard ['pəʊstkɑːd]   Postkarte
to say hello ['seɪ hə'ləʊ]   grüßen

Unit 9 / ⟨Revision 3⟩ / Unit 10

Vocabulary

Step D **Maxi's day at the seaside**

pet [pet]	Haustier
sandwich ['sænwɪdʒ]	belegtes Brot
to **understand** [ˌʌndə'stænd]	verstehen
glad [glæd]	froh
to **sleep** [sli:p]	schlafen
duck [dʌk]	Ente
to **bark** [bɑ:k]	bellen
rubbish ['rʌbɪʃ]	Abfall, Müll
to **show** [ʃəʊ]	zeigen
to **get lost** [get 'lɒst]	verloren gehen, sich verirren

⟨The fun run[1]⟩

[1]fun run ['fʌn 'rʌn] *Volkslauf* – [2]characters ['kærəktəz] *Personen* – [3]to hurry up [ˌhʌrɪ 'ʌp] *sich beeilen* – [4]school trip ['sku:l ˌtrip] *Schulausflug* – [5]Austria ['ɒstrɪə] *Österreich* – [6]to run [rʌn] *laufen* – [7]playing fields ['pleɪɪŋ fi:ldz] *Sportplatz* – [8]sponsor ['spɒnsə] *Förderer* – [9]one time [ˌwʌn 'taɪm] *einmal* – [10]costume ['kɒstju:m] *Kostüm* – [11]wheelchair ['wi:ltʃeə] *Rollstuhl* – [12]What's ... for? ['wɒts ... fɔ:] *Wozu ist ... gut?* – [13]clown [klaʊn] *Clown* – [14]back [bæk] *Rücken* – [15]sad [sæd] *traurig* – [16]to ski [ski:] *Ski laufen* – [17]starting point of the race ['stɑ:tɪŋ pɔɪnt əv ðə 'reɪs] *Ausgangspunkt des Rennens* – [18]saxophone ['sæksəfəʊn] *Saxofon* – [19]to carry ['kærɪ] *tragen* – [20]finish ['fɪnɪʃ] *Ziel, Ende* – [21]to run off [rʌn 'ɒf] *loslaufen* – [22]saints [seɪnts] *Heilige* – [23]break [breɪk] *Pause* – [24]on the plane [ɒn ðə 'pleɪn] *im Flugzeug* – [25]beautiful ['bju:təfʊl] *schön* – [26]mountains ['maʊntɪnz] *Berge* – [27]snow [snəʊ] *Schnee* – [28]to pay for ['peɪ fɔ:] *(be)zahlen für* – [29]fair [feə] *gerecht, fair* – [30]to collect [kə'lekt] *sammeln* – [31]cheers [tʃɪəz] *Hurrageschrei, Jubel*

⟨Revision 3⟩

Cleethorpes ['kli:θɔ:ps]	*englischer Seebadeort*
Debbie ['debi]	*weibl. Vorname*

Unit 10 On a Yorkshire farm

Eine Spielmöglichkeit ist die Vokabelkette, die du allein oder mit Freunden spielen kannst.
Einer nennt ein Wort. Der nächste muss ein zweites Wort finden, das mit dem letzten Buchstaben des ersten Wortes anfängt.
Schau dir Monnys Vokabelkette an.

Yorkshire ['jɔ:kʃə]	*Grafschaft in England*
farm [fɑ:m]	Bauernhof

Step A **Springfield farm**

Springfield ['sprɪŋfi:ld]	*Name eines Bauernhofs*

182 *one hundred and eighty-two*

Let's play with words

1 Word puzzle

Du kennst bereits viele englische Wörter, die im Deutschen gleich sind, wie z. B. COMPUTER. Kannst du alle Wörter aus dem Puzzle zusammensetzen?

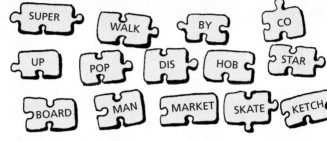

2 Word snakes

Welche Wörter findest du in den Schlangen? Schreibt man sie groß oder klein?

3 At the pond

Kannst du aus dem Teich die Wörter herausfischen, die zusammengehören? Bring sie auch in eine sinnvolle Reihenfolge. Welcher Fisch bleibt im Teich?

4 Word game

Denk an ein Wort. Wie viele andere Wörter kannst du finden, die etwas mit diesem Wort zu tun haben?

In dieser Spielwiese kannst du noch einmal mit den Wörtern spielen, die du in diesem Buch gelernt hast. Vielleicht kannst du auch selber solche Spiele mit anderen Wörtern zusammenstellen?

one hundred and eighty-three **183**

Unit 10

to **stay** [steɪ]		(zu Besuch) wohnen
Richards ['rɪtʃədz]		*Familienname*
guest house ['gest haʊs]	You can stay at a *guest house* at the seaside for a holiday.	Pension, Gästehaus
guest [gest]		Gast
Jack [dʒæk]		*männl. Vorname*
sheep *(sg + pl)* [ʃiːp]	one *sheep* two *sheep*	Schaf, Schafe
Sam [sæm]		*männl. Vorname*
sheepdog ['ʃiːpdɒg]		Hirtenhund
lamb [læm]	A *lamb* is a little sheep.	Lamm
lambing time ['læmɪŋ taɪm]		Zeit, in der Lämmer geboren werden
Lenny ['lenɪ]		*männl. Vorname*
animal ['ænɪməl]	Sheep, cats and dogs are *animals*.	Tier
cow [kaʊ]	We get milk from *cows*.	Kuh
pig [pɪg]	We get ham from *pigs*.	Schwein
hen [hen]	We get eggs from *hens*.	Henne
Grandpa ['grænpɑː]		Opa
to **feed** [fiːd]	Simon, Maxi and Mini are hungry. Can you *feed* them, please?	füttern
to **collect** [kə'lekt]		(ein)sammeln
to **lay** [leɪ]	Hens *lay* eggs.	legen

Step B Jack's special friend

enough [ɪ'nʌf]	Do we need sugar? No, we've got *enough*.	genug
to **drink** [drɪŋk]	You can *drink* tea, milk or lemonade.	trinken
all [ɔːl]		ganz

3 **post office** ['pəʊst ˌɒfɪs]		Post, Postamt
Northallerton [nɔː'θælətən]		*Ort in Yorkshire*
to **drive** [draɪv]	Can you *drive* a car? – No, I'm only 15.	fahren
⟨5⟩ **had** [hæd],		hatte
some [sʌm]		einige
chick [tʃɪk]		Küken
everywhere ['evrɪweə]		überall

Step B The tractor

tractor ['træktə]		Traktor, Trecker
who [huː]		wen/wem

Step C The seasons

ⓐ **season** ['siːzn]		Jahreszeit
spring [sprɪŋ]		Frühling
holidays ['hɒlədɪz]	The summer *holidays* are in July and August.	Ferien

Unit 10

summer ['sʌmə] — Sommer
autumn ['ɔːtəm] — Herbst
winter ['wɪntə] — Winter
snow [snəʊ] — *Snow* makes everything white in winter. — Schnee
night [naɪt] — day ⟷ *night* — Nacht
milkshake ['mɪlkʃeɪk] — Milchmixgetränk
how many [haʊ 'menɪ] — *How many* seasons are there? – Four. — wie viele

Step D Problems on the farm

Mary ['meərɪ] — *weibl. Vorname*
to be in trouble [bɪ ɪn 'trʌbl] — I'm late. I'm *in trouble* again. — Schwierigkeiten haben
trouble ['trʌbl] — Schwierigkeiten
tired ['taɪəd] — müde
shed [ʃed] — Stall, Schuppen

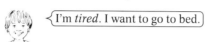

to wait [weɪt] — I'm not ready! Please *wait*. — warten
Alan ['ælən] — *männl. Vorname*
Smith [smɪθ] — *Familienname*
to examine [ɪg'zæmɪn] — untersuchen
inside [ɪn'saɪd] — outside ⟷ *inside* — drinnen
dead [ded] — tot
to save [seɪv] — Firemen often *save* people from fires. — retten
to stay [steɪ] — bleiben
to feel [fiːl] — fühlen, sich fühlen
to die [daɪ] — sterben
to trick [trɪk] — austricksen

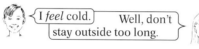

trick [trɪk] — Trick, Kunstgriff
skin [skɪn] — Haut
Walker ['wɔːkə] — *Familienname*
to bring [brɪŋ] — Please *bring* bread and milk from the shop. — mitbringen
free [friː] — kostenlos

⟨A holiday[1] in Scotland[2]⟩

[1] holiday ['hɒlɪdeɪ] *Ferien* – [2] Scotland ['skɒtlənd] *Schottland* – [3] Inverness [ˌɪnvə'nes] *Stadt in Schottland* – [4] McNeil [mək'niːl] *schottischer Familienname* – [5] farmhouse ['fɑːmhaʊs] *Bauernhaus* – [6] lovely ['lʌvlɪ] *hübsch, toll* – [7] Tulloch House [ˌtʌlək 'haʊs] *Name eines Hauses* – [8] Duncan ['dʌnkən] *schottischer Familienname* – [9] key [kiː] *Schlüssel* – [10] stream [striːm] *Bach* – [11] to run [rʌn] *rennen, laufen* – [12] excited [ɪk'saɪtɪd] *aufgeregt* – [13] to sniff [snɪf] *schnüffeln* – [14] to sleep [sliːp] *schlafen* – [15] to wake up [weɪk 'ʌp] *aufwachen* – [16] to run about [rʌn ə'baʊt] *herumrennen* – [17] tonight [tə'naɪt] *heute Nacht* – [18] to go to sleep [ˌgəʊ tə 'sliːp] *einschlafen* – [19] Loch Ness [ˌlɒk 'nes] *schottischer See* – [20] monster ['mɒnstə] *Ungeheuer* – [21] ghost [gəʊst] *Geist, Gespenst* – [22] someone ['sʌmwʌn] *jemand* – [23] storm [stɔːm] *Sturm, Unwetter* – [24] to look after [ˌlʊk 'ɑːftə] *aufpassen auf* – [25] shape [ʃeɪp] *Gestalt, Figur* – [26] to jump [dʒʌmp] *springen* – [27] Oh dear! [əʊ 'dɪə] *Oh! Oh je!*

Alphabetical word list

In dieser alphabetischen Liste ist das gesamte Vokabular von *Red Line New 1 Bayern* enthalten. Namen werden in einer gesonderten Liste nach dem Vokabular aufgeführt.

Der Wortschatz aus Übungen und Texten, die in Spitzklammern ⟨ ⟩ stehen, ist wahlfrei.

Die Zahlen verweisen auf das erstmalige Vorkommen der Wörter, z. B.
afternoon [ˌɑːftəˈnuːn] Nachmittag **LS**, 14 = Let's start, Seite 14
again [əˈgen] **2**, 33 = Unit 2, Seite 33

A

a [ə] ein/eine **LS**, 9
to talk **about** [ˈtɔːk‿əˌbaʊt] reden über, sprechen über **2**, 32
What about … ? [wɒt‿əˈbaʊt] Was ist mit … ? **3**, 38
accident [ˈæksɪdənt] Unfall **8**, 90
to **act** [ækt] spielen, nachspielen **2**, 32
activity [ækˈtɪvɪtɪ] Tätigkeit **4**, 50
after [ˈɑːftə] nach **7**, 80
afternoon [ˌɑːftəˈnuːn] Nachmittag **LS**, 14
Good afternoon. [gʊd ˌɑːftəˈnuːn] Guten Tag. (*Anrede am Nachmittag*) **LS**, 16
in the afternoon [ɪn ðiː‿ˌɑːftəˈnuːn] nachmittags, am Nachmittag **LS**, 14
this afternoon [ðɪs‿ˌɑːftəˈnuːn] heute Nachmittag **3**, 40
again [əˈgen] wieder, noch einmal **2**, 33
airport [ˈeəpɔːt] Flughafen **3**, 37
all [ɔːl] ganz **10**, 114
all over [ˈɔːl‿ˌəʊvə] überall auf **7**, 86
all [ɔːl] alle/alles **3**, 43
alphabet [ˈælfəbət] Alphabet **4**, 48
always [ˈɔːlweɪz] immer **7**, 82
ambulance [ˈæmbjʊləns] Krankenwagen **8**, 95
an [ən] ein/eine **1**, 23
and [ænd] und **LS**, 8
angry [ˈæŋrɪ] böse, verärgert **4**, 54
animal [ˈænɪməl] Tier **10**, 113
anorak [ˈænəræk] Anorak **6**, 73
another [əˈnʌðə] noch einen/eine/eins **5**, 64
answer [ˈɑːnsə] Antwort **LS**, 12
to **answer** [ˈɑːnsə] (be)antworten **6**, 73
Anything else? [ˈenɪθɪŋ ˈels] Sonst noch etwas? **7**, 85
apple [ˈæpl] Apfel **1**, 23
April [ˈeɪprəl] April **5**, 58
are [ɑː] bist/seid/sind **LS**, 11
arm [ɑːm] Arm **7**, 84
to **arrive** [əˈraɪv] ankommen **9**, 103
to **ask** [ɑːsk] fragen **1**, 21
to ask for [ˈɑːsk fɔː] bitten um **3**, 37
assembly [əˈsemblɪ] Versammlung **7**, 83
assistant [əˈsɪstənt] Helfer/in, Assistent/in **2**, 28
at [æt] , [ət] an **LS**, 9
at home [ət ˈhəʊm] zu Hause **1**, 18
at … o'clock [ət … əˈklɒk] um … Uhr **5**, 60
at the bottom of [ət ðə ˈbɒtəm‿əv] unten, am unteren Ende **6**, 72
at the top of [ət ðə ˈtɒp‿əv] ganz oben **2**, 33
August [ˈɔːgəst] August **5**, 58
aunt [ɑːnt] Tante **3**, 37
Aunty [ˈɑːntɪ] *Anrede für eine Tante* **3**, 39
autumn [ˈɔːtəm] Herbst **10**, 117

B

back [bæk] zurück **6**, 76
back door [ˈbæk ˈdɔː] Hintertür **8**, 96
bad [bæd] schlimm, schlecht **1**, 21
badminton [ˈbædmɪntən] Federballspiel **4**, 52
bag [bæg] Tasche **LS**, 10
ball [bɔːl] Ball **LS**, 10
balloon [bəˈluːn] Luftballon **5**, 59
banana [bəˈnɑːnə] Banane **7**, 85
bank [bæŋk] Bank **2**, 28
bank clerk [ˈbæŋk ˌklɑːk] Bankangestellte/r **2**, 28
bar [bɑː] Tafel **7**, 85
to **bark** [bɑːk] bellen **9**, 106
bath [bɑːθ] Bad, Badewanne **5**, 63
to have a bath [hæv‿ə ˈbɑːθ] baden **5**, 63
bathroom [ˈbɑːθrʊm] Badezimmer **5**, 63
to **be** [bɪ] sein **2**, 33
Be careful! [bɪ ˈkeəfʊl] Pass auf!, Vorsicht! **2**, 33
to be good at [bɪ ˈgʊd‿ət] gut sein in … **4**, 54
to be lucky [bɪ ˈlʌkɪ] Glück haben **3**, 38
to be on [bɪ ˈɒn] eingeschaltet sein **4**, 50
beach [biːtʃ] Strand **9**, 99
because [bɪˈkɒz] weil **6**, 72
bed [bed] Bett **1**, 18
bedroom [ˈbedrʊm] Schlafzimmer **5**, 63
beetle [ˈbiːtl] Käfer **7**, 84
behind [bɪˈhaɪnd] hinter **6**, 74
best [best] beste/bester/bestes **6**, 72
better [ˈbetə] besser **8**, 93
I hope you're better soon. [aɪ ˈhəʊp jʊə ˌbetə ˈsuːn] Ich hoffe, es geht dir bald besser. **8**, 93
big [bɪg] groß **1**, 21
bike [baɪk] Fahrrad **1**, 25
biro [ˈbaɪrəʊ] Kugelschreiber **LS**, 10
birthday [ˈbɜːθdeɪ] Geburtstag **5**, 57
biscuit [ˈbɪskɪt] Keks **1**, 18
a **bit** [əˈbɪt] etwas, ein bisschen **8**, 93
black [blæk] schwarz **2**, 28
blue [bluː] blau **2**, 28
boat [bəʊt] Boot **9**, 99
boating lake [ˈbəʊtɪŋ leɪk] Bootsteich **9**, 99
body [ˈbɒdɪ] Körper **7**, 84
book [bʊk] Buch **LS**, 10
boring [ˈbɔːrɪŋ] langweilig **4**, 48
bottle [ˈbɒtl] Flasche **7**, 85
box [bɒks] Schachtel, Kiste, Dose **LS**, 10
lunch box [ˈlʌntʃ bɒks] *Dose für belegte Brote zum Mittagessen* **LS**, 10
boy [bɔɪ] Junge **LS**, 12
bread [bred] Brot **3**, 42
breakfast [ˈbrekfəst] Frühstück **5**, 63
to **bring** [brɪŋ] bringen **LS**, 16; mitbringen **10**, 120

Alphabetical word list

British [ˈbrɪtɪʃ] britisch **3**, 37
broken [ˈbrəʊkən] kaputt, zerbrochen **1**, 23
brother [ˈbrʌðə] Bruder **1**, 18
brown [braʊn] braun **2**, 28
bubble bath [ˈbʌbl ˌbaːθ] Schaumbad **7**, 86
bucket [ˈbʌkɪt] Eimer **9**, 104
burglar [ˈbɜːɡlə] Einbrecher/in **8**, 97
bus [bʌs] Bus **6**, 72
　bus stop [ˈbʌs stɒp] Bushaltestelle **6**, 72
busy [ˈbɪzɪ] beschäftigt **5**, 59
but [bʌt] aber **1**, 18
butter [ˈbʌtə] Butter **3**, 42
to buy [baɪ] kaufen **7**, 79
by [baɪ] mit **3**, 41
Bye. [baɪ] Tschüs! (*kurze gesprochene Form von* Goodbye.) **8**, 91

C

cake [keɪk] Kuchen, Torte **5**, 57
calendar [ˈkælɪndə] Kalender **6**, 72
to call [kɔːl] rufen, anrufen **8**, 95
⟨**camcorder**⟩ [ˈkæmkɔːdə] Videokamera **R 2**, 69
camera [ˈkæmərə] Fotoapparat, Kamera **3**, 43
can [kæn] können **3**, 38
　cannot [ˈkænɒt], [kaːnt] nicht können **3**, 43
　can't [kaːnt] nicht können **3**, 38
candle [ˈkændl] Kerze **5**, 64
car [kaː] Auto **1**, 18
card [kaːd] Karte **8**, 94
Be **careful!** [bɪ ˈkeəfʊl] Pass auf!, Vorsicht! **2**, 33
case [keɪs] Etui, Hülle **LS**, 10
　pencil case [ˈpensl keɪs] Federmäppchen **LS**, 10
castle [ˈkaːsl] Burg **6**, 71
cat [kæt] Katze **2**, 28
CD [siː ˈdiː] CD **1**, 20
　CD player [siː ˈdiː pleɪə] CD-Spieler **1**, 20
centre [ˈsentə] Mitte, Zentrum **6**, 71
chair [tʃeə] Stuhl **LS**, 13
to check [tʃek] überprüfen, kontrollieren **LS**, 17
cheese [tʃiːz] Käse **3**, 42
⟨**chick**⟩ [tʃɪk] Küken **10**, 115
child [tʃaɪld], **children** (pl) [ˈtʃɪldrən] Kind, Kinder **2**, 28
chips (pl) [tʃɪps] Pommes frites **7**, 79
chocolate [ˈtʃɒklət] Schokolade **LS**, 15
church [tʃɜːtʃ] Kirche **6**, 71
cinema [ˈsɪnɪmə] Kino **6**, 72
city [ˈsɪtɪ] (Groß-)Stadt **6**, 71
⟨**to clap**⟩ [klæp] klatschen **1**, 19
class [klaːs] Klasse (*in einer deutschen Schule*) **LS**, 9
classroom [ˈklaːsrʊm] Klassenzimmer **LS**, 16
clerk [klaːk] Büroangestellte/r **2**, 28
　bank clerk [ˈbæŋk ˌklaːk] Bankangestellte/r **2**, 28
clever [ˈklevə] intelligent, klug **1**, 18
to climb up [ˌklaɪm ˈʌp] hochklettern, erklettern **8**, 97
to close [kləʊz] schließen, zumachen **8**, 96
clothes (pl) [ˈkləʊðz] Kleider **6**, 73
cold [kəʊld] kalt **4**, 53
to collect [kəˈlekt] abholen **7**, 81; (ein)sammeln **10**, 113
colour [ˈkʌlə] Farbe **2**, 28
to come [kʌm] kommen **4**, 50
　Come on! [kəmˈɒn] Komm schon!, Kommt schon! **2**, 33
　to come home [kʌm ˈhəʊm] nach Hause kommen **7**, 80
　⟨to come in⟩ [kʌmˈɪn] hereinkommen **1**, 26

comic [ˈkɒmɪk] Comic **LS**, 10
competition [kɒmpəˈtɪʃn] Wettbewerb, Preisausschreiben **7**, 79
computer [kəmˈpjuːtə] Computer **1**, 20
cornflakes (pl) [ˈkɔːnfleɪks] Cornflakes **7**, 81
to correct [kəˈrekt] korrigieren, verbessern **LS**, 16
to cost [kɒst] kosten **9**, 101
to count [kaʊnt] zählen **4**, 48
cousin [ˈkʌzn] Cousin/e **3**, 37
cow [kaʊ] Kuh **10**, 113
crab [kræb] Krebs **9**, 102
Crash! [kræʃ] Rums! **4**, 54
crayon [ˈkreɪən] Buntstift **2**, 28
crazy [ˈkreɪzɪ] verrückt **LS**, 10
cricket [ˈkrɪkɪt] *englischer Rasensport* **4**, 52
crisps (pl) [krɪsps] Kartoffelchips **7**, 79
⟨**'cross**⟩ [krɒs] über **4**, 53
cupboard [ˈkʌbəd] Schrank **8**, 93

D

Dad [dæd] Vati, Papa **1**, 19
to dance [daːns] tanzen **5**, 57
date [deɪt] Datum **5**, 60
day [deɪ] Tag **5**, 57
　in … days [ɪn … deɪz] in … Tagen **5**, 57
dead [ded] tot **10**, 118
dear [dɪə] liebe/lieber/liebes **5**, 58
　oh **dear** [əʊ ˈdɪə] Oh je! **7**, 82
December [dɪˈsembə] Dezember **5**, 58
desk [desk] Schreibtisch, Pult **LS**, 13
dialogue [ˈdaɪəlɒg] Dialog, Gespräch **2**, 32
dice (sg + pl) [daɪs] Würfel **2**, 30
to die [daɪ] sterben **10**, 118
different [ˈdɪfrənt] unterschiedlich, anders **3**, 45
dirty [ˈdɜːtɪ] schmutzig, dreckig **7**, 84
to do [duː] tun, machen **3**, 38
　to do the washing-up [ˈduː ðə ˌwɒʃɪŋˈʌp] spülen, abwaschen **7**, 82
doctor [ˈdɒktə] Arzt/Ärztin **8**, 95
dog [dɒg] Hund **LS**, 8
　dog biscuit [ˈdɒg ˌbɪskɪt] Hundekuchen **1**, 19
　dog-free zone [ˈdɒgfriː ˈzəʊn] hundefreie Zone **9**, 100
door [dɔː] Tür **7**, 82; (Garagen-)Tor **4**, 54
　back door [ˈbæk ˈdɔː] Hintertür **8**, 96
　front door [ˈfrʌnt ˈdɔː] Haustür **8**, 96
double [ˈdʌbl] zweimal, Doppel- **1**, 24
double decker [ˈdʌbl ˈdekə] Doppeldecker **6**, 72
down [daʊn] herunter, hinunter **6**, 74
　to sit down [sɪt ˈdaʊn] sich hinsetzen **LS**, 16
downstairs [ˌdaʊnˈsteəz] unten (im Gebäude) **5**, 63
drama group [ˈdraːmə gruːp] Theatergruppe **7**, 83
to draw [drɔː] zeichnen **2**, 28
to drink [drɪŋk] trinken **10**, 114
to drive [draɪv] fahren **10**, 115
driver [ˈdraɪvə] Fahrer/in **6**, 76
duck [dʌk] Ente **9**, 106

E

⟨**ear**⟩ [ɪə] Ohr **7**, 84
early [ˈɜːlɪ] früh **7**, 81
easy [ˈiːzɪ] einfach, leicht **LS**, 14
to eat [iːt] essen **6**, 75

one hundred and eighty-seven **187**

Alphabetical word list

egg [eg] Ei **1**, 23
else [els] sonst (noch) **7**, 85
end [end] Ende **6**, 72
ending ['endɪŋ] Ende, Schluss (*bei Geschichten*) **8**, 97
English ['ɪŋglɪʃ] englisch, Englisch **LS**, 10
enough [ɪ'nʌf] genug **10**, 114
evening ['i:vnɪŋ] Abend **4**, 49
　in the evening [ɪnðɪ_'i:vnɪŋ] abends, am Abend **4**, 49
every ['evrɪ] jede/jeder/jedes **7**, 80
⟨**everybody**⟩ ['evrɪbɒdɪ] jede/jeder **9**, 99
everyone ['evrɪwʌn] jede/jeder, alle **5**, 59
everything ['evrɪθɪŋ] alles **2**, 33
⟨**everywhere**⟩ ['evrɪweə] überall **10**, 115
to **examine** [ɪg'zæmɪn] untersuchen **10**, 118
example [ɪg'zɑ:mpl] Beispiel **1**, 18
exciting [ɪk'saɪtɪŋ] aufregend, spannend **4**, 50
Excuse me, please. [ɪk'skju:z mɪ pli:z] Entschuldigung., Entschuldigen Sie bitte. **6**, 74
exercise ['eksəsaɪz] Übung, Aufgabe **4**, 55
　exercise book ['eksəsaɪz ˌbʊk] Heft **7**, 84
extra ['ekstrə] zusätzlich **7**, 86
eye [aɪ] Auge **7**, 84

F

to **fall over** [fɔ:l̩_'əʊvə] hinfallen **7**, 86
family ['fæməlɪ] Familie **2**, 28
farm [fɑ:m] Bauernhof **10**, 113
father ['fɑ:ðə] Vater **1**, 19
favourite ['feɪvərɪt] Lieblings- **6**, 72
February ['februərɪ] Februar **5**, 58
to **feed** [fi:d] füttern **10**, 113
to **feel** [fi:l] fühlen, sich fühlen **10**, 118
feeler ['fi:lə] Fühler **7**, 84
⟨**feet**⟩ *(pl)* [fi:t] Füße **1**, 19
ferry ['ferɪ] Fähre **3**, 41
to **find** [faɪnd] finden **LS**, 15
　to find out [faɪnd_'aʊt] herausfinden **4**, 50
I'm fine. [aɪm 'faɪn] Mir geht's gut. **5**, 58
to **finish** ['fɪnɪʃ] beenden, aufhören **7**, 80
fire brigade ['faɪə brɪˌgeɪd] Feuerwehr **8**, 95
fireman ['faɪəmən] Feuerwehrmann **8**, 95
firm [fɜ:m] Firma **8**, 96
first [fɜ:st] erste/erster/erstes **5**, 58
fish [fɪʃ] Fisch **8**, 96
　fish finger [fɪʃ 'fɪŋgə] Fischstäbchen **8**, 96
flat [flæt] Wohnung **1**, 22
flat [flæt] flach, platt **2**, 30
　flat tyre [ˌflæt 'taɪə] platter Reifen, Platten **2**, 30
floor [flɔ:] Boden **4**, 54
flowerpot ['flaʊəpɒt] Blumentopf **4**, 54
folder ['fəʊldə] Mappe, Hefter **LS**, 10
football ['fʊtbɔ:l] Fußball **1**, 20
for [fɔ:], [fə] für **1**, 18
　to ask for ['ɑ:sk fɔ:] bitten um **3**, 37
form [fɔ:m] Form **3**, 39
free [fri:] kostenlos **10**, 120
free [fri:] frei **4**, 48
Friday ['fraɪdeɪ] Freitag **6**, 72
friend [frend] Freund/in **LS**, 9
frog [frɒg] Frosch **1**, 25
from [frɒm] aus, von **LS**, 8
　from … to [frəm … tə] von … nach **3**, 41
front door ['frʌnt 'dɔ:] Haustür **8**, 96
　in **front of** [ɪn 'frʌnt ɒv] vor **6**, 71
fun [fʌn] Spaß **8**, 98
funny ['fʌnɪ] lustig, komisch **LS**, 16

G

game [geɪm] Spiel **LS**, 13
garage ['gærɑ:dʒ] Garage **2**, 30
garden ['gɑ:dən] Garten **1**, 21
⟨**gay**⟩ [geɪ] fröhlich **9**, 99
German ['dʒɜ:mən] deutsch, Deutsch, Deutsche/r **LS**, 12
to **get** [get] bekommen **4**, 51; holen **2**, 33
　Get out! [get 'aʊt] Hinaus mit dir!, Hinaus mit euch! **7**, 84
　Get well soon! ['get wel 'su:n] Gute Besserung! **8**, 94
　to get lost [get 'lɒst] verloren gehen, sich verirren **9**, 106
　to get ready [get 'redɪ] (sich) vorbereiten **5**, 59
　to get stuck [get 'stʌk] stecken bleiben **8**, 97
　to get the bus [ˌget ðə 'bʌs] den Bus nehmen **6**, 72
　to get there ['get ðeə] hinkommen **3**, 41
　to get up [get_'ʌp] aufstehen **7**, 80
girl [gɜ:l] Mädchen **LS**, 11
to **give** [gɪv] geben **3**, 40
　give my love to … [ˌgɪv maɪ 'lʌv tə] grüß/grüßt … recht herzlich **8**, 96
　to give … a lift [lɪft] … im Auto mitnehmen **6**, 76
glad [glæd] froh **9**, 106
to **go** [gəʊ] gehen, fahren **2**, 30
　to go for a walk [ˌgəʊ fər_ə 'wɔ:k] spazieren gehen **4**, 53
　to go home [gəʊ 'həʊm] nach Hause gehen **8**, 92
　to go on [gəʊ_'ɒn] weitermachen **LS**, 10
　to go swimming [gəʊ 'swɪmɪŋ] schwimmen gehen **9**, 99
　to go to bed [gəʊ tə 'bed] ins Bett gehen, schlafen gehen **7**, 80
　to go to the shops [gəʊ tə ðə 'ʃɒps] einkaufen gehen **3**, 40
　to go together [gəʊ tə'geðə] zusammenpassen **7**, 85
goal [gəʊl] Tor (*beim Sport*) **4**, 54
good [gʊd] gut **LS**, 12
　Good afternoon. [gʊd ɑ:ftə'nu:n] Guten Tag. (*Anrede am Nachmittag*) **LS**, 16
　Good morning. [gʊd 'mɔ:nɪŋ] Guten Morgen. **LS**, 12
　It's good to see you. [ɪts ˌgʊd tə 'si: jʊ] Schön dich/euch zu sehen. **8**, 93
　to be good at [bɪ 'gʊd_ət] gut sein in … **4**, 54
Goodbye. [gʊd'baɪ] Auf Wiedersehen., Tschüs. **LS**, 10
has got [hæz gɒt] hat **1**, 20
　hasn't got ['hæznt gɒt] hat nicht/kein **1**, 20
　have got ['hæv gɒt] haben, besitzen **1**, 21
Grandma ['grænmɑ:] Oma **6**, 75
Grandpa ['grænpɑ:] Opa **10**, 113
great [greɪt] toll, großartig **2**, 29
Greek [gri:k] griechisch, Griechisch **3**, 37
green [gri:n] grün **2**, 28
group [gru:p] Gruppe **LS**, 9
　tutor group ['tju:tə ˌgru:p] Klasse (*in einer englischen Schule*) **LS**, 9
guest [gest] Gast **10**, 113
　guest house ['gest haʊs] Pension, Gästehaus **10**, 113
guitar [gɪ'tɑ:] Gitarre **5**, 57

H

⟨**had**⟩ [hæd] hatte **10**, 115
half [hɑ:f] halb; Hälfte **5**, 61
hall [hɔ:l] Diele, Flur **5**, 63
ham [hæm] gekochter Schinken **3**, 42
hand [hænd] Hand **7**, 84

Alphabetical word list

happy ['hæpɪ] fröhlich, glücklich **5**, 64
Happy birthday! [ˌhæpɪ 'bɜ:θdeɪ] Herzlichen Glückwunsch zum Geburtstag! **5**, 64
has got … [hæz gɒt] hat … **1**, 20
    hasn't got … ['hæznt gɒt] hat nicht/kein … **1**, 20
    ⟨hat⟩ [hæt] Hut **9**, 99
to **have** [hæv] haben **3**, 42
    have got ['hæv gɒt] haben, besitzen **1**, 21
    haven't got … ['hævnt gɒt] nicht haben **1**, 21
    to have a bath [hæv ə 'bɑ:θ] baden **5**, 63
    ⟨to have on⟩ [hæv ˈɒn] anhaben, tragen **9**, 99
he [hi:] er **LS**, 9
    Is he …? ['ɪz 'hi:] Ist er …? **LS**, 9
head [hed] Kopf **7**, 84
headteacher [ˌhed'ti:tʃə] Schuldirektor/in **7**, 86
healthy living ['helθɪ 'lɪvɪŋ] gesunde Lebensweise **7**, 79
Hello. [hə'ləʊ] Hallo., Guten Tag. **LS**, 7
    to say hello ['seɪ hə'ləʊ] grüßen **9**, 105
Help! [help] Hilfe! **8**, 95
to **help** [help] helfen **3**, 37
hen [hen] Henne **10**, 113
her [hɜ:] ihr/ihre **LS**, 12; ihr/sie **3**, 40
here [hɪə] hier **LS**, 10
    Here you are. ['hɪə juˌ'ɑ:] Hier, bitte schön. **2**, 28
    here's (= here is) [hɪəz] hier ist **LS**, 10
Hey! [heɪ] He! **LS**, 13
Hi! [haɪ] Hallo! **1**, 25
hill [hɪl] Hügel **6**, 74
    ⟨on the hillside⟩ [ˌɒn ðə 'hɪlsaɪd] am Hang **2**, 35
him [hɪm] ihm/ihn **3**, 40
    ⟨hip, hip, hurray⟩ [hɪp hɪp hʊ'reɪ] hipp, hipp, hurra! **9**, 99
his [hɪz] sein/seine **LS**, 12
Hmm. Hm., Tja. **LS**, 15
hockey ['hɒkɪ] Rasenhockey **7**, 83
hole [həʊl] Loch **1**, 21
    ⟨holiday⟩ ['hɒlədɪ] Urlaub(stag) **9**, 99
holidays ['hɒlədɪz] Ferien **10**, 117
home [həʊm] Heim, Zuhause **1**, 22
    at home [ət 'həʊm] zu Hause **1**, 18
    to come home [kʌm 'həʊm] nach Hause kommen **7**, 80
    to go home [gəʊ 'həʊm] nach Hause gehen **8**, 92
homework ['həʊmwɜ:k] Hausaufgaben **LS**, 16
to **hope** [həʊp] hoffen **8**, 93
hospital ['hɒspɪtl] Krankenhaus **8**, 93
hot [hɒt] heiß **6**, 75
hour ['aʊə] Stunde **9**, 101
house [haʊs] Haus **1**, 22
housework ['haʊswɜ:k] Hausarbeit **7**, 82
hovercraft ['hɒvəkrɑ:ft] Luftkissenboot **3**, 41
how [haʊ] wie **LS**, 11
    How are you? [haʊˌˈɑ: ju:] Wie geht es dir/euch/Ihnen? **5**, 58
    how many [haʊ 'menɪ] wie viele **10**, 117
    How much? [haʊ 'mʌtʃ] Wie viel? **7**, 79
hungry ['hʌŋgrɪ] hungrig **1**, 19
to **hurt** [hɜ:t] weh tun, schmerzen **8**, 93

I

I [aɪ] ich **LS**, 7
    Am I …? ['æmˌaɪ] Bin ich …? **LS**, 10
    I'm (= I am) [aɪm] ich bin **LS**, 7
    I've got ['aɪv gɒt] Ich habe **1**, 21
ice cream [ˌaɪs 'kri:m] Eiskrem **8**, 96
idea [aɪ'dɪə] Idee **1**, 21

in [ɪn] in **LS**, 7
    in … days [ɪn … deɪz] in … Tagen **5**, 57
    in front of [ɪn 'frʌnt əv] vor **6**, 71
    in the afternoon [ɪn ðiˌ_ɑ:ftə'nu:n] nachmittags, am Nachmittag **LS**, 14
    in the evening [ɪn ðiˌ_'i:vnɪŋ] abends, am Abend **4**, 49
    in the morning [ɪn ðə 'mɔ:nɪŋ] morgens, am Vormittag **LS**, 14
inside [ɪn'saɪd] drinnen **10**, 118
into ['ɪntʊ] in, hinein **6**, 72
invitation [ˌɪnvɪ'teɪʃn] Einladung **5**, 57
to **invite** [ɪn'vaɪt] einladen **5**, 57
irregular [ɪ'regjʊlə] unregelmäßig **7**, 81
is [ɪz] ist **LS**, 8
it [ɪt] es/er/sie **LS**, 13; ihn/sie/es; ihm/ihr **4**, 51
    it's (= it is) [ɪts] es ist, er ist, sie ist **LS**, 13
Italian [ɪ'tæljən] italienisch, Italienisch, Italiener/in **3**, 37
its [ɪts] sein, seine/ihr, ihre **2**, 29

J

January ['dʒænjʊərɪ] Januar **5**, 58
jeans *(sg + pl)* [dʒi:nz] Jeans **6**, 73
job [dʒɒb] Beruf, Arbeit **4**, 50
July [dʒʊ'laɪ] Juli **5**, 58
June [dʒʊ:n] Juni **5**, 58
just [dʒʌst] eben, gerade, nur **4**, 50
    ⟨just the same⟩ [ˌdʒʌst ðə 'seɪm] genau gleich **2**, 35

K

to **kick** [kɪk] treten, mit dem Fuß stoßen **4**, 54
kitchen ['kɪtʃɪn] Küche **1**, 19
kite [kaɪt] Drachen **4**, 48
    ⟨knee⟩ [ni:] Knie **7**, 84
knife [naɪf], **knives** *(pl)* [naɪvz] Messer *(Sg/Pl)* **2**, 29
to **know** [nəʊ] wissen, kennen **8**, 90

L

ladder ['lædə] Leiter **8**, 96
lake [leɪk] (der) See, Teich **9**, 99
lamb [læm] Lamm **10**, 113
lambing time ['læmɪŋ taɪm] Zeit, in der Lämmer geboren werden **10**, 113
last [lɑ:st] letzter/letzte/letztes **4**, 48
late [leɪt] spät, zu spät **LS**, 10
    to work late ['wɜ:k leɪt] länger arbeiten **4**, 50
to **laugh** [lɑ:f] lachen **4**, 54
to **lay** [leɪ] legen **10**, 113
lb (= **pound**) [paʊnd] *Abkürzung für* pound *(Gewicht)* **7**, 86
to **learn** [lɜ:n] lernen **LS**, 14
to **leave** [li:v] abfahren **9**, 103
left [left] (nach) links **6**, 74
    on the left/right [ɒn ðə 'left], [ɒn ðə 'raɪt] links/rechts, auf der linken/rechten Seite **6**, 74
leg [leg] Bein **3**, 43
lemonade [leməˈneɪd] Limonade **7**, 85
to **lend** [lend] leihen, verleihen **7**, 79
lesson [lesn] Unterrichtsstunde **LS**, 16
Let's [lets] Lasst uns **LS**, 14
letter ['letə] Brief **5**, 58

one hundred and eighty-nine **189**

Alphabetical word list

letter ['letə] Buchstabe **4**, 48
to **lie** [laɪ] liegen **5**, 59
to give … a **lift** [lɪft] … im Auto mitnehmen **6**, 76
to **like** [laɪk] mögen, gern haben **8**, 90
like [laɪk] (so) wie **3**, 44
   What's … like? [wɒts … laɪk] Wie ist … ? **4**, 53
list [lɪst] Liste **5**, 59
to **listen** ['lɪsn] zuhören **LS**, 10
   listening practice ['lɪsnɪŋ ˌpræktɪs] Hörverstehens-
   übung **LS**, 15
little [lɪtl] klein **2**, 32
to **live** [lɪv] leben, wohnen **9**, 102
living-room ['lɪvɪŋrʊm] Wohnzimmer **2**, 33
locked [lɒkt] abgeschlossen **8**, 96
long [lɒŋ] lang **6**, 76
to **look** [lʊk] sehen, anschauen **LS**, 9; aussehen
   9, 104
   Looking at the UK [ˌlʊkɪŋ ət ðə juː ˈkeɪ] Ein Blick auf
   das Vereinigte Königreich! **1**, 22
   to look at ['lʊk ət] anschauen **LS**, 9
a **lot of** [ə'lɒt əv] viel/viele, eine Menge **6**, 71
love [lʌv] alles Liebe (als Briefschluss) **5**, 58
lucky ['lʌkɪ] glücklich, Glücks- **7**, 86
   to be lucky [bɪ 'lʌkɪ] Glück haben **3**, 38
   You're lucky. [jɔː 'lʌkɪ] Du hast Glück. **3**, 38
lunch [lʌntʃ] Mittagessen **LS**, 10
   lunch box ['lʌntʃ bɒks] Dose für belegte Brote zum
   Mittagessen **LS**, 10

M

⟨**made out of**⟩ [ˌmeɪd 'aʊt əv] gemacht aus, hergestellt
   aus **2**, 35
magazine [ˌmægə'ziːn] Zeitschrift **8**, 90
to **make** [meɪk] machen **LS**, 9
man [mæn] , **men** (pl) [men] Mann, Männer **2**, 28
how **many** [haʊ 'menɪ] wie viele **10**, 117
map [mæp] Landkarte **3**, 41
March [mɑːtʃ] März **5**, 58
market ['mɑːkɪt] Markt **6**, 71
mascot ['mæskət] Maskottchen **7**, 88
May [meɪ] Mai **5**, 58
maybe ['meɪbiː] vielleicht **3**, 40
me [miː] mir/mich **3**, 40
mechanic [mɪ'kænɪk] Mechaniker/in **8**, 90
to **meet** [miːt] (sich) treffen **9**, 100
mess [mes] Unordnung **7**, 82
milk [mɪlk] Milch **3**, 42
milkshake ['mɪlkʃeɪk] Milchmixgetränk **10**, 117
Never **mind**. ['nevə ˌmaɪnd] Mach dir nichts daraus.,
   Macht euch nichts daraus. **9**, 99
minute ['mɪnɪt] Minute **4**, 50
   In a minute. [ɪn ə 'mɪnɪt] Augenblick noch!, Warte/t
   mal einen Moment. **4**, 50
Monday ['mʌndeɪ] Montag **6**, 72
money ['mʌnɪ] Geld **7**, 79
month [mʌnθ] Monat **5**, 58
more [mɔː] mehr, weitere **1**, 25
morning ['mɔːnɪŋ] Morgen **LS**, 12
   Good morning. [gʊd 'mɔːnɪŋ] Guten Morgen. **LS**, 12
   in the morning [ɪn ðə 'mɔːnɪŋ] morgens, am
   Vormittag **LS**, 14
mother ['mʌðə] Mutter **1**, 19
mouth [maʊθ] Mund **7**, 84
Mr ['mɪstə] Herr (Anrede für Männer) **LS**, 12
Mrs ['mɪsɪz] Frau (Anrede für verheiratete Frauen)
   LS, 12

Mum [mʌm] Mama, Mutti **1**, 21
music ['mjuːzɪk] Musik **4**, 52
   pop music ['pɒp 'mjuːzɪk] Popmusik **4**, 52
must [mʌst] müssen **3**, 40
my [maɪ] mein/meine **LS**, 8

N

name [neɪm] Name **LS**, 8
   My name is … ['maɪ neɪm ɪz] Ich heiße … **LS**, 8
near [nɪə] in der Nähe von **6**, 71
⟨**near**⟩ [niːə] nahe **4**, 53
to **need** [niːd] brauchen, benötigen **8**, 90
neighbour ['neɪbə] Nachbar/in **2**, 31
never ['nevə] nie **7**, 82
   Never mind. ['nevə ˌmaɪnd] Mach dir nichts daraus.,
   Macht euch nichts daraus. **9**, 99
new [njuː] neu **LS**, 8
next [nekst] nächste/nächster/nächstes **5**, 58
nice [naɪs] nett, schön **LS**, 9
night [naɪt] Nacht **10**, 117
no [nəʊ] kein/keine **4**, 54
no [nəʊ] nein **LS**, 10
nobody ['nəʊbədɪ] niemand, keiner **4**, 49
noise [nɔɪz] Lärm, Krach, Geräusch **2**, 33
⟨**nose**⟩ [nəʊz] Nase **7**, 84
nosy ['nəʊzɪ] neugierig **2**, 31
not [nɒt] nicht **LS**, 11
   not … yet [nɒt … jet] noch nicht **1**, 25
nothing ['nʌθɪŋ] nichts **2**, 33
November [nəʊ'vembə] November **5**, 58
now [naʊ] jetzt, nun **LS**, 16
number ['nʌmbə] Nummer, Zahl **1**, 24
nurse [nɜːs] Krankenschwester/Krankenpfleger **8**, 93
nursery school ['nɜːsərɪ ˌskuːl] Kindergarten **7**, 81

O

o [əʊ] null (bei Telefonnummern) **1**, 24
at … **o'clock** [ət … ə'klɒk] um … Uhr **5**, 60
October [ɒk'təʊbə] Oktober **5**, 58
of [ɒv] , [əv] von **3**, 42
   of course [əv 'kɔːs] natürlich, selbstverständlich **4**, 48
office ['ɒfɪs] Büro, Amt **6**, 75
police officer [pə'liːs ˌɒfɪsə] Polizist/in **8**, 95
often ['ɒfn] oft **7**, 82
oh [əʊ] oh **LS**, 8
   Oh dear! [əʊ 'dɪə] Oh je! **7**, 82
OK [əʊ'keɪ] OK; in Ordnung **LS**, 12
old [əʊld] alt **LS**, 11
on [ɒn] auf **LS**, 13
   ⟨on the hillside⟩ [ɒn ðə 'hɪlsaɪd] am Hang **2**, 35
   on (the radio) [ɒn] im (Rundfunk) **4**, 50
   on the seventh of [ɒn ðə 'sevnθ əv] am siebten **5**, 60
   on the telephone [ɒn ðə 'telɪfəʊn] am Telefon **3**, 40
   to be on [bɪ 'ɒn] eingeschaltet sein **4**, 49
   on the left/right [ɒn ðə 'left] , [ɒn ðə 'raɪt] links/
   rechts, auf der linken/rechten Seite **6**, 74
one [wʌn] ein/eine/eins **1**, 18
only ['əʊnlɪ] nur, erst **3**, 43
Oops! [uːps] Hoppla! **1**, 21
to **open** ['əʊpən] öffnen, aufmachen **8**, 96
open ['əʊpən] offen, geöffnet **8**, 96
opposite ['ɒpəzɪt] Gegenteil **4**, 56
or [ɔː] oder **LS**, 14
word **order** ['wɜːd ˌɔːdə] Satzstellung **7**, 82

Alphabetical word list

Vocabulary

other [ˈʌðə] andere, weitere **2**, 31
our [ˈaʊə] unser/unsere **1**, 19
out [aʊt] draußen, heraus **4**, 51
⟨made out of⟩ [ˌmeɪd ˈaʊt̮ əv] gemacht aus, hergestellt aus **2**, 35
outside [ˌaʊtˈsaɪd] draußen **2**, 33
over [ˈəʊvə] über **5**, 57
over there [əʊvə ˈðeə] da drüben, dort **1**, 23

P

packet [ˈpækɪt] Päckchen **7**, 79
page [peɪdʒ] Seite **LS**, 9
pair [peə] Paar **LS**, 14
parents *(pl)* [ˈpeərənts] Eltern **2**, 29
park [pɑːk] Park **1**, 25
partner [ˈpɑːtnə] Partner/in **1**, 21
party [ˈpɑːtɪ] Party, Feier **5**, 57
to **pass** [pɑːs] reichen, weitergeben **3**, 42
past [pɑːst] nach *(bei Uhrzeiten)* **5**, 61
pen [pen] Füller **LS**, 10
pence (= **p**) *(pl)* [pens] Pfennige *(britisches Geld)* **7**, 79
pencil [ˈpensl] Bleistift **LS**, 10
pencil case [ˈpensl keɪs] Federmäppchen **LS**, 10
people *(pl)* [ˈpiːpl] Leute **3**, 37
person [ˈpɜːsn] Person **6**, 75
pet [pet] Haustier **9**, 106
to **phone** [fəʊn] anrufen **3**, 40
photo [ˈfəʊtəʊ] Foto **3**, 41
to take a photo of [teɪk ə ˈfəʊtəʊ əv] ein Foto machen von **3**, 43
picture [ˈpɪktʃə] Bild **LS**, 14
pig [pɪg] Schwein **10**, 113
⟨pink⟩ [pɪŋk] rosa **2**, 35
pint [paɪnt] *etwa 0,5l* **7**, 85
plan [plæn] Plan **5**, 63
plane [pleɪn] Flugzeug **3**, 41
to **play** [pleɪ] spielen **LS**, 13
playground [ˈpleɪgraʊnd] Schulhof, Spielplatz **LS**, 15
please [pliːz] bitte **LS**, 9
pocket [ˈpɒkɪt] Tasche *(bei Kleidung)* **8**, 90
pocket money [ˈpɒkɪt ˌmʌnɪ] Taschengeld **8**, 90
police [pəˈliːs] Polizei **8**, 95
police officer [pəˈliːs ˌɒfɪsə] Polizist/in **8**, 95
pond [pɒnd] Teich **1**, 21
poor [pɔː] arm **1**, 25
pop music [ˈpɒp ˈmjuːzɪk] Popmusik **4**, 52
popular [ˈpɒpjʊlə] beliebt **8**, 92
post office [ˈpəʊst ˌɒfɪs] Post, Postamt **10**, 115
postcard [ˈpəʊstkɑːd] Postkarte **9**, 105
poster [ˈpəʊstə] Poster, Plakat **LS**, 9
potato, potatoes *(pl)* [pəˈteɪtəʊ] Kartoffel, Kartoffeln **6**, 75
pound (= **lb**) [paʊnd] Pfund *(Gewicht)* **7**, 85
pound (= **£**) [paʊnd] Pfund *(britisches Geld)* **7**, 79
Word **power** [ˈwɜːd ˌpaʊə] Die Kraft der Wörter **1**, 23
practice [ˈpræktɪs] Übung, Training **LS**, 10
listening practice [ˈlɪsnɪŋ ˌpræktɪs] Hörverstehens-übung **LS**, 15
sound practice [ˈsaʊnd ˌpræktɪs] Aussprache-übung **LS**, 10
present [ˈprezənt] Geschenk **3**, 39
prize [praɪz] Preis, Gewinn **7**, 79
problem [ˈprɒbləm] Problem **5**, 57
promenade [ˌprɒməˈnɑːd] Promenade **9**, 104
pullover [ˈpʊlˌəʊvə] Pullover **6**, 73

pump [pʌmp] Luftpumpe **2**, 30
pupil [ˈpjuːpl] Schüler/in **7**, 83
to **put** [pʊt] setzen, stellen, legen **2**, 33
to put in [ˈpʊt̮ ɪn] einsetzen, hineintun **1**, 27

Q

quarter [ˈkwɔːtə] Viertel **5**, 61
question [ˈkwestʃən] Frage **LS**, 15
quiet [ˈkwaɪət] still, ruhig **LS**, 16
quiz [kwɪz] Quiz, Ratespiel **3**, 38

R

radio [ˈreɪdɪəʊ] Radio **1**, 20
to **rain** [reɪn] regnen **4**, 53
to **read** [riːd] lesen **4**, 48
ready [ˈredɪ] fertig, bereit **1**, 25
to get ready [get ˈredɪ] (sich) vorbereiten **5**, 59
really [ˈrɪəlɪ] wirklich **9**, 101
red [red] rot **2**, 28
reduced in size [rɪˌdjuːst̮ ɪn ˈsaɪz] verkleinert **7**, 79
to **remember** [rɪˈmembə] behalten, sich merken, sich erinnern **5**, 58
to **repair** [rɪˈpeə] reparieren **4**, 48
request [rɪˈkwest] Bitte, Wunsch **8**, 94
restaurant [ˈrestərɒnt] Restaurant **6**, 71
⟨revision⟩ [rɪˈvɪʒn] Wiederholung **R1**, 47
rhyme [raɪm] Reim **4**, 48
right [raɪt] (nach) rechts **6**, 74
on the left/right [ɒn ðə ˈleft], [ɒn ðə ˈraɪt] links/rechts, auf der linken/rechten Seite **6**, 74
right [raɪt] richtig **LS**, 12
right away [ˈraɪt̮ əˈweɪ] sofort **3**, 43
ring [rɪŋ] Ring **2**, 33
road (= **Rd.**) [rəʊd] Straße **1**, 22
rock [rɒk] Fels **9**, 102
role play [ˈrəʊl pleɪ] Rollenspiel **1**, 24
room [ruːm] Raum, Zimmer **1**, 20; Platz **9**, 102
round [raʊnd] um … herum **4**, 51
rubbish [ˈrʌbɪʃ] Abfall, Müll **9**, 106

S

⟨to sail⟩ [seɪl] segeln **4**, 53
salad [ˈsæləd] gemischter Salat **3**, 42
same [seɪm] gleich **4**, 52
⟨all the same⟩ [ˌɔːl ðə ˈseɪm] alle gleich **2**, 35
⟨just the same⟩ [ˌdʒʌst ðə ˈseɪm] genau gleich **2**, 35
sandcastle [ˈsændkɑːsl] Sandburg **9**, 104
sandwich [ˈsænwɪdʒ] belegtes Brot **9**, 106
Saturday [ˈsætədeɪ] Samstag, Sonnabend **4**, 54
sausage [ˈsɒsɪdʒ] Würstchen, Wurst **7**, 79
to **save** [seɪv] sparen **8**, 90
to **save** [seɪv] retten **10**, 118
to **say** [seɪ] sagen **LS**, 10
to say hello [ˈseɪ həˈləʊ] grüßen **9**, 105
scene [siːn] Szene **R2**, 69
school [skuːl] Schule **LS**, 8
sea [siː] Meer **1**, 21
at the **seaside** [ˈsiːsaɪd] an der See **9**, 99
season [ˈsiːzn] Jahreszeit **10**, 117
seat [siːt] Sitz, Sitzplatz **9**, 99
to **see** [siː] sehen **2**, 33
to **sell** [sel] verkaufen **8**, 90
sentence [ˈsentəns] Satz **LS**, 14

one hundred and ninety-one **191**

Alphabetical word list

September [sep'tembə] September **5**, 58
she [ʃiː] sie **LS**, 9
  she isn't (= she is not) [ʃiː‿'ɪznt] sie ist nicht **LS**, 15
  she's (= she is) [ʃiːz] sie ist **LS**, 9
shed [ʃed] Stall, Schuppen **10**, 118
sheep (sg + pl) [ʃiːp] Schaf, Schafe **10**, 113
sheepdog ['ʃiːpdɒg] Hirtenhund **10**, 113
shelf [ʃelf], **shelves** (pl) [ʃelvz] Regal, Regale **2**, 29
shirt [ʃɜːt] Hemd(bluse) **6**, 73
shoe [ʃuː] Schuh **4**, 48
shop [ʃɒp] Geschäft, Laden **2**, 31
  shop assistant ['ʃɒp‿ə‿sɪstənt] Verkäufer/in **8**, 90
  to go to the shops [gəʊ tə ðə 'ʃɒps] einkaufen gehen **3**, 40
shopping ['ʃɒpɪŋ] Einkaufs-, Einkaufen **5**, 59
  shopping centre ['ʃɒpɪŋ ˌsentə] Einkaufszentrum **6**, 71
  shopping list ['ʃɒpɪŋ lɪst] Einkaufsliste **5**, 59
short [ʃɔːt] kurz **9**, 101
⟨**shoulder**⟩ ['ʃəʊldə] Schulter **7**, 84
to show [ʃəʊ] zeigen **9**, 106
silly ['sɪlɪ] dumm, albern **2**, 33
to sing [sɪŋ] singen **5**, 57
sister ['sɪstə] Schwester **1**, 21
to sit [sɪt] sitzen **4**, 53
  Sit down. [sɪt 'daʊn] Setz dich., Setzt euch. **LS**, 16
  to sit down [sɪt 'daʊn] sich hinsetzen **LS**, 16
size [saɪz] Größe **7**, 79
skateboard ['skeɪtbɔːd] Skateboard **1**, 20
skin [skɪn] Haut **10**, 119
to sleep [sliːp] schlafen **9**, 106
small [smɔːl] klein **9**, 104
snack bar ['snæk bɑː] Imbissstube **9**, 100
snake [sneɪk] Schlange **LS**, 13
snow [snəʊ] Schnee **10**, 117
so [səʊ] also **3**, 39
soap [səʊp] Seife **7**, 86
⟨**some**⟩ [sʌm] einige **10**, 115
sometimes ['sʌmtaɪmz] manchmal **7**, 82
song [sɒŋ] Lied **8**, 91
soon [suːn] bald **8**, 93
Sorry! ['sɒrɪ] Entschuldigung!, Tut mir Leid. **LS**, 11
sound practice ['saʊnd ˌpræktɪs] Aussprache-übung **LS**, 10
souvenir [ˌsuːvə'nɪə] Souvenir, Andenken, Mitbringsel **9**, 105
spade [speɪd] Spaten **4**, 51
Spanish ['spænɪʃ] spanisch, Spanisch **3**, 37
to speak [spiːk] sprechen **3**, 38
special ['speʃəl] besondere/r/s; Spezialität des Hauses **6**, 75
to spell [spel] buchstabieren **4**, 48
spoon [spuːn] Löffel **2**, 29
spring [sprɪŋ] Frühling **10**, 117
square ['skweə] Platz **6**, 71
⟨**to stamp**⟩ [stæmp] stampfen **1**, 19
  ⟨**Stamp your feet.**⟩ [ˌstæmp jɔː 'fiːt] Stampf/t mit deinen/euren Füßen. **1**, 19
to stand [stænd] stehen **6**, 76
to start [stɑːt] anfangen, beginnen **3**, 37
  Let's start. [ˌlets 'stɑːt] Lasst uns anfangen. **LS**, 7
station ['steɪʃn] Bahnhof **9**, 100
statue ['stætʃuː] Statue, Denkmal **6**, 71
to stay [steɪ] (zu Besuch) wohnen **10**, 113; bleiben **10**, 118
step [step] Schritt, Stufe **1**, 18
stone [stəʊn] Stein **4**, 51
to stop [stɒp] anhalten **6**, 76

⟨**stormy**⟩ ['stɔːmɪ] stürmisch **4**, 53
story ['stɔːrɪ] Geschichte, Erzählung **3**, 43
straight on [streɪt 'ɒn] geradeaus **6**, 74
street [striːt] Straße **6**, 71
sugar ['ʃʊgə] Zucker **3**, 42
summer ['sʌmə] Sommer **10**, 117
⟨**sun**⟩ [sʌn] Sonne **9**, 99
Sunday ['sʌndeɪ] Sonntag **6**, 72
sunny ['sʌnɪ] sonnig **4**, 53
superdogs (pl) ['suːpədɒgz] Superhunde **1**, 18
supermarket ['suːpəˌmɑːkɪt] Supermarkt **7**, 85
sure [ʃɔː] sicher **LS**, 15
  I'm not sure. [aɪm nɒt 'ʃɔː] Ich bin mir nicht sicher. **LS**, 15
surprise [sə'praɪz] Überraschung **5**, 57
sweatshirt ['swetʃɜːt] Sweatshirt **4**, 52
sweet [swiːt] Bonbon **8**, 90
to go swimming [gəʊ 'swɪmɪŋ] schwimmen gehen **9**, 99

T

T-shirt ['tiːʃɜːt] T-Shirt **4**, 52
table ['teɪbl] Tisch **1**, 25
to take [teɪk] nehmen **7**, 86; bringen **8**, 95
  to take a photo of [teɪk ə'fəʊtəʊ‿əv] ein Foto machen von **3**, 43
  to take home [teɪk 'həʊm] nach Hause bringen **7**, 82
to talk about ['tɔːk‿ə‿baʊt] reden über, sprechen über **2**, 32
tea [tiː] Mahlzeit am frühen Abend **3**, 42; Tee **3**, 42
teacher ['tiːtʃə] Lehrer/in **LS**, 10
team [tiːm] Mannschaft **4**, 54
telephone ['telɪfəʊn] Telefon **1**, 24
  on the telephone [ɒn ðə 'telɪfəʊn] am Telefon **3**, 40
to tell [tel] erzählen **3**, 38; sagen, mitteilen **6**, 74
  to tell the time ['tel ðə 'taɪm] die Uhrzeit angeben **5**, 61
tennis ['tenɪs] Tennis **4**, 52
terrible ['terəbl] schrecklich, furchtbar **3**, 40
text [tekst] Text **8**, 97
Thank you. ['θæŋk‿jʊ] Danke schön. **LS**, 10
Thanks! [θæks] Danke! **1**, 19
that's (= that is) [ðæts] das ist **LS**, 8
the [ðə] der/die/das **LS**, 12; **the** [ðiː] der/die/das **LS**, 14
their [ðeə] ihr/ihre (Pl) **1**, 19
them [ðem] sie/ihnen **4**, 51
then [ðen] dann **4**, 48
there [ðeə] da, dort **1**, 23
  over there [ˌəʊvə 'ðeə] da drüben, dort **1**, 23
  there are [ðeər‿'ɑː] es gibt, es sind **3**, 37
  there is [ðeər‿'ɪz] es gibt, es ist **3**, 37
these [ðiːz] diese hier **2**, 32
they [ðeɪ] sie (Pl) **LS**, 12
  they aren't (= they are not) [ðeɪ‿'ɑːnt] sie sind nicht **LS**, 15
  they're (= they are) [ðeə] sie sind **LS**, 12
thing [θɪŋ] Ding, Sache **1**, 26
to think [θɪŋk] denken, glauben **4**, 48
  to think of ['θɪŋk‿əv] ausdenken **4**, 50
this [ðɪs] dies/dieser/diese/dieses **1**, 22
  this afternoon [ðɪs‿ɑːftə'nuːn] heute Nachmittag **3**, 40
those [ðəʊz] die da drüben **2**, 32
through [θruː] durch **3**, 41
to throw [θrəʊ] werfen **2**, 30

Alphabetical word list

Vocabulary

Thursday [ˈθɜːzdeɪ] Donnerstag **6**, 72
ticket [ˈtɪkɪt] Fahrkarte **9**, 99
⟨ticky tacky⟩ [ˈtɪkɪ ˈtækɪ] billiges Material **2**, 35
tidy [ˈtaɪdɪ] ordentlich, aufgeräumt **7**, 82
to **tidy up** [ˈtaɪdɪ ˌʌp] aufräumen **7**, 82
time [taɪm] Zeit **4**, 48
  It's time for … [ɪts ˈtaɪm fə] Es ist Zeit für … **4**, 48
  to tell the time [ˈtel ðə ˈtaɪm] die Uhrzeit angeben **5**, 61
What **time is it**? [ˌwɒt ˈtaɪm ˌɪz ˌɪt] Wie spät ist es?, Wie viel Uhr ist es? **5**, 61
timetable [ˈtaɪmteɪbl] Fahrplan **9**, 103
tired [ˈtaɪəd] müde **10**, 118
to [tʊ] zu **3**, 40; vor **5**, 61
  from … to [frəm … tə] von … nach **3**, 41
today [təˈdeɪ] heute **2**, 29
⟨toe⟩ [təʊ] Zeh **7**, 84
together [təˈgeðə] zusammen **1**, 24
toilet [ˈtɔɪlɪt] Toilette **5**, 63
tomato, tomatoes *(pl)* [təˈmaːtəʊ] Tomate, Tomaten **6**, 75
tomorrow [təˈmɒrəʊ] morgen **5**, 62
too [tuː] auch **LS**, 9; allzu, zu **6**, 72
town [taʊn] Stadt **6**, 71
tractor [ˈtræktə] Traktor, Trecker **10**, 116
train [treɪn] Zug **3**, 41
tree [triː] Baum **1**, 21
trick [trɪk] Trick, Kunstgriff **10**, 119
to **trick** [trɪk] austricksen **10**, 118
to **trip** [trɪp] stolpern **7**, 86
trouble [ˈtrʌbl] Schwierigkeiten **10**, 118
  to be in trouble [bɪ ˌɪn ˈtrʌbl] Schwierigkeiten haben **10**, 118
trousers *(sg + pl)* [ˈtraʊzəz] Hose, Hosen **6**, 73
to **try on** [traɪ ˌɒn] anprobieren **6**, 73
Tuesday [ˈtjuːzdeɪ] Dienstag **6**, 72
tunnel [ˈtʌnl] Tunnel **3**, 41
Turkish [ˈtɜːkɪʃ] türkisch, Türkisch **3**, 37
Your **turn**. [ˈjɔː tɜːn] Du bist an der Reihe. **LS**, 8
to **turn** [tɜːn] abbiegen **6**, 74
tutor [ˈtjuːtə] Klassenlehrer/in, Betreuungslehrer/in **LS**, 9
  tutor group [ˈtjuːtə ˌgruːp] Klasse (*in einer englischen Schule*) **LS**, 9
TV [ˈtiːˈviː] Fernsehen **4**, 48
twin [twɪn] Zwilling **6**, 75
twin town [ˈtwɪn ˈtaʊn] Partnerstadt **6**, 75
Twinning Office [ˈtwɪnɪŋ ˌɒfɪs] Städtepartnerschaftsbüro **6**, 75
tyre [ˈtaɪə] Reifen **2**, 30

U

uncle [ˈʌŋkl] Onkel **3**, 37
under [ˈʌndə] unter **LS**, 13
to **understand** [ˌʌndəˈstænd] verstehen **9**, 106
uniform [ˈjuːnɪfɔːm] Uniform **3**, 40
unit [ˈjuːnɪt] Lektion, Kapitel **1**, 18
untidy [ʌnˈtaɪdɪ] unordentlich **2**, 29
upstairs [ˌʌpˈsteəz] oben (im Gebäude) **5**, 63
us [ʌs] uns **4**, 51
to **use** [juːz] benutzen **8**, 94
usually [ˈjuːʒʊəlɪ] gewöhnlich, normalerweise **8**, 96

V

verb [vɜːb] Verb **7**, 87
very [ˈverɪ] sehr **2**, 29
vet [vet] Tierarzt/Tierärztin **2**, 28
  vet's assistant [ˈvets əˌsɪstənt] Tierarzthelfer/in **2**, 28
video [ˈvɪdɪəʊ] Video **5**, 64

W

to **wait** [weɪt] warten **10**, 118
  to wait for [ˈweɪt fɔː] warten auf **8**, 96
walk [wɔːk] Spaziergang **4**, 53
  to go for a walk [ˌgəʊ fər ə ˈwɔːk] spazieren gehen **4**, 53
to **walk** [wɔːk] (zu Fuß) gehen **6**, 72
to **want** [wɒnt] (haben) wollen **8**, 90
warm [wɔːm] warm **4**, 53
to **wash up** [wɒʃ ˈʌp] abwaschen, (Geschirr) spülen **4**, 50
washing-up [ˌwɒʃɪŋˈʌp] Abwasch **7**, 82
to **watch** [wɒtʃ] (zu)schauen, gucken **4**, 48
water [ˈwɔːtə] Wasser **9**, 102
⟨waters⟩ [ˈwɔːtəz] Gewässer **4**, 53
way [weɪ] Weg **6**, 74
  ⟨all the way⟩ [ˌɔːl ðə ˈweɪ] den ganzen Weg **1**, 19
we [wiː] wir **LS**, 12
  we're (= we are) [wɪə] wir sind **LS**, 12
to **wear** [weə] tragen, anhaben **6**, 73
weather [ˈweðə] Wetter **4**, 53
Wednesday [ˈwenzdeɪ] Mittwoch **6**, 72
week [wiːk] Woche **6**, 72
Welcome to … [ˈwelkəm tʊ] Willkommen in … **3**, 37
well [wel] gut, nun, na ja **4**, 48
  Get well soon! [ˈget wel ˈsuːn] Gute Besserung! **8**, 94
  Well done! [wel ˈdʌn] Gut gemacht!, Bravo! **7**, 82
wet [wet] nass **4**, 53
what [wɒt] was **LS**, 8
  What's … like? [wɒts … laɪk] Wie ist … ? **4**, 53
  What a … [ˈwɒt ə] Was für ein/e … **2**, 29
when [wen] wann **5**, 60
where [weə] wo **LS**, 13
  where's (= where is) [weəz] wo ist **LS**, 13
white [waɪt] weiß **7**, 79
who [huː] wer **3**, 38; wen/wem **10**, 116
why [waɪ] warum **6**, 72
window [ˈwɪndəʊ] Fenster **8**, 96
windy [ˈwɪndɪ] windig **4**, 53
winner [ˈwɪnə] Gewinner/in **7**, 84
winter [ˈwɪntə] Winter **10**, 117
with [wɪð] bei, mit **1**, 18
without [wɪðˈaʊt] ohne **5**, 58
woman [ˈwʊmən], **women** *(pl)* [ˈwɪmɪn] Frau, Frauen **2**, 28
word [wɜːd] Wort **LS**, 14
  word order [ˈwɜːd ˌɔːdə] Satzstellung **7**, 82
  Word power [ˈwɜːd ˌpaʊə] Die Kraft der Wörter **1**, 23
to **work** [wɜːk] arbeiten **1**, 21
worried [ˈwʌrɪd] besorgt, beunruhigt **6**, 76
to **write** [raɪt] schreiben **LS**, 14
wrong [rɒŋ] falsch **LS**, 16

one hundred and ninety-three **193**

Alphabetical word list

Y

year [jɪə] Jahr, Jahrgang **LS**, 14
yellow ['jeləʊ] gelb **2**, 28
yes [jes] ja **LS**, 8
not … **yet** [nɒt … jet] noch nicht **1**, 25
you [juː] du, Sie **LS**, 10; ihr/Sie **LS**, 12; dich/euch/
Sie; dir/euch/Ihnen **4**, 51
 Are you … ? [ɑː juː] Bist du … ?/Sind Sie …? **LS**, 11
 you're (= you are) [jʊə] du bist/Sie sind **LS**, 11
 you're (= you are) [jʊə] ihr seid/Sie sind **LS**, 12
your [jɔː] dein/deine, Ihr/Ihre **LS**, 8; euer/eure; Ihr/
Ihre **LS**, 12

Boys' names

Alan ['ælən]
Colin ['kɒlɪn]
David ['deɪvɪd]
Eddy ['edɪ]
Jack [dʒæk]
Lenny ['lenɪ]
Mark [mɑːk]
Michael ['maɪkəl]
Peter ['piːtə]
Robert ['rɒbət]
Sam [sæm]
Simon ['saɪmən]
Tim [tɪm]

Girls' names

Anna ['ænə]
Annabel ['ænəbel]
Audrey ['ɔːdrɪ]
Becky ['bekɪ]
Debbie ['debɪ]
Helen ['helɪn]
Janet ['dʒænɪt]
Jenny ['dʒenɪ]
Kim [kɪm]
Margaret ['mɑːgrɪt]
Mary ['meərɪ]
Pat [pæt]
Sarah ['seərə]
Suvina [sə'viːnə]
Victoria [vɪk'tɔːrɪə]

Surnames

Adib [ə'dɪb]
Barker ['bɑːkə]
Benson ['bensn]
Burton ['bɜːtn]
Cooper ['kuːpə]
Croft [krɒft]
Dane [deɪn]
Dixon ['dɪksn]
Hilton ['hɪltən]
Hunt ['hʌnt]
Miller ['mɪlə]
Nosy ['nəʊzɪ]
Penrose ['penrəʊz]
Richards ['rɪtʃədz]

Smith [smɪθ]
Walker ['wɔːkə]
Wall [wɔːl]
White [waɪt]
Wood [wʊd]

Geographical names

Africa ['æfrɪkə]
⟨Albania⟩ [æl'beɪnjə]
Angel Row ['eɪndʒəl 'rəʊ]
Arndale Road ['ɑːndeɪl 'rəʊd]
Arnot Hill Park [ˌɑːnət hɪl 'pɑːk]
⟨Austria⟩ ['ɒstrɪə]
Beastmarket Hill ['biːstmɑːkɪt 'hɪl]
Beeston ['biːstən]
Belgium ['beldʒəm]
⟨Belorussia⟩ [ˌbeləʊ'rʌʃə]
Berlin [bɜː'lɪn]
Bestwood ['bestwʊd]
⟨Bosnia Herzegovina⟩ ['bɒznɪə ˌheətsəgəʊ'viːnə]
⟨Bulgaria⟩ [bʌl'geərɪə]
Castle Gate ['kɑːsl 'geɪt]
Channel Tunnel ['tʃænl 'tʌnl]
Cleethorpes ['kliːθɔːps]
⟨Croatia⟩ [krəʊ'eɪʃə]
⟨Czech Republic⟩ [ˌtʃek rɪ'pʌblɪk]
⟨Denmark⟩ ['denmɑːk]
Edward's Lane ['edwədz ˌleɪn]
England ['ɪŋglənd]
⟨Estonia⟩ [es'təʊnjə]
⟨Europe⟩ ['jʊərəp]
Exchange Walk [ɪks'tʃeɪndʒ 'wɔːk]
⟨Finland⟩ ['fɪnlənd]
France [frɑːns]
Friar Lane ['fraɪə 'leɪn]
Germany ['dʒɜːmənɪ]
⟨Greece⟩ [griːs]
Heathrow [ˌhiːθ'rəʊ]
the **High Street** ['haɪ striːt]
⟨Hungary⟩ ['hʌŋgərɪ]
⟨Iceland⟩ ['aɪslənd]
⟨Ireland⟩ ['aɪələnd]
⟨Italy⟩ ['ɪtəlɪ]
Larwood Grove ['lɑːwʊd 'grəʊv]
⟨Latvia⟩ ['lætvɪə]
⟨Lithuania⟩ [ˌlɪθjuː'eɪnjə]
London ['lʌndən]
⟨Luxembourg⟩ ['lʌksəmbɜːg]
Maid Marian Way [ˌmeɪd 'mærɪən 'weɪ]
⟨Malta⟩ ['mɔːltə]
Mansfield Road ['mænsfiːld 'rəʊd]
⟨Moldavia⟩ [mɒl'deɪvjə]
⟨Montenegro⟩ [ˌmɒntɪ'niːgrəʊ]
Mount Street ['maʊnt striːt]
the **Netherlands** [ðə 'neðələndz]
North Sea [nɔːθ 'siː]
Northallerton [nɔː'θælətən]
⟨Norway⟩ ['nɔːweɪ]
Nottingham ['nɒtɪŋəm]
Old Market Square [əʊld 'mɑːkɪt 'skweə]
Parliament Street ['pɑːləmənt ˌstriːt]
Poland ['pəʊlənd]
⟨Portugal⟩ ['pɔːtʃʊgl]
⟨Romania⟩ [ru:'meɪnjə]
⟨Russia⟩ ['rʌʃə]
⟨Serbia⟩ ['sɜːbjə]

Alphabetical word list

Sherwood [ˈʃɜːwʊd]
Skegness [skegˈnes]
⟨Slovakia⟩ [sləʊˈvækjə]
⟨Slovenia⟩ [sləʊˈviːnjə]
South Parade [ˈsaʊθ pəˈreɪd]
⟨Spain⟩ [speɪn]
⟨Sweden⟩ [ˈswiːdn]
⟨Switzerland⟩ [ˈswɪtsələnd]
⟨Turkey⟩ [ˈtɜːkɪ]
the **UK** (= the **United Kingdom**) [juː ˈkeɪ] , [juːˈnaɪtɪd ˈkɪŋdəm]
⟨Ukraine⟩ [juːˈkreɪn]
Yorkshire [ˈjɔːkʃə]

Other names

Greenwood [ˈgriːnwʊd]
Haywood School [ˈheɪwʊd ˈskuːl]
Maxi [ˈmæksɪ]
7MD [ˌsevn emˈdiː]
Mini [ˈmɪnɪ]
Monny [ˈmɒnɪ]
Robin Hood [ˈrɒbɪn ˈhʊd]
Sneaky Snake [ˈsniːkɪ ˌsneɪk]
Springfield [ˈsprɪŋfiːld]
St. Peter's Church [snt ˌpiːtəz ˈtʃɜːtʃ]
Tabby [ˈtæbɪ]

Vocabulary

⟨In the classroom⟩

Vocabulary

What you can say to your friends or to the teacher

Before and after the lesson

- Good morning, Mr/Mrs … .
Good-bye. Bye.
Thanks. Thank you (very much).

  Guten Morgen, Herr/Frau … .
  Auf Wiedersehen. Tschüs.
  Danke. Vielen Dank.

- I'm sorry I'm late.
I'm not feeling well.
Can I open the window?

  Tut mir Leid, dass ich mich verspätet habe.
  Ich fühle mich nicht gut.
  Kann ich das Fenster aufmachen?

- What's that in English/German?
What does … mean?

  Was heißt das auf Englisch/Deutsch?
  Was bedeutet …?

- Can I have your crayon/ruler/…?
How do you do this exercise?
Can you help me, please?
I'm not sure.
Sorry I don't know.
Is this right?
I don't think this is right/wrong.
Can you repeat the sentence, please?
Pardon?
Can you write it on the board?

  Kann ich deinen Buntstift/dein Lineal/ … haben?
  Wie macht man/geht diese Übung?
  Können Sie/Kannst du mir bitte helfen?
  Ich bin nicht sicher.
  Tut mir Leid, das weiß ich nicht.
  Ist das richtig?
  Ich glaube nicht, daß dies richtig/falsch ist.
  Können Sie/Kannst du bitte den Satz wiederholen
  Wie bitte?
  Können Sie es an die Tafel schreiben?

- Let's act the story/play a game.
Can we sing a song?

  Wir möchten die Geschichte/ein Spiel spielen.
  Können wir ein Lied singen?

- What's for homework?

  Was haben wir als Hausaufgabe auf?

… and what the teacher says to you

- Open your books at page … .
Read the text on page … .

  Öffnet eure Bücher auf Seite … .
  Lies den Text auf Seite … .

- Please get me some chalk.
Would you collect the exercise books/
worksheets/workbooks, please?
Do this exercise for homework.
Who would like to write on a
transparency?

  Bitte hol mir Kreide.
  Würdest du bitte die Übungshefte/Arbeitsblätter/
  Arbeitsbücher einsammeln?
  Macht diese Übung als Hausaufgabe.
  Wer möchte auf Folie schreiben?

- Good. Very good. That's good.
You can do better. Try again.
That's it. Well done.

  Gut! Sehr gut! Das ist gut.
  Das kannst du besser. Versuch es noch einmal.
  So ist es richtig. Gut gemacht.

- Be quiet.
Sit down, please.
Please speak up.

  Sei/Seid ruhig.
  Setz dich/Setzt euch, bitte.
  Sprich/Sprecht lauter, bitte.